STORIES FROM THE MAHABHARATA

STORIES FROM THE MAHABHARATA

Sri Swami Sivananda

Published by

THE DIVINE LIFE SOCIETY

P.O. SHIVANANDANAGAR—249 192

Distt. Tehri-Garhwal, Uttaranchal, Himalayas, India

Price] **2007** **[Rs. 100/-**

First Edition: 1943
Second Edition: 1984
Third Edition: 1994
Fourth Edition: 2000
Fifth Edition: 2007
[1,000 Copies]

ISBN 81-7052-026-6
ES 168

Published by Swami Vimalananda for
The Divine Life Society, Shivanandanagar, and printed by him at
the Yoga-Vedanta Forest Academy Press,
P.O. Shivanandanagar, Distt. Tehri-Garhwal, Uttaranchal,
Himalayas, India

OM

Dedicated to

Lord Krishna

and

The Heroes of the

Mahabharata

and Bhagavan Sri Vyasa

OM

SRI SWAMI SIVANANDA

Born on the 8th September, 1887, in the illustrious family of Sage Appayya Dikshitar and several other renowned saints and savants, Sri Swami Sivananda had a natural flair for a life devoted to the study and practice of Vedanta. Added to this was an inborn eagerness to serve all and an innate feeling of unity with all mankind.

His passion for service drew him to the medical career; and soon he gravitated to where he thought that his service was most needed. Malaya claimed him. He had earlier been editing a health journal and wrote extensively on health problems. He discovered that people needed right knowledge most of all; dissemination of that knowledge he espoused as his own mission.

It was divine dispensation and the blessing of God upon mankind that the doctor of body and mind renounced his career and took to a life of renunciation to qualify for ministering to the soul of man. He settled down at Rishikesh in 1924, practised intense austerities and shone as a great Yogi, saint, sage and Jivanmukta.

In 1932 Swami Sivananda started the Sivanandashram. In 1936 was born The Divine Life Society. In 1948 the Yoga-Vedanta Forest Academy was organised. Dissemination of spiritual knowledge and training of people in Yoga and Vedanta were their aim and object. In 1950 Swamiji undertook a lightning tour of India and Ceylon. In 1953 Swamiji convened a 'World Parliament of Religions'. Swamiji is the author of over 300 volumes and has disciples all over the world, belonging to all nationalities, religions and creeds. To read Swamiji's works is to drink at the Fountain of Wisdom Supreme. On 14th July, 1963 Swamiji entered Mahasamadhi.

ॐ

9th December, 1942

Children of Light,

Mahabharata is said to be the fifth Veda. It contains the essence of all scriptures. If you cannot find anything here, you cannot find it anywhere else.

Stick to Dharma. Be truthful and righteous. This is the message of Mahabharata.

May you all imbibe the righteousness of Yudhishthira, the purity of Bhishma, the valour of Arjuna and the liberality of Karna.

Sivananda

ॐ

PRAYER

यो नित्यो यमुपासतेऽखिलजना येनेदमावास्यते
यस्मै कर्म करोति सात्त्विककुलं यस्माज्जगज्जायते ।
यस्यैश्वर्यमवेद्यनैजविभवं यस्मिन्हि विश्वं स्थितं
तं दूरे पुनरन्तिकेऽपि विदितं ध्यायामि नारायणम् ॥

He who is worshipped by all men, who is eternal, by whom this world is indwelt, by whose power sentient beings perform actions, from whom this world has come out, in whom this world exists, who is known and realised (by Yogins and sages), far as well as near, depending on whose lordship and glory everything else (in this world) shines: on that Lord Narayana I meditate.

PUBLISHERS' NOTE

This *epic* is held in great reverence and esteem by the millions of Hindus and is generally known as the fifth Veda, for it contains the Gita, acknowledgment of a belief in which as 'the Scripture' is the hallmark of every true Hindu. For thousands of years and even today, the Hindu prefaces his worship, his ceremonies and his celebrations with the announcement that he is a dweller in the land of *Bharatavarsha* and *Bharatakhanda.*

The *epic* contains the life history of the *Bharatas*, for more than four generations beginning with Santanu onwards to Parikshit and Janamejaya and commonly known as 'Pandavas' and 'Kauravas.' It includes the biographies and episodes of various other important people connected with the *Bharatas* besides folk-tales, legends and moral stories innumerable. Many great heroes and heroines take part in it – from Bhishma who took the vow of celibacy for the sake of his father, to Karna who gave up everything, even his life-protecting *Kavacha* and *Kundalas* for charity, from Gandhari who covered up her eyes because her husband was blind, to Draupadi, the delicately nurtured princess, who followed her husbands to exile in the forest voluntarily, to Savitri and Damayanti who recovered their husbands from death and dishonour through the power of their supreme chastity. Every stratum of society – kings, peasants and beggars, saints, villains and sinners and other characters of every shade and variety – plays its part in this *epic*. Yudhishthira, Arjuna, Drona, Asvatthama, Kripa and others are too well-known to need mention here. So much so that every kind of complicated situation in life comes up for issue and is resolved in tune with the best Hindu ideals of Satya and Dharma (Truth and Righteousness). In the midst of all these, the ever glorious Sri Krishna Paramatma moves majestically holding the life-line in His hands and with His master-key, the Gita, opens up every moral and spiritual problem that can possibly arise in human life. To every man born of woman, of whatever caste or creed, of whatever age or clime, the only prayer, if it were possible for formulation definitely, cannot be better expressed than in the words of our oldest Upanishad and there cannot be a more satisfying and better answer to this prayer than our *epic* (Mahabharata), bestowed on us by the Almighty in His boundless love for all beings.

असतो मा सद्गमय ।
तमसो मा ज्योतिर्गमय ।
मृत्योर्माऽमृतंगमय ॥

From unreal, lead me to the Real;
From darkness, lead me to the Light;
From death, lead me to Immortality.
(*Brihadaranyaka Upanishad: 1-3-38.*)

The facile pen of Sri Swami Sivanandaji Maharaj has issued an unending series of books and pamphlets on spiritual and religious matters; and there has been such warm and welcome response of appreciation from the beginning that he has continued in this service with great pleasure. The impact of Western civilisation, ideas and ideals, though providing us with great comforts and conveniences, has created false standards of easy *conscience* and morality and our young men and women, especially after the advent of cinemas and talkies with their vivid and expressive pictures, have been misguided and corrupted. It has given our Gurudev pain of mind to see our youth going down the smooth and pleasant path of vice and easy virtue. Against this spread of vice, Swamiji Maharaj has ever been waging war relentlessly with great zeal and devotion; and he has no doubt become a great moral force among us and nothing has given him greater happiness than their grateful acknowledgments.

Numerous branches of "The Divine Life Society" have been formed all over the country under his aegis and even in distant places as Sri Lanka, Malaysia, South Africa, Europe, Australia and America. The sole end and aim of his life had ever been to serve humanity and guide them in the right path, both morally and spiritually, as far as it lay in his powers. His Ashram at Rishikesh is at the service of every spiritual aspirant and many a wrecked soul, with his peace of mind shattered by the battle of life and eager for rest, has returned happy and more than satisfied.

—THE DIVINE LIFE SOCIETY

INTRODUCTION

Mahabharata—the very mention of the name gives a thrill of holy ideas. This is a great *epic* heroic poem. It contains the essence of all scriptures. It is an encyclopaedia of ethics, knowledge, politics, religion, philosophy and Dharma. If you cannot find anything here, you cannot find it anywhere else. It contains one hundred thousand verses.

It contains eighteen Parvas or sections, viz., Adi Parva, Sabha Parva, Vana Parva, Virata Parva, Udyoga Parva, Bhishma Parva, Drona Parva, Karna Parva, Salya Parva, Sauptika Parva, Sthree Parva, Santi Parva, Anusasana Parva, Asvamedha Parva, Asramavasika Parva, Mausala Parva, Mahaprasthanika Parva and Svargarohanika Parva. Each Parva contains many sub-Parvas or sub-sections.

This wonderful book was composed by Sri Vyasa (Krishna Dvaipayana) who was the grandfather of the heroes of the *epic*. He taught the *epic* to his son Suka and his disciples Vaisampayana and others. King Janamejaya, son of Parikshit, the grandson of the heroes of the epic, performed a great sacrifice. The *epic* was recited by Vaisampayana to Janamejaya at the command of Vyasa. Later on Suta recited the Mahabharata as was done by Vaisampayana to Janamejaya, to Saunaka and others, during a sacrifice performed by Saunaka in Naimisaranya, which is near Sitapur in Uttar Pradesh.

The *Svayamvara* of Draupadi, the coronation of Yudhishthira, the game of dice, the forest life of the Pandavas, the fight between Arjuna and Karna, between Arjuna and Bhishma, the speeches of the warriors in the council of war, are amazing. They command the admiration of the readers and produce an indelible impression in their minds.

It is very interesting to remember the opening and closing lines of this great *epic*. It begins with: "Vyasa sang of the ineffable greatness and splendour of Lord Vasudeva, who is the source and support for everything, who is eternal, unchanging, self-luminous, who is the Indweller in all beings, and of the truthfulness and righteousness of the Pandavas." It ends with: "With raised hands, I shout at the top of my voice, but alas, no one hears my words which can give them Supreme Peace, Joy and Eternal Bliss. One can attain wealth and all objects of desire through Dharma (righteousness). Why do not people practise Dharma? One should not abandon Dharma at any cost, even at the risk of his life. One should not relinquish Dharma out of passion or fear or covetousness or for the sake of preserving one's life. This is the *Bharata Gayatri*. Meditate on this daily, O man! when you retire to sleep and when you rise from your bed every morning. You will attain everything. You will attain glory, fame, prosperity, long life, eternal bliss, everlasting peace and immortality."

The Mahabharata, the most renowned *epic* of India, is the only book of its kind in the whole world. It contains countless stories besides the main episode – the Mahabharata – which teach moral lessons or illustrate distinguishing characteristics of the ancients of India. It contains the history of ancient India and all the details of its political, social and religious life. The stories, songs, nursery tales, anecdotes, parables, the discourses and sayings contained in this *epic* are marvellous and highly instructive. It contains the brilliant records of mighty heroes, warriors of great prowess, deep thinkers, profound philosophers, sages and ascetics and devoted wives of chastity. The beauty and charm of the language is extremely striking and attractive.

One is struck with amazement and becomes tongue-tied when he reads of the marvellous strength of Bhima, of the wonderful skill in archery and bowmanship of Arjuna, of the dexterity of Sahadeva in the use of swords and of the profound knowledge of Nakula in astronomy and of the extreme righteous conduct and justice of Yudhishthira in all matters. The deeds of heroism done by Bhishma, Karna, Drona, Parasurama, Jayadratha, Dhrishtadyumna and many others are superhuman. These heroes did severe Tapas and obtained rare boons from the Lord. That is the reason why they did marvellous heroic deeds which baffle description.

Yudhishthira did not wield arms. He did not take active part in the war-front. He did not use bow and arrows. He had neither the strength of Bhima nor the skill of Arjuna in archery. But he was an embodiment of righteousness. He was an incarnation of Dharma. That is the reason why he is called as Dharmaputra. He was a wise and ideal king. He established peace and order. He guided his brothers in the path of truth and righteousness and checked them whenever they went astray. Arjuna bore manfully the insults which Draupadi was subjected to before his eyes. He could not disobey Yudhishthira and show him the least disrespect. All the brothers were meek and submissive before Yudhishthira, however mighty and heroic they were. They could crush mountains and dry up oceans with their arrows. They were terrible before their opponents but they were mild and gentle before Yudhishthira and were ever ready to obey his commands. They would never speak a word in opposition. Such was the awe-inspiring personality of Yudhishthira. Had it not been for Yudhishthira, Arjuna and his brothers would not have won the war.. Yudhishthira was the founder of an empire. He is an inspiring example, even now, for the rulers of kingdoms and states. He was an embodiment of justice, patience, steadiness, purity, truthfulness and forbearance.

Draupadi, Savitri, Kunti, Madri and Damayanti were highly devoted to their husbands. They were bold and fearless when they were under extreme difficulties, hardships, sufferings and privations. They were pious. They bore the sufferings through the force of their chastity and moral strength. They were ideal wives and ideal mothers. That is the reason why they have left an immortal name behind them.

The Mahabharata still exerts a marvellous influence over the millions of Hindus. The lustre and high renown of these brilliant personages of Mahabharata has not suffered a diminution, in spite of the ravages of cruel time. Their character was untainted and sublime. Hence their deeds also were admirable, laudable and sublime. Determination has ever been the key to success in the lives of great men of all countries. Heroes would not move an inch from the path of their duty when they are called upon to perform it. They were fiery in their determination. They had iron will.

The noble and heroic grandsire Bhishma—who had control over his death and who was unconquerable in war even by the gods—still inspires us with the spirit of self-sacrifice, undaunted courage and purity. Yudhishthira is still a model of justice and righteousness. Remembrance of his very name generates a thrill in our hearts and goads us to tread the path of truth and virtue. Karna still lives in our hearts on account of his extreme munificence and liberality. Karna's name has become proverbial. People even now say, whenever they come across a very generous man, "He is like Karna in gifts."

Even now, we admire Arjuna as a perfect man and worship Lord Krishna as our Protector and Saviour. Whenever we are in trouble and distress we pray to Him, "O Lord! Save us just as you saved Draupadi and Gajendra in days of yore."

The sufferings of the Pandavas and Draupadi, Nala and Damayanti, Savitri and Satyavan, clearly explain to us the fact or hard truth that the goal of life or perfection can only be attained through pain and suffering. Pain is the means through which man is moulded, disciplined and strengthened. Just as impure gold is turned into pure gold by melting it in the crucible, so also the impure and imperfect weak man is rendered pure, perfect and strong, by being melted in the crucible of pain and suffering. Therefore, one should not be afraid of pain and suffering. They are blessings in disguise. They are eye-openers. They are silent teachers. They turn the mind towards God and instil mercy in the heart, strengthen the will and develop patience and power of endurance, which are the pre-requisites for God-realisation.

The message of the Mahabharata is the message of Truth and Righteousness. The great *epic* produces a moral awakening in the readers and exhorts them to tread the path of Satya and Dharma. It urges them strongly to do good deeds, practise Dharma, cultivate dispassion by realising the illusory nature of this universe and its vain glories and sensual pleasures, and attain Eternal Bliss and Immortality. It induces people to do what Yudhishthira did and abandon what Duryodhana did. Stick to Dharma tenaciously. You will attain material and spiritual prosperity. You will attain everlasting happiness and Moksha, the *summum bonum* of life. This is the final purport or central teaching of the Mahabharata.

The blind Dhritarashtra represents Avidya or ignorance; Yudhishthira represents Dharma; Duryodhana Adharma; Draupadi Maya; Bhishma dispassion; Dussasana evil quality; Sakuni jealousy and treachery; Arjuna the individual soul; and Lord Krishna the Supreme Soul. Antahkarana is the Kurukshetra.

The Mahabharata war was a just war. If you go through the speech given by Bhishma to Yudhishthira, you will know the usages of righteous war. A brave hero would fight only with an enemy of equal strength and on equal vantage. This was the motto of every brave soldier who engaged himself in warfare in days of yore in India. Perfect justice and fairness in everything was rigidly observed on both sides. There was no fighting during nights; when the enemy had no arms in his hands, no arrows were aimed at him.

The kings had a complete knowledge of the scriptures and of right and wrong. They practised rigid austerities also. That is the reason why Yudhishthira and Nala were able to bear the privations and hardships. They rolled in wealth and yet they had the strength and power of endurance to walk barefooted in forests and sleep on a bed of stones. They had such a rigorous training and discipline in suffering.

The Mahabharata is the history of the Great War of India between the Pandavas and the Kauravas. The two brothers Dhritarashtra and Pandu were born through sage Vyasa after the death of Vichitravirya. Dhritarashtra being blind, Pandu succeeded to the throne but he entrusted the kingdom to his elder brother and himself proceeded to forest where his five sons Yudhishthira, etc., were born and were called the "Pandavas." Dhritarashtra also had one hundred children in Duryodhana and others, who were called the "Kauravas." Pandu died during the infancy of his sons and Dhritarashtra continued to rule the kingdom with the help of their grand uncle Bhishma, who had pledged himself to lifelong celibacy. The Pandava and Kaurava princes were brought up together and also educated and trained alike through Dronacharya. Both sets of princes considered themselves entitled to the kingdom and looked upon the other with hostility and their feelings and relations grew strained from day to day. On account of persecution by the Kauravas, the Pandavas left their home and suffered much hardship and pain, but on their marriage with the daughter of Drupada, king Dhritarashtra sent for the Pandavas and made over half the kingdom to them. The Pandavas improved their country and established their capital at Indraprastha and then performed the horse sacrifice with great pomp. The Kauravas were also invited there but on seeing the good fortune of the Pandavas and being offended by jokes made at them, they were overcome with jealousy and resentment and returned home with feelings of enmity and revenge. They then conspired against the Pandavas and invited them to gamble and thereby they won all their wealth, kingdom and their persons and also insulted and ill-treated their wife, Draupadi, in the presence of all. In the end, it was settled that the Pandavas should go out in exile to the forest for twelve years and pass another year in secrecy and on return from the exile be entitled to get back their lost kingdom. The Pandavas did all this but on their return the Kauravas refused to return the kingdom. This gave rise to the great family war in which all the Kauravas and the two armies were annihilated and the Pandavas alone survived and got the victory.

The Pandavas were assisted by Sri Krishna and other relations, Drupada, Virata, etc., and their forces numbered seven battalions (Akshauhinis). The Kauravas were also assisted by their relations and friends and their forces numbered eleven battalions. The Pandavas were successful on account of their righteous cause and divine grace.

Arjuna was the bravest of all the five Pandavas. Arjuna had got Draupadi by winning in the selection match and he had defeated the Kauravas on several occasions. He was a devoted friend of Sri Krishna who had married him to His sister Subhadra, even against the wishes of His elder brother Balarama. Sri Krishna assisted the Pandavas in the great war on account of Arjuna and by acting as his charioteer, led him to victory.

May the teachings of this illustrious and ancient *epic* guide you in every walk of your life. May you stick to Dharma. May the great characters of the Mahabharata inspire you! May you imbibe the righteousness of Yudhishthira, the purity of Bhishma, the courage of Arjuna and the liberality of Karna! Glory to Sri Bhagavan Vyasa, the grandsire of the heroes, the author of the Mahabharata, a Chiranjeevi and an Avatara of Lord Hari. May His blessings be upon you all!

Ananda Kutir,
1st January, 1943

Sivananda

CONTENTS

STORIES FROM
THE MAHABHARATA

PART I

WILDERNESS OF LIFE

Dhritarashtra said: "O Venerable Vidura! Tell me at full length the story of the Brahmin who was caught in the wilderness of life."

Vidura said: "Once a certain Brahmin was caught in a vast thick forest which was inhabited by wild beasts like lions, tigers, leopards and other kinds. The Brahmin became perturbed and frightened. He went hither and thither to find out some place of refuge. He did not succeed. He found the forest enmeshed in a net. He saw a terrible woman standing there with outstretched hands. Many five headed snakes also lived in that terrible forest. There was a pit within the forest which was covered by trees, herbs and creepers. The Brahmin fell into the pit in the course of his wanderings. He got himself entangled in the spreading branches of a big tree. He was hanging there with feet upwards and head downwards.

"In this position, he saw a big snake within the pit. He also saw a huge six-faced, twelve-footed elephant slowly approaching the pit and a number of black and white mice and rats gnawing and eating the very roots of the tree. Bees swarmed in large numbers to drink the honey in the comb that was hanging from a branch of the tree. The honey was trickling down in drops. The man who was thus hanging from the tree drank the honey but his thirst was not quenched. He did not obtain any satisfaction. On the other hand the thirst became more and more intense. He was restless and discontented. He was not disgusted with life. He was still clinging to life. The thirst for life became intense. His desire to continue his existence even in such miserable conditions was growing stronger and stronger.

"Imagine the miserable plight of the Brahmin! He got terrified of the carnivorous beasts, of the gigantic woman with outstretched arms, of the huge snake at the bottom of the pit, of the elephant near the tree, of the impending fall of the tree through the action of the rats and lastly of the bees flying about to taste the honey. But the ignorant Brahmin continued to dwell in this miserable condition. He lost his power of discrimination. He was lost to all sense of right understanding and intelligence. But he did not lose, at any time, the hope of prolonging his life."

Dhritarashtra said: "O learned Vidura! Tell me, what is that wilderness you refer to? What is the snake that dwells in the bottom of the pit? What is that six-faced elephant? Please explain to me in detail all about this excellent parable."

Vidura replied: "The 'wilderness' is this mysterious universe. The limited sphere of one's own life is the enmeshed 'forest' within it. The 'beasts' that dwell in this forest are the various diseases to which man is subject to. The 'gigantic woman' who resides in this forest is decrepitude which destroys beauty. The 'pit' is this physical body. The 'huge snake' that dwells in the bottom of that pit is time, the universal destroyer of all creatures. Desire for life is the 'tree' that grows in the pit. Man is attached to the spreading branches of this 'tree' and hangs down.

"The 'six-faced elephant' is the year. This marches towards the tree that stands at the mouth of the pit. The 'six faces' are the seasons. Its 'twelve legs' are the twelve months. The 'rats and the mice' that are cutting off the tree are the days and nights that are continually lessening the span of life of all creatures. The 'bees' are our desires. The 'drops of honey' that are oozing out are the sensual pleasures derived from the gratification of our desires. The ignorant man clings to the sensuous objects. He is thus caught in the wheel of births and deaths. The sages know life's course to be even such. They tear off the bonds of this mundane life through discrimination, dispassion and knowledge of the Self and enjoy Eternal Bliss and Immortality."

(*Santi Parva, Section VI*)

THE CAT AND THE MOUSE

There was a large banyan tree in the midst of a vast forest. A wise mouse named Palita lived at the foot of the tree. Here also lived a cat named Lomasa on the branches of the tree. One day the cat was caught in a snare spread by a hunter named Parigha. When the cat—the enemy of the mouse—was caught in the net, the mouse, Palita came out of the hole and moved about joyfully without any fear. It began to eat the flesh which the hunter had spread about there as a lure. While he was eating the meat, he saw a mongoose named Harita. The mongoose was getting ready to devour the mouse. The mouse saw also an owl named Chandrak sitting on a branch of the banyan tree. The mouse was greatly alarmed at the sight of his two enemies, the mongoose and the owl.

Now the mouse reflected within himself thus: "There is danger for me on all sides. There is fear in every direction. Death itself is staring me in the face. At such a perilous moment how should one act? One should certainly save one's life by warding off the dangers by all means. I have got three enemies now who are ready to pounce upon me. If the cat frees himself from the net, he is sure to devour me. An intelligent and wise man who has knowledge of the 'science of diplomacy', never sinks in despair however great and formidable may be the danger that threatens him. Three enemies are surrounding me now. How should I now act to save my life? At this juncture, I ought to make friendship with the cat, though he is my enemy. He is in great distress now. If I help him now, he may make peace with me. The wise declare that a person should make peace with even an enemy when he is attacked by another common enemy and his own life is in danger. I should make the cat understand his own interests. By making friendship with the cat I can escape from all the three. It is better to have a learned and wise man for an enemy than a fool for a friend. My life now rests entirely in the hands of my enemy, the cat. I shall suggest to the cat my plans for his liberation."

The intelligent mouse was well versed in diplomacy. He knew quite well when war should be declared and when peace should be made. He said to the cat: "O cat! How do you do? Thou art my friend. I am thy comrade. Do not be afraid. I shall rescue you if you do not kill me. I have hit upon a plan. This will save both our lives. You cannot come out of the net without my help. I shall cut the net with my teeth in no time if you solemnly promise that you will not kill me. Let us love each other. Let us be united now. You should trust me and I should trust you. He who never trusts another and is not trusted is seldom praised by men of wisdom. Such a person is unhappy and miserable. There is no use attempting to escape when the opportunity has slipped away. Now is the proper time for a right understanding between us. I earnestly wish you should live and I am sure you also wish that I live. Our mutual agreement will surely bring happiness and joy to both of us. I shall rescue you and you in turn must rescue me." Palita spoke these convincing words of wisdom to Lomasa and waited anxiously for a favourable reply.

Lomasa replied: "O my dear Palita! I am immensely pleased with thee. Thou art my amiable friend indeed. I am all the more delighted with thee as thou now evincest an interest in my welfare. I am really in great distress and so art thou. Let us be united now. If you set me free I shall rescue you from your dangers. I am at thy service."

Palita said: "Your reply is really very encouraging. Save me now from the mongoose and the owl. They are intent on killing me. I will lie beneath your body. Do not kill me. I shall cut the noose that entangles you with my sharp teeth in the twinkling of an eye. Believe me, my beloved friend; I swear by Truth, my dear Lomasa."

Lomasa replied: "O Palita! Thou art very dear to me. Come, come, quick! Through thy assurance I have almost got back my life. Let there be peace between us now. I shall really serve thee. I am thy obedient servant and friend. I shall worship and honour thee always in return for thy services. He who does good to others is eulogised by the wise, the man who does abundant services in return for good done to him can never equal the person who does him good in the first instance. The former repays for the services he has received, while the latter serves voluntarily. I assure you solemnly, my beloved Palita, that I shall, with all my friends and relatives, do all that will be agreeable and beneficial to thee."

The mouse hid itself under the body of the cat. The mongoose and the owl realised that the mouse and the cat were closely united with each other and so they would not be able to devour the mouse. They both left the place quickly and repaired to their respective abodes.

Palita came out and began to cut the strings of the net slowly. The cat became impatient and said: "How is it, my friend, that you are cutting the strings very very slowly? You are saved now. Since your object has been accomplished, your avowed interest in me has slackened. Cut these strings quickly. The hunter may come at any moment."

The wise mouse replied: "Be not worried. Do not be afraid, my friend, wait a bit. Be patient. Every action should be at its proper time. Then only it will produce good results. If you were freed at an improper time, my life would be in danger. I will be afraid of you. The moment I perceive the hunter, I shall cut the strings. At that particular moment you will ascend the tree and will not think of anything else except the safety of your life. I shall also enter my hole at the foot of the tree."

The cat said: "O my amiable friend, mouse Palita! I saved your life with considerable promptness. In the same manner you should also do everything quickly for me. Delay is dangerous. You must be honest in your dealings. You must keep your promise. If you think only of your former hostility and postpone your promised help, you will be doing immense harm to me. If I have done you wrong, you should forget and forgive."

The mouse replied: "Listen to me, my friend! In this world people are united out of selfish motives. Persons become friends for achieving some object. There is no suspicion in the friendship of magnanimous souls. If there is fear in friendship and if the friendship cannot be kept up without fear, that friendship should be maintained with great caution like the hands of a snake-charmer from the poisonous fangs of the snake. If a weak man makes compact with a strong man, he should always be on the alert. Otherwise the compact will do him more harm than good. No one pays any heed to the person who helps in a difficult time after the occasion is over. Therefore some portion of the act should always be left undone. If I free you when the hunter is coming, then the moment I set you free, you will run away to save your life on account of the fear of the hunter and you will have no thought of devouring me. Just see this net. I have cut all the strings save one. I will cut this one string also as soon as I behold the hunter. Meanwhile rest in peace, my dear Lomasa!"

The hunter Parigha came to the spot in the early morning accompanied by a pack of dogs. The cat was extremely frightened. He said to the mouse: "What will you do now?" The intelligent mouse cut the string immediately. The cat was thus freed from the noose. He ran quickly and ascended the banyan tree. The mouse also immediately entered his hole. The hunter was disappointed and returned to his house.

The cat now addressed the mouse: "My amiable friend! How is it you have suddenly run away without talking to me further? I trust you do not suspect me of any evil intention. I am very grateful to you for the most valuable service you have rendered me. You have saved my life. We are friends now. We should enjoy the sweetness of friendship. I shall honour and worship you, so also all my friends and relations. You are my friend, father, counsellor and the lord of my body and home. Take possession of all my wealth. He who forgets his friend after receiving favours from him is a wicked person. He fails in enlisting the help of friends at times of danger and need. Do not be afraid of me in the least, I swear by my life, my amiable comrade Palita. Believe me. Believe me."

The mouse gave a very intelligent reply. He spoke very sweetly: "Look here, my dear Lomasa! This is a mysterious world. People become friends and enemies from consideration of gain and loss. Self-interest plays a very prominent part. Self-interest is very powerful. It can turn a friend into an enemy in no time and an enemy also into a friend. There is no such thing in existence as a friend or an enemy. Force of circumstances creates friends and enemies. One should carefully examine and study one's friends and enemies; but it is the most difficult thing in this world. Even people of great intelligence fail in this respect. Friends put on the guise of enemies. Enemies also assume the guise of friends. When friendship is formed between two parties, it is difficult to determine whether the other party has selfish motives or not. One takes another as friend so long as he helps one, so long as one's interests are ensured. The moment the interests clash, the other man becomes an enemy. Such is the world. There is no such thing as a permanent friend or foe.

"One should not trust a person who is not deserving of trust. There is great danger in trusting a man blindly. The beings of this world are moved by the desire of gain in some form or other. People look to their own interests only. This is a world of self-interest.

"If a man who is saved from some danger, tries to seek the happiness of the helper, and if the latter is his natural enemy, he will be caught in the clutches of that enemy. His chances of escape are few. O Lomasa! You are a foolish person. That is the reason why you were caught in the net of the hunter. Such a man cannot protect himself. Then how can he protect others? He is bound to fail in all his attempts. He ruins himself.

"You told me that I am very dear to you. One becomes dear for an adequate cause. One also becomes an enemy for the same reason. One never becomes dear to another without a motive. Remember this point well. The friendship between persons depends upon interest. I do not know of any kind of friendship, love or affection between any two persons that does not depend upon some self-interest or gain.

"One becomes dear to another for his good nature, or for his spirit of service, or for his learning. Generally, a person becomes dear to another for the help he has received. The love between us arose from an adequate cause. That cause exists no longer and automatically that love between us has come to an end. I am very dear to you now because you wish to eat me. I am fully aware of this. You seek your own interest. The circumstances under which peace or war is declared are changed as quickly as the clouds change their form. You are my enemy by nature. You became my friend when your life was in danger.

You are my enemy again. That interim friendship has now vanished. The old state of enmity has returned.

"Why should I fall into the net that is spread for me by you? You have served me. I have served you. I am weak. You are strong. I understand you fully well. I know that you are hungry. You want to make a meal of me. We cannot have any lasting friendship. You are praising me in order that you may succeed in your object of eating me. I cannot agree to your proposal. I do not wish to prolong our friendship. No sane rat will place himself under a cat who is unrighteous, who is hungry and who is in search of prey. O beloved Lomasa! Be happy! I will presently leave you. I am afraid to look at you even from a distance. When I wander about carelessly, you can protect me. This will also be an act of gratitude. A weak person should not dwell in the vicinity of another who is endowed with strength and power. Even if the danger has passed away, I should always entertain fear of one who is more powerful than myself.

"I shall certainly give you everything except my life. One should sacrifice one's all—one's dominion, property, etc.—for the sake of protecting one's own self. If he survives, he may get back all the mundane things he has sacrificed."

The cat replied: "O my dear friend Palita! Do not suspect me like this. I swear; I will not injure you. You are my beloved comrade as you have saved my life. I am prepared to lay down my very life in your service. I know my duty. It is not good for you to take me for what I am not."

The mouse reflected a little and said: "O my friend, Lomasa! Thou art extremely good. Thank you very much indeed for all the kindness shown. However, I cannot place any confidence in you. You cannot tempt me to retain friendship with you either by praising me or by offering gifts. A wise man should not place himself under the power of his enemy. A weak man should not place himself under the power of a strong man. I have already told you that one should never trust a man who does not deserve to be trusted. One should never place trust in one's enemies. The basic truth of all treaties is distrust. Distrust produces highest good. If weak people would only distrust strong people, the latter cannot get them in their power. O cat, one like myself should always be on the guard against persons like you. If you are wise, you also will protect your life from the hunter, Parigha."

While the mouse spoke thus, the cat got frightened at the mention of the hunter. He left the branch of the tree and ran away in all haste. Wise Palita who was endowed with knowledge of the science of diplomacy entered his hole peacefully, after exhibiting his power of understanding and wisdom.

Bhishma said: "O Yudhishthira! The mouse Palita, though weak and alone, succeeded in combating against his powerful enemies by reason of his wisdom. The mouse and the cat saved their lives owing to their reliance upon each other's services.

"If two persons who were once enemies make a compact with each other before a common danger, it is certain that each of them has in his heart the subjugation of the other. A man of wisdom and discretion succeeds in bringing the other in his power. A careless and thoughtless man is easily subdued by the wise and cautious.

"When one is in fear he should appear to be fearless. One should seem to be trustful while really mistrusting others. Such a man is never ruined. One should make peace with an enemy or wage war as occasion arises.

"You have listened to the story of the 'Cat and the Mouse'. Now act wisely. Learn the difference between friend and foe and the proper time for war and peace. Thus you can save yourself when you are in danger. Make peace with one who is powerful in the face of common danger. You should be very careful in continuing it with your enemy after the common danger has passed away. You should not trust your enemy again after you have gained your object.

"O King Yudhishthira! Protect your subjects! Attain prosperity! Be guided by the *Brahmanas* and the Scriptures. Brahmanas are teachers of duty and morality. They are wise persons. Worship them. They will do you good. Thus, you will obtain kingdom, fame and great achievements. Remember always the story of the 'Cat and the Mouse' and conduct yourself in the midst of your foes accordingly."

(*Santi Parva, Section CXXXVIII*)

THE PIOUS CAT

If one conceals one's evil actions, if his standard of righteousness is always unsteady like a piece of straw or cotton floating in the air, his conduct is certainly similar to that of the cat whose story is narrated by *Deva Rishi* Narada.

Once upon a time, a wicked lazy cat went to the bank of the Ganga and stood there with upraised hands. It pretended to be very pious and devotional. In order to inspire confidence in the surrounding animals and birds, it proclaimed: "I shall practise penance and virtue." The innocent birds assembled together and praised the cat. The cat then reflected thus: "I have now achieved my object. I have realised now the fruit of my pretended devotion."

The practising of virtue and rigorous penance by the cat was witnessed by the mice of the locality. They discussed between themselves: "We have many enemies. We will regard this holy cat as our maternal uncle. It will surely protect all of us, young and old." They approached the cat with reverence and said: "Through your grace and help, we wish to roam about care-free. You are pious. You are doing severe austerities. You have developed much devotion. You are virtuous and noble. You are our sole prop and refuge. You are our best friend and guide. We all place ourselves under your benign protection. Protect us."

The cunning cat replied: "I do not see any connection between my penance and my protecting you but I shall try to do you good. You should all obey me. You should follow my advice implicitly. On account of practice of rigid austerities, I am physically weak now but I will stick to my resolve. I cannot move about now. My beloved friends, you will escort me everyday to the river side. I will take fresh air. My health will improve quickly."

The mice said: "Very well, sir, since you are to protect all of us, we will obey you implicitly and carry out your instructions." The wicked cat began to feed on the mice every day and began to grow fat and strong. The number of mice decreased steadily.

The mice assembled and pondered: "Our pious and virtuous maternal uncle is growing fat day by day but our numbers are diminishing quickly. What is at the bottom of this?"

Dindika, the wisest among the mice, said: "You all go together in advance to the river side. I shall accompany our maternal uncle." All other mice highly appreciated the words of wisdom uttered by Dindika and acted according to the suggestion.

The wicked cat ate up Dindika also that day. It had a sumptuous meal. Then the mice re-assembled. One of the oldest mice named Kilika said: "This wretched cat, our maternal uncle, is a cut-throat. Do not believe this cat any more. It is only pretending to be virtuous and pious. It is like a tiger in the garb of a cow. Our maternal uncle is not at all practising any virtue and penance. We all have been totally deceived by its external appearance. Its desire is not to practise penance. It is only a pretence. We should be vigilant and cautious henceforward at least. The excreta of a cat subsisting on roots and fruits cannot contain hair. Its body is growing fat day by day and our number is decreasing daily. Moreover our Dindika too is not to be seen these days. This wretched cat is not certainly living on roots and fruits. It subsists on our members only."

All the mice heard the wise words of Kilika and ran away immediately. The wicked cat also went to its own abode.

Many people in this world behave just as the cat behaved to the mice. Their words mean one thing while their actions are quite different. They do not say what they mean nor mean what they say. Some talk at great length on philosophy, the Gita and the Upanishads. They deliver lectures but their actions are not consistent with their speech. The public is deceived by such people. Some pose to be pious. They wear many *Tulsi Malas* or *Rudraksha Malas* around their neck, grow long beard and matted locks and utter '*Siva, Siva*', '*Hare Rama*', '*Hare Krishna*,' but their actions belie their words. Just as the mind of a vulture is ever fixed on the flesh, though it soars very high in the sky, so also the minds of these people are fixed on sensual enjoyments in spite of their lengthy discourses on piety. Do not be deceived like the mice in the story by external appearances. Do not be carried away by prostrations and crocodile tears. Watch the actions, speeches and behaviour of such persons minutely. Judge them correctly after due reflection and mature deliberation.

(Ulukadutagamana of the Udyoga Parva, Ch. CLX-160)

THE THREE FISH

Bhishma said: O King Yudhishthira! He who provides for the future and he who is endowed with the presence of mind always enjoys happiness. He who is given to procrastination is lost. Listen to this interesting story attentively.

In a small shallow lake which abounded with fish, there lived three *Sakula* fish. They were intimate friends. One of them had much forethought. He always liked to provide for the future. Another was endowed with great presence of mind. The third was a procrastinator.

One day a fisherman came to the lake and tried to empty the water through various channels. The fish that had foresight said to his two friends: "There is immediate danger for us. Let us quickly move to some other place. He who takes measures against future evil with a wise policy never meets with any serious calamity or danger. Listen to my advice. Be vigilant and cautious now. Let us all leave this place immediately."

The fish who was a procrastinator said: "Friend! your advice is really good. You are doubtless wise. There is, however, no need for such haste. This is my opinion. You are unnecessarily alarmed."

The third fish said: "When the time comes, I shall act with great presence of mind."

The fish who had forethought immediately moved along the current of water and reached another deep lake.

After draining the water in the lake the fisherman began to catch the fish. The procrastinating *Sakula* was caught with many others. The fisherman tied them to a long string. The *Sakula* who possessed presence of mind thrust himself into the company of those that had been tied and remained quietly among them biting the string. The fisherman thought that all the fish attached to the string had been caught. Afterwards he carried the fish to another lake which contained deep water for washing them. Just as that time the *Sakula* which possessed presence of mind left the string and quickly escaped. The procrastinating *Sakula* was unable to escape and met with his death.

Thus every one who procrastinates, like the procrastinating fish, meets with destruction. The *Rishis* and sages have pronounced that the man of forethought and the man of presence of mind are the best of men.

He who does everything after deep thinking and scrutiny succeeds in attaining the object. He who acts with due regard to time and place succeeds in achieving result better than the man of forethought and the man of presence of mind.

(Santi Parva, Ch. 137)

THE FOOLISH CAMEL

Yudhishthira said: O Venerable Lord! What acts should a king do by performing which he may become happy? Enlighten me in detail on this point. You are endowed with the knowledge of everything. You are perfectly conversant with the duties of a king.

Bhishma said: O my beloved Yudhishthira! Kindly hearken with rapt attention to the story of the camel. There was a huge camel in the *Krita* age. It could recollect all the actions of its former life. It observed rigid vows and practised severe austerities in the forest. Brahma was very much pleased with its penance. He appeared before the camel and said: "Ask any boon and it shall be granted."

The camel said: "O Lord! Grant this boon. Let my neck become long enough so that I may catch any food that may lie at the end of even a hundred *Yojanas*."

Brahma said: "Be it so."

After getting the boon, the camel lived in the forest. It became very idle from the day it obtained the boon from the Lord. It did not go out for grazing at all. It extended its long neck anywhere up to a hundred *Yojanas* and obtained food without any exertion. One day there was a great storm. The camel placed its head and a portion of the neck within the cave of a mountain and waited till the storm abated. There was very heavy rain. So it could not obtain its food. It had to starve. A jackal that was drenched by rain entered the cave in which the camel had placed its head and neck. It was very hungry. It began to eat as much of the neck of the camel as it could. The camel in vain endeavoured to shorten its neck. But the jackal continued to eat the neck of the camel with great avidity and joy. The camel died in the end. The jackal had a good meal that day. The rain ceased and the jackal came out of the cave joyfully. Thus did the camel meet with its death on account of its foolishness.

O Yudhishthira! Mark! What disastrous results accrue to one who leads a life of sloth and idleness! Therefore, abandon idleness. Subdue the senses. Use your intelligence. Do everything in this world with intelligence. Then alone you will succeed in achieving all desired objects. Manu himself has said that one becomes victorious with the help of intelligence. Those who listen to the counsels of wise persons and act after proper scrutiny, reflection and mature deliberation always succeed in achieving all their objects. Exercise your intelligence and act in this world. Be happy, O King.

(Santi Parva, Section CXII)

THE JACKAL AND THE APE

Yudhishthira said: O Grandsire! May I know the end of those wicked persons who do not give after having promised to give?

Bhishma said: The hopes of a man who does not give after making a promise become fruitless like the hopes of a *eunuch* in respect of progeny. Just listen, O King, to the old discourse between a jackal and an ape. They were intimate friends when they were both human beings. After death one of them became a jackal and the other an ape. The ape saw the jackal one day eating the carcass of a beast. He then remembered his own and his friend's former births as human beings. The ape said to the jackal: "Friend, what terrible sins did you commit in your previous birth in consequence of which you are forced to eat the carcass of an animal?"

The jackal replied: "I made a promise to give a gift unto a *Brahmana*. I did not make him the gift. It is for that sin I have taken the birth of a jackal and I eat the carcass of an animal."

The jackal said: "O friend ape! What sin did you commit in your previous birth in consequence of which you have become what you are?"

The ape replied: "In my former life I used to appropriate the fruits belonging to *Brahmanas*. That is the reason why I have become an ape."

Therefore it is clear that one should never appropriate what belongs to *Brahmanas* or to others. If anyone makes a promise to give something to a man, he should certainly make the promised gift unto him. O King, I heard this from my preceptor. I heard this from Krishna also. Gift is the highest form of action. By giving gifts to a *Brahmana*, the deities and the ancestors are pleased. Therefore one should ever make gifts to the *Brahmanas*.

Be slow to make a promise but be quick to carry it out. He who breaks his promise will be treated with contempt. People will have no confidence in such a man. He who keeps up to his promise is honoured by the people. Celestial regions are reserved for him.

THE OCEAN AND THE RIVERS

Yudhishthira said: O, Venerable Grandsire! Tell me how a king should behave towards a powerful enemy?

Bhishma said: Just listen to the discourse between the ocean and the rivers. You will get a solution to your problem.

The Ocean said: "Ye rivers! All of you bring to me trunks of large trees. You root them out with branches and leaves. But you do not ever bring a cane! May I know the reason for this?"

The River Ganga said: "The trees resist our currents. They do not bend. They are proud. They are unyielding. They do not know to move with the time and to adapt themselves to circumstances. On account of this disposition they are uprooted and washed away by our current. But the cane behaves in quite a different manner. It sees the advancing current and bends to it. After the current passes away, it resumes its former position. It is humble. It is yielding. It adjusts itself to time and tide. Therefore it stands in its own place. We are not able to root it out. Further we do not wish to do any harm to those that are humble, obedient and yielding. We like the cane for its good qualities. We destroy the big trees as they are arrogant and proud of their might and strength."

He who does not yield to a powerful enemy competent to imprison or kill him meets with destruction quickly like the big trees. Whereas the wise man who acts prudently after judging fully his own strength and weakness and that of his adversary rarely undergoes any trouble or suffering. When a wise man realises that his enemy is more powerful than himself, he behaves like the cane. This is certainly an indication of wisdom. He who adapts himself to circumstances and conditions always attains success and prosperity.

(Santi Parva, Chapter 113).

THE SALMALI TREE

Yudhishthira said: O Grandfather! If a weak and worthless person provokes a powerful neighbour who is ever on the alert, by his insolent and boastful speeches, how should the former act when the latter gets angry and proceeds to destroy him?

Bhishma said: Just listen to the old discourse between *Salmali* and *Pavana*. There was a very huge tree (Salmali) on one of the peaks of the Himalayas. He stood like a lord of trees in the forest. He had spread out his branches wide around. His branches and leaves were countless. He existed for many centuries. Elephants and many other animals used to rest under his shade. The circumference of his trunk was 400 cubits. Various kinds of birds had their abode in this magnificent tree. He was loaded with flowers and fruits. Ascetics, pilgrims and traders used to rest under the shade of that king of trees.

One day *Deva Rishi* Narada approached the tree and said: "O *Salmali*, king of all trees! I am delighted at the sight of thee. Thou art very charming and graceful. I do not see any of thy branches broken by *Pavana*, the Wind God. Is it because he is pleased with thee? Is he thy amiable friend? I think *Pavana* protects thee through *Prem* and love. *Pavana* is a mighty God. He destroys even the tallest and strongest trees. He dries up the rivers, lakes and seas. He moves even the summits of mountains. He destroys huge mansions and big palatial buildings. Thy proximity resembles heaven itself. Ascetics, Yogis and sages practise meditation under thy shade. Birds rest peacefully in thy branches and sing melodiously."

Narada continued: "O *Salmali! Pavana* certainly likes thee immensely. There is doubtless close affinity between thee and the Wind God. Thou hast apparently told him: 'I am thine'. That is why he protects thee."

The *Salmali* replied: "O Venerable *Rishi*! The Wind is neither my friend nor well-wisher, nor ordainer that he should protect me. I am more powerful than the Wind God! His strength is about only an eighteenth part of mine! When he comes in a rage, uprooting trees, I attack him and resist his strength with my power. He cannot certainly stand against me. On the other hand he is terribly afraid of me. He has been curbed by me several times. I am not afraid of him in the least."

Narada said: "O *Salmali!* Your understanding is perverted. You brag too much. You are nothing before the Wind God. Even *Indra, Yama* or *Varuna* is not equal to the God of Wind in strength. You are only an ordinary tree. *Pavana* gives life and Prana to all creatures. All beings find ease and comfort when the wind blows. You are haughty and arrogant. You speak ill of a mighty God who should be worshipped. You are speaking at random. I am displeased with you. I shall myself report to the Wind God about your insolent and contemptuous speech. Even

Sandal trees, *Salas, Devadarus, Sanalas, Syndanas, Vetasas* and *Dhanvanas* that are far stronger than you have never uttered such invectives against the *Vayu*. They all bow down their heads in humble submission. They are fully aware of the might of the Wind God. You do not realise the infinite power and strength of the wind on account of your vanity and perverted mentality. I shall presently go to the Wind God and report your contempt for him."

Narada repaired to the Wind God and represented unto him all that the *Salmali* had boasted. Narada said: "There is a huge tree *Salmali* on one of the heights of the *Himavat* (Himalayas). He is charming and beautiful. He is adorned with countless branches, flowers and fruits. That tree is extremely proud. He treats thee with contempt. He censures thee. It is not proper, O Wind, to repeat them in your presence."

The God of Wind immediately repaired to the spot where *Salmali* stood and addressed him in great rage: "O *Salmali*! You have spoken ill of me before Narada. You have treated me with contempt. I know you well. Know that I am the mighty God of Wind. Up to this time I had a soft corner for you in my heart, because *Brahma* took rest under you while engaged in creating the Universe. I have hitherto shown you grace on account of this incident. It is for this alone that thou standest here unharmed and not on account of thy own might. I will crush thee now. Be prepared for my attack."

The *Salmali* replied: "What can you do to me by showing your temper, O Wind? I am not at all afraid of you. I am superior to you in might. Remember this point well. He who is possessed of strong understanding is really strong. He who is endowed with physical strength alone cannot be regarded as strong."

The Wind God said: "Beware. Do not brag too much. Be on the alert. I shall test thy strength tomorrow."

Salmali reflected within himself: "All that I said to Narada is false; I am undoubtedly inferior in might to the Wind. Truly he is very strong and powerful. Verily I am weaker than other trees. But no tree is equal to me in intelligence. I shall use my intelligence now to save myself."

The *Salmali* therefore caused all his branches leaves and flowers to be cut off. In the morning he looked steadily at the Wind when he marched towards him. The Wind was filled with immense joy. He said: "O *Salmali*, thou art now divested of thy proud top, branches, leaves and flowers. I would have done thee exactly what thou hast done to thyself by cutting off all thy branches. Thou hast been brought under my power on account of thy own perverted understanding and vanity. Do not boast. Be careful in future."

Bhishma said: The *Salmali* was very much ashamed. He repented very much for his folly.

Even thus, O Yudhishthira, a weak and foolish man is at last forced to repent like the *Salmali* in the story by provoking a powerful man. Though one may possess equal might, he should not wage war with another without fore-thought. He should show his might mildly and gradually. Just as fire penetrates a heap of dry grass, so also the intelligence of a clever man penetrates the person upon whom it is directed. Intelligence is the most precious possession that a man can acquire.

Likewise a man can have nothing here more precious than might. Just as one overlooks the acts of a child, so also one should overlook the wrongs done by a man of superior strength.

(Santi Parva, Sec. CLIV-CLVII)

PART II

KING YAYATI

Emperor Yayati was the son of Nahusha. Yayati had five sons—Yadu, Turvasu, Druhyu, Anu and Puru. He ruled over his subjects in a righteous manner for many years. At last when overcome with old age, he called his eldest son Yadu and spoke to him: "O Child! old age, wrinkles and white hair have come over to me. But I have not yet got over the longings of youth. O Yadu! take upon yourself my decrepitude and consequent old age in exchange for your youth. I shall then enjoy the pleasures with your youth. When one thousand years will be completed I shall return to you your youth and take back my decrepitude and its consequent weakness."

Yadu replied: "O venerable father, there are many inconveniences in old age in regard to eating and drinking. Therefore, O King! I shall not take your decrepitude upon me. This is my determination. White hair, cheerlessness, wrinkles all over the body, deformities, infirmities, inability to work are the consequences of decrepitude. Even friends and dependents forsake an old decrepit man."

His other sons Turvasu, Druhyu, Anu also did not agree to exchange their youth for their father's old age. The youth Puru told Yayati: "O Great King! I shall do as you command me. I shall take upon myself your old age and its consequences. Take my youth and enjoy the pleasures of life. At your command I shall assume your old age and occupy the throne."

Yayati said: "My child! I am much pleased with you. I grant you with great willingness the following boon. The people of your kingdom will have their desires fulfilled." Yayati remembered the great ascetic Sukra and transfered his decrepitude to the body of the high-souled Puru.

Yayati became a youth of Puru's age. Puru took Yayati's age and governed the kingdom. Yayati was extremely delighted. He again plunged into the pleasures of life. He enjoyed life a long time. He enjoyed himself to the utmost extent; yet he was not satisfied. Then he spoke:

"O son! desires never die. They are never satisfied by indulgence. By indulgence they flame up like the sacrificial fire fed with ghee. If one becomes the sole lord of all the earth with its paddy, oats, gems, beasts and women, still it will not be enough for him. Therefore wisdom lies in the thirst for enjoyment being abandoned. The thirst for enjoyment, which is not quenched even as the power to enjoy is reduced, is verily a fatal disease in man. To get rid of this thirst is to achieve real happiness. My mind was immersed in the pleasures of the senses for full one thousand years. Yet my thirst for them has not abated. On the other hand it is increasing daily. Therefore I shall renounce this craving and fix my mind on *Brahman*. Devoid of attachment I shall pass the rest of my days peacefully in the forest with the innocent deer. O Puru! I am extremely delighted with you. Take back your own youth. May you prosper! Take this kingdom also! You are the only son whose conduct has pleased me."

Yayati then received back his own old age and his son Puru also got back his youth. Yayati gave the kingdom to Puru and lived for a long time in the forest. He lived on fruits and roots and attained self-control and peace. His fame spread far and wide. At last he reached *Svarga*, the abode of the gods. He lived in heaven for a long time.

Sensual enjoyments cannot give satisfaction. One can never become satiated with sensual pleasures. Enjoyment aggravates the desires, just as ghee, when poured into the fire, aggravates the flame. The more one indulges in sensual pleasures, the greater the desires grow. Renunciation alone leads to peace and happiness. The *Srutis* emphatically declare, "Not by work, not by progeny, not by wealth, but by renunciation alone, one attains peace and *Brahman*." Whenever you are tormented by passion, remember the story of Yayati and his words. You will attain solace and peace of mind. Dispassion and discrimination will dawn in your mind.

The great king Yayati once happened to go to Indra. Indra said: "O King, after accomplishing all your duties you retired to the forest, leaving your home. You practised austerities. Tell me with whom you can compare in ascetic merits?"

Yayati replied: "O Indra! I do not find among men, the celestials, the *Gandharvas*, great *Rishis* and sages, any one equal to me in austerity."

Indra said: "O King! You disregard your superiors, equals and inferiors without knowing their merits. Your virtues will, therefore, suffer a diminution and you will fall from heaven."

Thereupon Yayati fell from heaven. He was seen thus falling by that royal sage Ashtaka, the protector of religion.

Ashtaka said: "Who are you, young man, effulgent like fire, dropping down from the intense darkness of the rain cloud? We have all come to meet you and ascertain the truth about your downfall."

Yayati said: "I am Yayati, the son of Nahusha and the father of Puru. I am falling down from the region of the celestials, the *Siddhas* and the *Rishis*, for the diminution of my virtues. I am falling because I slighted every creature in the Universe. I have come to this plane, where you offer sacrifices, guided by the sacrificial fire."

Ashtaka said: "O Yayati, do not fall down. I bestow on you those high abodes which are mine. Ascend to them quickly. Get on the chariot and go to heaven."

Madhavi, daughter of Yayati, a Tapasvini, who was walking near the sacrifice saw her father come back to the earth. She said to her sons: "Listen, my children! Why has my father, who has attained great fame, come here in this manner?" One of her sons said: "Mother! he has been banished from heaven."

Madhavi told her father: "Accept the gift of those worlds which are mine, which are won by my rigorous penances. Ascend to the heaven by virtue of our austerity."

Yayati said: "I have been saved by the Tapas of my daughter and my daughter's sons. Let us all now go together to heaven."

All the princes ascended their chariots. By virtue of their Dharma all reached heaven. King Yayati was saved by the sons of his daughter. He reached heaven filling the earth and sky with the glory of his meritorious deeds.

Vanity is a vice which leads to hell. Humility is the greatest of all virtues. It brings eternal happiness. Vanity leads to downfall and destruction. A proud man is treated by people with contempt. Yayati had a set back on account of his pride.

Devotion and obedience to parents are the highest virtues. They bring great merits. Parents are visible gods on earth. Srutis declare, '*Matri devo bhava*—let your mother be your God, *Pitri devo bhava*—let your father be your God.' How devoted and obedient Puru, the son of Yayati, was to his father. He even took upon himself the infirmities of old age to please his father. Madhavi and her sons helped Yayati to regain lost heaven.

(Adi Parva, Ch. 69-93)

KING SIBI AND THE PIGEON

The story of Sibi is told by sage Lomasa to Yudhishthira when in the course of their pilgrimage the Pandavas came to the place of the confluence of the Yamuna with the tributaries, Jala and Upajala. Here, king Sibi, while performing a sacrifice, was tested by Indra and Agni.

One day the celestials resolved that they should go to the earth-plane and try the virtues of king Sibi. Agni and Indra went to the kingdom of Sibi (known also as Ushinara), to the spot where Sibi was performing a sacrifice.

Agni assumed the form of a pigeon, Indra took the form of a hawk and chased the pigeon. The pigeon fell on the lap of king Sibi for protection. It was almost dead with fright.

The hawk said: "All the kings of the earth call you virtuous. I am tormented by severe hunger. I want to eat this pigeon now. Do not think that you will gain virtue by saving the life of this pigeon. Pray, do not hinder me from eating my ordained food."

The king said: "O hawk! This little bird is trembling with fear. It has come to me for protection. It is not proper for me to forsake it. He who kills a *Brahmana* or a cow and he who forsakes one who seeks his protection both commit equal sin.

He does not get protection when he is in need of it. The clouds do not shower rain for him in season. The seeds, though sown, do not grow for him. The gods refuse to accept his libations of ghee into the sacrificial fire. The ancestors of such a man can never reside in heaven."

The hawk said: "O king! All creatures subsist on food. A man can live many days even after abandoning his dear and near ones, but he cannot live long after abstaining food. O king! my life will depart today, if I do not appease my hunger. If I die, my wife and children too will perish. By protecting the pigeon, you will be the cause of destroying many lives. The virtue which stands in the way of another virtue is really unrighteous. That only is the real virtue which does not conflict. After comparing the opposing virtues and weighing their pros and cons, one ought to embrace that which is absolute. One should adopt that virtue which does not conflict with others.

"That Dharma which injures many is not Dharma at all. It is wicked conduct. That action which does not conflict with another righteous action is Dharma. If the actions conflict with one another, one must consider which is weightier and wherein no injury is done and adopt that as Dharma."

The king said: "O bird! Why do you regard it virtuous to forsake one who has sought my protection? You want only food. I am perfectly willing to procure for you any sort of delicious food, whether it be an ox, or a boar, or a deer, or a buffalo."

The hawk said: "I do not want to eat a boar, or an ox, or any other kind of beast. Give me, therefore, this pigeon which is the food ordained for me by nature. Hawks eat pigeons. This is ordained and an eternal law. Do not climb a plantain tree without knowing its strength to support you."

The king said: "O bird! I am willing to give you this kingdom and all the wealth and also all that you wish to have. I will give up my own life but I will not give up this pigeon."

The hawk said: "If you have so much affection for the pigeon, then give me as much flesh from your body as would be equal in weight to the pigeon. Then you would do what would be agreeable to me and at the same time your subjects will praise and bless you in joy."

The king said: "I regard this, O excellent bird, a special favour that you should ask this of me. Therefore I shall this day give you my flesh, weighing it in the scale."

Thereupon the king who knew the highest Dharma cut off a piece of flesh and weighed it against the pigeon, but the pigeon weighed heavier. He cut off another piece of flesh, but still the pigeon weighed heavier. Then he cut off pieces of flesh from all parts of his body and placed them on the scale, but the pigeon still weighed heavier. Thereupon the king himself got on the scale. He did not feel the least compunction for it.

The hawk said: "O virtuous king! You are wise in Dharma. I am Indra. The pigeon is Agni. We came to this place of sacrifice in order to test your virtues. As a result of your action in being prepared to sacrifice your own body, your glory will be resplendent. You are the foremost of men. These pieces of flesh that you have cut off from your body to save the pigeon have made deep open wounds in your body. I shall make those marks auspicious. They will be handsome, golden-coloured and sweet-scented. You will earn great and undying fame and will rule over your kingdom for a long time. Eternal region would be reserved for you. You will get out of your own body a son named Kapotaramana. He will be a hero. He will be very handsome. He will earn great fame."

Having said this to the king, Indra returned to heaven. King Sibi ruled the earth for a long time. He then went to heaven, retaining his mortal body.

What a magnanimous soul was Sibi! He was an embodiment of Dharma. He fulfilled his promise at the risk of his life. He had an extremely compassionate heart. To save the life of a pigeon, he cut off pieces of flesh from his own body. Dharma and mercy saved him, earned for him eternal fame and helped him to attain the eternal regions. He who sticks to Dharma and is merciful and he who fulfils his promise is adored by the gods. He surely attains Immortality and Eternal Bliss.

You should protect that man who has taken shelter under you. This is your Dharma. You will earn great merit like Sibi.

(Vana Parva, Ch. 197)

JAJALI AND TULADHARA

Once upon a time a Brahmin lived in a forest as a forest-recluse. His name was Jajali. He went on a certain occasion to the sea-shore and practised rigorous austerities. He observed many vows and restraints. He fasted. He had matted locks on his head. He observed vow of silence and practised Yoga and meditation. He used to live sometime within the waters of the sea. He was able to roam through all the worlds through his Yogic power and beheld everything he wished to see.

One day, he reflected within himself thus: "There is none equal to me in this world. Who can roam with me along with the stars and planets in the sky or dwell within the waters of the ocean?" The Rakshasas said to him: "Do not think like this, O Jajali. There is a famous man named Tuladhara who was a trader. Even he is not worthy of uttering such words as you say." Jajali said: "I shall certainly see that famous Tuladhara of great wisdom." Those Rakshasas raised him from the sea and said: "Go along this road."

Yudhishthira said: Kindly tell me, O Venerable Sir, what are those difficult penances which Jalali had performed in order to acquire such great powers?

Bhishma said: In summer he exposed himself to the sun and wind. In winter he remained under water. In the rains he slept under the canopy of the open sky. He used to sleep on various kinds of painful bed. He gave up food entirely for some time and lived on air alone. Sometimes he stood in the forest like a wooden post without stirring an inch. While he stood there like a post, a pair of birds built their nest in the matted locks of his head. The bird also laid eggs in the nest. The young ones also grew up in the nest. Jajali did not move even a bit. He left the place only after the birds and the young ones had vacated the nest.

Jajali thought that he had attained great ascetic success. Pride slowly entered his heart. He proclaimed loudly: "I have won great merits through my penance." Then an invisible voice arose in the sky: "O Jajali, do not get puffed up with pride. Thou art not equal to Tuladhara in righteousness. He is a man of great wisdom. He lives at Varanasi. Even he is not fit to say what thou sayest." Jajali bacame angry and proceeded towards the city of Varanasi and reached the place. He saw Tuladhara in his shop engaged in selling miscellaneous articles. Tuladhara stood up as soon as he saw the Brahmin and worshipped him with proper rites.

Tuladhara said: "You have performed severe penances. But you had no consciousness of having achieved righteousness or merit. Pride, however, penetrated your heart when you thought that you had attained great ascetic merits by standing in one place without moving an inch till the birds and young ones left the nest that was built in your matted locks. Then you heard a voice in the sky that referred to me. On hearing these words you became angry and so you have come to me. Tell me please, O venerable Brahmin, how could I serve you?"

Jajali said: "O Tuladhara, you are a *Vaishya*. You are a trader only. You sell all kinds of juice, scents, herbs and roots. How did you succeed in attaining wisdom or poised understanding?"

Tuladhara who had full knowledge of the fundamental principles of life, then talked to Jajali on the ways of morality: "O Jajali! I know morality which is eternal with all its mysteries. Morality consists of universal friendliness and beneficence to all creatures. One should not do any harm to any creature. This is the highest morality. Complete harmlessness should be practised. I practise this, O Jajali. I purchase scents, juices, etc., and sell them without cheating. I never quarrel with anyone. He who is always the friend of all creatures in thought, word and deed, knows morality or righteousness. I entertain no dislike or hatred for any one. Also I do not desire for anything. I have equal vision on all creatures. I neither praise nor blame the actions of others. I see no difference between a lump of earth, a block of stone and a lump of gold. I keep all my senses under perfect restraint. I have no relish for wealth or pleasure or enjoyments.

"If a person is absolutely fearless and does not cause fear to others, if he is freee from desires and if he has no aversion for anything, then he is one who has attained Brahman. If a person does not conduct himself sinfully towards any creature in thought, word or deed, then he has attained Brahman. I always follow the practices of sages and the rules laid down in the scriptures. If a person subdues his senses, practises harmlessness, treads the path of righteousness, adopts the conduct followed by high-souled men, he is sure to attain the final emancipation or deliverance from the rounds of births and deaths. He who practises universal harmlessness will enjoy whatever fruits one enjoys by austerities, sacrifices, charity and speaking the truth. It is very difficult to get oneself established in perfect harmlessness to others at once. It takes a long time. From the beginning, one should try to do as little as possible even in cases of necessity. Gradually if he keeps a careful watch over his conduct towards others, he will attain perfect success in the practice of harmlessness.

"He who practises the great vow of Ahimsa, obtains the merit of all the sacrifices. He becomes absolutely fearless. There is certainly no duty superior to the duty of refraining from injury to others. Of all the attainments, the assurance of harmlessness to all creatures is indeed of the highest form. I have neither liking nor dislike for anybody. He who praises me and he who injures me are one and the same to me."

Jajali said: "Your doctrine belong to the school of atheism. This world will come to an end if the means by which life is sustained have to be abandoned."

Tuladhara said: "I shall now speak on the subject of the means of subsistence. O Jajali! I am not an athiest. I do not speak ill of sacrifices. The man who truly possesses knowledge of sacrifices is extremely rare. My silent prostrations unto those who are truly conversant with sacrifice! The Brahmanas have abandoned the sacrifice that is prescribed for them. They perform the sacrifices that are ordained for Kshatriyas. Many greedy persons have no understanding and knowledge of the right significance of the declarations of the Srutis. They proclaim things that are really false. They have introduced many kinds of sacrifices in order to obtian wealth. They say: 'This should be given in this sacrifice. This sacrifice brings great fruits.' On account of this many evil practices have srung up. This is priest-craft. Priests obtain wealth in an illicit manner. This is another form of theft. The sacrificial offerings which are obtained by righteous means can propitiate the gods. Unrighteous persons get wicked offsprings. Greedy persons beget greedy children. Contented persons produce contented children. The oblations that are poured on the sacrificial fire, rise to the sun. From the sun comes rain. From the rain comes food. From food are born living beings.

"In days of yore men had intense faith in sacrifices. They were righteously devoted to sacrifices and so they obtained whatever they wished. The earth yielded crops without tillage. The blessings of Rishis and sages produced herbs and plants. In former days men never performed sacrifices from a desire for benefits. Those who perform sacrifices whithout faith and who do not believe in their efficacy take birth in their next lives as dishonest greedy men. Those who condemn scriptures and who do not follow the ordinances of the scriptures, who say that the scriptures contain some useless and evil things, go into the realms of the sinful. They do not attain peace and knowledge. If a man performs daily the obligatory acts which are prescribed in the scriptures as his duty, if he entertains fear when he fails to perfom them any day, if he thinks and feels that all the essentials of sacrifice are identical with Brahman, if he thinks and feels that he is not the actor, he is truly a Brahmana. If the acts of such a person become incomplete, even then those acts are highly efficacious. If those acts are performed with a desire of gaining some benefits and if impediments arise in their completion, then expiation would be necessary.

"Those who long for obtaining the final emancipation, who are free from greed, jealousy, who do not provide themselves for the future, who practise truth and self-restraint as their sacrifice, those who know the distinction between body and soul, who practise Yoga and contemplation on the Pranava or OM are able to please others. When a man who has attained knowledge of Brahman eats and is gratified, all the deities become gratified and contented. Knowledge of Brahman gives eternal satisfaction which is a source of perfect bliss for the knower or sage. The wise men who tread the path of righteousness, who take delight in righteousness who are the refuge of righteousness have definite knowledge of right and wrong, good and evil and what is to be done and what should not be done.

"They consider that all things of the universe have sprung from their own selves. Some who are dispassionate and are endowed with discrimination and faith try to reach the other shore of this ocean of life. They eventually succeed, through incessant meditation and purity, in attaining the immortal abode of Brahman, where there is neither pain nor sorrow, whence there is no return. Such men do not wish to obtain heaven, because heaven also is a place of sensuous enjoyment and is not an eternal abode. They do not worship Brahma by sacrifices. They perform sacrifices without injuring any creature. Herbs, fruits and roots are their only sacrificial offerings. Greedy priests do not officiate at the sacrifices of these men. These virtuous persons have done all acts and perform sacrifices in order to do good to all creatures. They pour their own selves as sacrificial offerings. They perform sacrifice of wisdom. They do mental sacrifices. The greedy priests officiate at the sacrifices of only those misguided persons who do not wish to attain the final emancipation, but who wish to attain heaven. Those who perform sacrifices from desire of fruit, return to this earth from the region which they reach. Those wise persons who do sacrifices without desire for fruit do not return again to the world of death.

"He who has abandoned all desires for fruit, who rests in his own inner Self, who never praises others, who keeps an equal eye towards all creatures, who is free from lust, anger, jealousy and egoism is a Brahmana or an emancipated sage."

Jalali said: "O Tuladhara! I have never heard before of these profound secret and abstruse doctrines of ascetics who perform only moral sacrifices. It is difficult to have a comprehensive understanding of these doctrines. The sages of olden days did not follow these doctrines of Yoga. Therefore they have not propounded them to the public. Tell me, O wise Tuladhara, by what act could people attain happiness?"

Tuladhara said: "If people have no faith in sacrifices, then the sacrifices performed by such faithless persons, do not become effective. They are not worthy of performing any sacrifice internal or external. The Vedas declare that sacrifices should not be performed by an unmarried man. One should not kill animals for sacrifice. He can offer clarified butter, herbs, etc., as oblations in the sacrifice. He can make faith as his wedded wife for giving such innocent offerings to the gods. The rice-ball is a worthy offering in sacrifices. One is sure to attain Brahma by performing sacrifices with innocent offerings.

"All rivers are as sacred as the Sarasvati. The soul is itself the greatest Tirtha. Do not roam about visiting sacred places. He who observes these duties which I have spoken of, and which do not involve injury to other creatures, and who tries to achieve merit according to his ability, attains blessed regions hereafter."

Bhishma said: "O Yudhishthira! These are the duties which Tuladhara applauded. These duties are consistent with reason also. They are always observed by virtuous and wise persons."

Tuladhara said: "The virtuous people adopted this path of duty that I have spoken of. O Jajali, many birds are hovering in the sky. Amongst them are those that were reared on thy head. They are showing their love for thee as their father. Call thy children."

Jajali summoned them. They gave answer which was in accordance with injunctions of that religion which proclaims: "Do not injure any creature on this earth." Tuladhara continued: "All acts that are done without injuring any creature cause happiness both here and hereafter. Those acts which cause injury to others destroy faith. If faith is destroyed, the performer of actions is ruined. Those who perform sacrifices from a sense of duty but not from desire for fruit, who are endowed with faith and tranquil mind, who have subjugated the senses, enjoy happiness both here and hereafter.

"Faith in Brahman is the daughter of Surya. She is the Proctectress. She bestows good birth. Faith is even superior to the merit obtained from the recitation of the Vedas and meditation. Faith saves an action that is spoiled by defect of speech or the defect of mind. But an action that is tainted by lack of faith cannot be saved by either speech or mind. He who is destitute of faith is not fit to give offerings to the gods. The food of such a man is not fit to be eaten. Lack of faith is regarded as a great sin. Faith is a purifier of sins. He who has faith is purified. Faith is of three kinds, viz., Sattvic, Rajasic and Tamasic.

"We have got all this on the subject of duties from the sage Dharmadarsana. O Jajali, cultivate faith. He who has faith in the declaration of the Srutis, and who acts in accordance with the injunctions of the Srutis with the faith that they are good for him is a righteous person. He will soon attain Eternal Bliss."

Bhishma continued: "Tuladhara had perfect knowledge of the religion of abstention from injury (Ahimsa). Jajali heard the words of wisdom uttered by Tuladhara, practised tranquillity, cultivated faith and was endowed with great wisdom. Eventually, Tuladhara and Jajali ascended to heaven and enjoyed happiness."

SAGE DURVASA AND THE PANDAVAS

Duryodhana heard that the Pandavas were leading a very happy life even in the forest, doing meritorious deeds and communing with great Rishis. He with Karna, Dussasana and others longed to harm them. When those wicked men were hatching various evil designs, the great ascetic Durvasa came to the city of Kurus with ten thousand disciples. Duryodhana welcomed them respectfully and gave them a sumptuous feast.

Durvasa said: "O Duryodhana! I am very much pleased with you. Ask for any boon that is not opposed to religion."

Duryodhana said: "O great sage, the great king Yudhishthira

is the eldest and the best of our family. That virtuous-minded one is now living in the forest with his brothers. O Brahmin, as you have been my guest for some time, it is my earnest desire that you become the guest of that illustrious person. Kindly go unto him with all thy disciples at a time when that excellent lady Draupadi, after having served the Brahmins, her husband and finished her own dinner, may lie down to rest." Duryodhana's motive in asking this boon was that Durvasa and his numerous disciples will be too heavy guests on the Pandavas, especially if they go at a late hour, and that the ascetic will curse the Pandavas as they will not be able to feed him and his disciples.

Durvasa said: "O Duryodhana! I shall do it for your satisfaction. I have granted you this boon."

The Rishi and his ten thousand disciples went to the forest and presented themselves before the Pandavas late at night. Yudhishthira suspected nothing. He with his brothers gave the Rishi and his disciples a fit and hearty welcome and said: "Return soon, Venerable Sir, after performing your ablutions and reciting your prayers." The Rishi went to bathe in the neighbouring river along with his disciples wondering, 'How will he feed me and my disciples!'

In the interval, Draupadi, the best of women, ever devoted to her husband, began to think how she could provide food. She could not find any means. She prayed to Lord Krishna: "O Krishna of mighty arms, O Eternal, O son of Devaki, whose power is inexhaustible, O Vasudeva, Lord of the Universe, who removes the difficulties of those who bow down to Thee, O sole creator and destroyer of the Universe, O Lord, the Protector of the afflicted, O the Highest of the high, O the Source for everything, O Worshipful One, O endless giver of boons! Thou art the refuge of the helpless! Thou art the ancient Purusha, the vital breath, O the Lord of All, the most excellent Lord! I seek Thy protection. Kindly protect me. Thou art fond of Your devotees. Thou art the beginning and the end of creation. Thou art the supreme light and essence of the Universe. Thou art the supreme gem and the repository of all wealth. Under Thy protection, O Lord of gods, none need be afraid of anything.

Thou didst protect me before from Dussasana in the assembly. Dost Thou save me now from this difficulty!"

Lord Kesava of mysterious movements, the God of gods, the Lord of the Universe, thus addressed by Draupadi, perceived Draupadi's difficulty and instantly appeared before her. Draupadi in great delight bowed down to the Lord and informed Him of the untimely arrival of Durvasa and his ten thousand disciples. Thereupon Krishna said to her: "I am very hungry. Give me some food at once from the Akshayapatra given by the Sun. Afterwards I shall do everything for you."

Draupadi replied: "The vessel given by the Sun remains full till I take my meals. O Venerable Lord! I have taken my meals and there is no food." Then the Lotus-eyed said to Draupadi: "This is not the time for joking. I am very much afflicted with hunger and fatigue. Go thou quickly, fetch the vessel and show it to me." Draupadi said: "My Lord, there is nothing in the vessel. I shall prepare food for Thee in no time. Dost Thou wait a few seconds." Lord Krishna said: "I cannot wait. I am extremely hungry. You bring that vessel. Let me see if there is nothing in it." Draupadi replied: "I assure Thee, the vessel is empty. There is nothing in it." She brought the vessel. Krishna quickly snatched it from Draupadi's hand, looked into it and said: "You look here. There is a particle of rice and vegetable sticking at a corner." He ate it up and said to her: "This little bit of rice is more than enough for me. My hunger is satisfied. May Lord Hari, the Soul of the Universe, be pleased with it and may that God who partakes at sacrifices be satisfied with this."

Lord Krishna said to Sahadeva: "Bring the Rishis here and feed them." Thereupon Sahadeva ran with great speed to invite them for taking food. The ascetic Durvasa and others were standing in the river and taking bath. Suddenly they felt their stomachs to be full. They were not able to breathe freely. They were struck with wonder. They stared at one another. They were not able to speak. The disciples turned their faces towards their Guru and said: "We asked the King to get our meals ready. We are now full to satiety. How can we eat anything now, O Revered Guru? The food has been uselessly prepared for us. What shall we do now?"

Durvasa said: "We have really done a great wrong to that royal sage by making him prepare food uselessly. The Pandavas will destroy us by looking down upon us with angry eyes. I know the royal sage is endowed with great ascetic powers. I am terribly afraid of those men who are devoted to Hari's feet. All those Pandavas are high-souled, pious, heroic and learned. They do severe austerities and observe vows. They always observe the rules of good conduct. They are highly devoted to Vasudeva. If provoked, they can consume us with their anger, as fire does cotton. So, O disciples, shall we run away quickly without seeing them!"

The disciples said: "Our stomachs are full. We cannot rise up. How then could we run? We find it extremely difficult even to talk or breathe. We are full to the neck. O Venerable Guru, save us from this trouble." Durvasa did not know what to do. He regretted very much for granting the boon to that wicked Duryodhana.

Sahadeva appeared on the spot and said to Durvasa: "Come, O Rishi, with all thy disciples. My brothers, Draupadi and Krishna are waiting to receive thee." Poor Durvasa trembled in fear at the very mention of Krishna's name. He felt greatly ashamed to see the Pandavas. Therefore, he said to his disciples: "Exert yourselves. Apply your strength. Rise up from the water. Let us walk slowly to the abode of the Pandavas. There is no other go." With great difficulty they reached the abode of the Pandavas. They were duly welcomed by Yudhishthira and others.

Krishna showed special attention to Durvasa. Durvasa was in a miserable plight. The face of the poor Rishi became pale and small. He was very much ashamed. He bowed to Krishna and said: "O Lord, forgive me. I did a very foolish act. I regret it very much now. I gave a promise to the wicked Duryodhana. The Pandavas are virtuous and pious. They are highly devoted to Thee. Therefore no harm could ever come to them." Then he related the whole story and how he and his disciples had already been punished.

Then Draupadi said: "O my Venerable Lord, Krishna! Prostrations unto Thee. Now only I can understand Thy mysterious far-seeing action. Thou art Omniscient and Omnipotent. I can see why Thou feigned hunger for a grain of rice. All these Rishis were satisfied by your eating that little bit of rice. This clearly shows that Thou art the Soul of the Universe in whom all creatures live, move and have their being. Thou art the Sutratman, the thread-Soul of this world. All this is threaded on Thee, as rows of pearls or flowers on a string. Thou art in this world as fragrance in the flower, as butter in milk, as coolness in the ice. Glory unto Thee! Thou art our sole refuge, teacher, friend, relative, father and mother. No harm can come to the followers of Hari. No danger can come to the worshippers of Lord Krishna."

Durvasa and his disciples were forgiven. All sang the glory of Lord Krishna. Glory unto Lord Krishna and His Name. May His blessings be upon you all!

(Draupadi Harana Parva of the Vana Parva, Ch. 262)

YUDHISHTHIRA AND THE SERPENT

Yudhisthira saw his beloved brother Bhimasena in the coils of a snake and said: "My dear Bhimasena! How have you met with this disaster? Who is this serpent whose body is as huge as a mountain?"

Bhimasena said: "O venerable brother! This huge serpent has seized me for his food. He is the royal sage Nahusha living in the form of a serpent."

Yudhishthira said: "O serpent! Kindly free my brother. I will give you some other food to appease your hunger."

The serpent replied: "Leave the place. If you remain here I will eat you also tomorrow. I will not liberate your brother. I do not want any other food."

Yudhishthira said: "O serpent! Tell me whether you are a god or a demon or a *Uraga.* For what have you caught Bhimasena? What food shall I give you to satisfy your hunger? Under what conditions will you liberate him?"

The serpent replied: "O king! I was thy ancestor, the son of Ayu and fifth in descent from Soma. I was known by the name of king Nahusha. I attained mastery of the three worlds by sacrifices, penance, study of the Vedas, self-restraint and power. I was puffed up with pride. Many Brahmanas used to carry my palanquin. I insulted the twice-born and was therefore brought to this miserable condition by Agastya. Even now I have got my memory. I have got your younger brother for my food by the grace of Agastya. If you anwer my questions today I will let your brother free."

Yudhishthira said: "Ask me, O serpent, whatever you like. I will answer your questions, if I can."

The serpent said: "O king, who is a Brahmana? What is it that ought to be known?"

Yudhishthira said: "O king of serpents, if the qualities of truthfulness, charity, forgiveness, good conduct, benevolence, asceticism and mercy are found in a man, he is a Brahmana. That which ought to be known is the Supreme Self or Para Brahman who is destitute of the feelings of pleasure and pain. If one attains Him, he is freed from birth, death, sorrow, pain and misery."

The serpent said: "O Yudhishthira, even amongst the Sudras are found the qualities of a Brahmana. You have said that what is to be known is devoid of pleasure and pain but I have not come across any such thing in which these feelings are absent."

Yudhishthira said: "O serpent! If these qualities are present in a Sudra, he is no longer a Sudra. He is a Brahmana. If these qualities are absent in a twice-born, he is not a Brahmana. It seems at first sight that existence is impossible without the feelings of pleasure and pain. Just as cold is characterised by the absence of heat and heat by the absence of cold, so there can exist an object in which the feelings of pleasure and pain will be absent."

The serpent said: "If a Brahmana is known by certain virtues, then the distinction of castes is of no purpose so long as he does not possess these qualities."

Yudhishthira said: "O wise serpent! It is extremely difficult to find out one's caste in this world owing to promiscuous intercourse of all the orders. Men of all the four orders are, without restriction, incessantly producing children from women of all the castes. On account of this, the wise have said that the character is the most essential thing. Every man is regarded as a Sudra before initiation into the Vedas. He who observes the principles of right conduct or good behaviour is a Brahmana."

The serpent said: "O Yudhishthira! I have listened to your words of wisdom. I am highly thankful to you. You are a wise sage. You know the right significance of the Vedas. How can I now devour your brother Bhimasena?"

Yudhishthira said: "O serpent! You are well-versed in the Vedas and the Vedangas. Please tell me by what sort of acts one can obtain heaven?"

The serpent said: "O king! One can obtain heaven by giving alms to deserving persons, truthfulness, unenviousness and kind words."

Yudhishthira said: "O serpent! Which is more superior or praiseworthy—benevolence or truthfulness? Which is more important—unenviousness or good behaviour?"

The serpent replied: "The superiority or inferiority in benevolence or truthfulness is estimated by the benefit produced by each of these. Sometimes truthfulness is regarded as superior to some charitable acts. Sometimes charity is considered more laudable than truthfulness. Similarly, O king, good behaviour is sometimes regarded to be more important than unenviousness. Sometimes unenviousness is deemed to be more praiseworthy or important than good behaviour. Their superiority or greater importance or inferiority or lesser importance depends on their utility. This is the fundamental point to be noted."

Yudhishthira said: "O serpent! Tell me how one attains heaven, how he reaps the fruits of his actions?"

The serpent replied: "One attains heaven by charity, self-exertion and unenviousness. He who is subject to lust, anger and malice, takes his birth among the lower animals. The embodied soul takes birth again and again to reap the fruits of his Karmas. But the liberated sage or Jivanmukta rests peacefully for ever in the Eternal Brahman."

Yudhishthira said: "O serpent! Tell me how the man becomes

aware of sound, touch, form, smell and taste? Do we not simultaneously feel the sensations of sound, touch, form, etc. by means of the senses?"

The serpent replied: "The Jiva or the individual soul who is encased in this physical frame enjoys the objects of senses through the five organs of knowledge viz., ear, skin, eye, tongue and nose. The senses, the mind and the intellect assist the soul in his enjoyment of the objects. They are called Karanas or instruments. The mind is the cause of all perceptions. It cannot, at one and the same time, perceive manifold objects. It cannot simultaneously feel the sensations of touch, taste, etc. It can only do one thing at a time. The soul assisted by the mind, which acts through the organs of sense, which are the recipients of all sensations, perceives all objects. The soul, which is located between the eyebrows, sends the intellect to different objects of senses. The Yogi stops the thought-waves, controls the mind and the senses and attains knowledge of the Supreme Soul by entering into Nirvikalpa Samadhi."

Yudhishthira said: "Tell me the chief characteristics of the mind and the intellect respectively. The knowledge of their functions helps one to attain the knowledge of Brahman or the Supreme Being."

The serpent replied: "The soul comes under the domination of intellect on account of cloudiness of understanding. That is the reason why the intellect guides the soul, though it is subordinate to the latter. The intellect exists by acts of perception but the mind exists of itself. The mind and not the intellect has the power of producing the feelings of pleasure and pain."

Yudhishthira said: "You are exceedingly wise. You have performed meritorious acts. You have obtained a place in heaven also. How is it you became subject to illusion and attained the form of a serpent? I am at a great loss to understand this point."

The serpent replied: "Those who lead a life of luxury and who are puffed up with pride, lose their understanding and sense. O King, I too was intoxicated with pride on account of prosperity. Therefore I have fallen into this degraded and highly deplorable state. I have recovered my reason now. O wise monarch! You have done me a great service. You have helped me much. I have been freed from this dreadful curse on account of my conversation with your pious self.

"O Yudhishthira! I shall narrate to you my story. In olden times I was in a very prosperous conditon. I used to mount on a celestial chariot and roam about in the heaven at my own will. I was elated with pride. I had great influence over the Brahmarishis, the celestials and the Gandharvas. Many Brahmarishis were engaged in carrying my palanquin. This sin brought about my fall from my exalted position. One day when Rishi Agastya was carrying my palanquin, my feet touched his body. He became very angry and cursed me: 'You will be turned into a serpent.' Then I prayed to the Rishi: 'Kindly pardon me. I was under the intoxication of pride. Kindly free me from the terrible curse.' He being moved by pity said: 'Yudhishthira, the wise monarch, will liberate you from this curse, when this horrible sin of pride in you will vanish and you will enjoy the fruits of your virtue.' I fell down from my palanquin and in the course of my fall I found myself turned into a serpent with my head downwards.

"Through the sight of thy magnanimous personality, I am blessed now. I will reassume my original form through thy grace. It is for this reason that I have put you these questions that relate to Brahman and the Brahmanas.

"Truthfulness, self-control, asceticism, benevolence, unenviousness, right conduct, adherence to virtue, devotion and meditation are the means by which one can attain the final emancipation, or freedom from births and deaths. Final emancipation cannot be had by birth in a good race or in an illustrious family.

"O mighty monarch, may you be happy! May your younger brother Bhimasena prosper gloriously! I shall now go to heaven again."

(Ajagara of the Vana Parva, Ch. 181)

PROUD DAMBHODBHAVA

In days of yore, there was a king named Dambhodbhava. He was a great and heroic car-warrior. He was the ruler of a vast dominion. There was none equal to him. He was intoxicated with great vanity and pride. He used to ask the Brahmanas and Kshatriyas: "Please tell me, is there anybody in this world who is more accomplished or even equal to me in battle?"

Several revered Brahmanas who were well-versed in the Vedas said: "O king! Do not be puffed up with vanity. Do not brag too much of yourself. There are two persons who are the best among men. They have achieved many victories in battle. You are certainly no equal to them."

The king said: "O Brahmanas! Where are these two heroes? Who are they? What victories have they achieved?"

The Brahmanas replied: "These two persons are the devotees of Nara and Narayana, who have taken their birth in this world. Fight with them. They are practising rigorous penance in some caves in the Gandhamadana mountain."

The king collected a large army, went to the Gandhamadhana, searched for the devotees and at last found them out. They were in an emaciated condition on account of their severe austerities. They received the king with roots and fruits and offered him a seat and water. They asked the king: "O king! What can we do for you? How can we serve you?"

The king replied: "I have conquered the whole earth. I have killed all my enemies. I have come here to fight with you."

Nara and Narayana said: "O king! This is a peaceful retreat for Tapas and meditation. There is neither hatred nor greed here. There is no warfare in this peaceful abode. There are neither weapons nor arrows, neither soldiers nor car-warriors. There are many potent Kshatriyas on the face of this earth. Fight with them."

The king again and again summoned these two devotees of rare Tapas and effulgence to fight.

Nara took a handful of blades of grass and said: "Come and fight, O you Kshatriya! Take up arms and mobilise your army. I shall destroy your thirst for war."

Dambhodbhava shot forth his arrows to kill Nara. But Nara destroyed the arrows by the blades of grass. The eyes, ears and noses of the king's soldiers were cut off by the blades of grass through the spiritual power of Nara.

The king fell at the feet of Nara and said: "O devotee! Glory unto thee. I am defeated. I am struck with wonder. How powerful are the blades of grass!"

Nara said: "Give up your false pride and vanity from this moment onward. Follow the wise instructions of the Brahmanas. Never insult anybody in any way, whether he is your inferior or your superior. Do not insult anybody without knowing his strength and weakness. Acquire mastery over the lower self. Annihilate your desires. Be humble. Develop forgiveness. Be serene and tranquil. Attain wisdom or knowledge of the Self. Abandon covetousness and vanity. Protect your subjects well. Be just and righteous. Respect the Brahmanas who are well-versed in the Vedas. Enquire of the Brahmanas about their welfare. May good betide you! May you prosper gloriously!"

Then the king prostrated at the feet of Nara and Narayana, returned to his own capital and henceforward acted most righteously.

Those who are under the influence of vanity and greed move about intoxicated. Their senses are turbulent and impetuous. They do not prosper. They are shunned by the people. They are ever restless and discontented. They come to grief and destruction. Therefore give up vanity and greed. Develop the opposite Sattvic qualities, humility and contentment. You will enjoy Supreme Peace.

(Bhagavadyana of the Udyoga Parva, Ch. CXVI)

KING AMBARISHA AND CUPIDITY

In days of yore, there was a king named Ambarisha. He rid himself of his faults and defects, worshipped the righteous and acquired great success and fame.

He reflected within himself and said: "I have got rid of many faults. But I have got one great vice, viz., cupidity, which should be eradicated. I am not yet able to destroy it. Man fails to free himself from desire on account of this vice only. It is cupidity which impels one to indulge in forbidden acts. I will sever this cupidity with sharp-edged swords.

"Desire springs from cupidity. Anxiety originates from desire. He who becomes a victim of desire acquires many evil qualities. He falls into ditches without knowing them.

"He takes births again and again on account of cupidity. He is united with a body and is moved to action owing to this cupidity. He dies when his Prarabdha Karma is exhausted and again takes birth.

"One should destroy cupidity by intelligence, dispassion, discrimination and meditation on the Supreme Self. One should desire for the sovereignty of his soul alone. This is the true aim. The soul is the real King of kings. He who realises the Atman is the real Emperor of emperors."

Ambarisha applied himself diligently in eradicating this cupidity and destroyed this evil trait completely. He practised regular meditation and attained Self-realisation.

(Asvamedha Parva, Ch. 31)

GAUTAMI AND THE SNAKE

Bhishma said: Why, Yudhishthira, do you consider your soul, which is dependent on God, Destiny and Time, to be the cause of your actions? The manifestation of its inaction is subtle and imperceptible to the senses. Just listen to this ancient story—conversation between Mrityu, Gautami and Kala.

There was an old lady named Gautami. She was endowed with great patience and serenity of mind. One day her son was bitten by a serpent and died. A fowler named Arjunaka tied the serpent with a string and brought it before Gautami. He then said to her, "This serpent has been the cause of your son's death. Tell me quickly how this serpent should be killed. Shall I throw it into the fire or shall I cut it into pieces?"

Gautami: You are a man of no understanding. Release this serpent. It does not deserve death at your hands. My son will not be restored to life by killing this serpent.

The fowler: Deluded people abstain from acts like the one I proposed as they fear the loss of happiness in the next world. Those who want to attain peace of mind attribute everything to 'fate', 'destiny' and 'Kala' as the cause, but practical men soon allay their grief by revenge. Therefore, O lady, allow me to destroy this wretched serpent and allay your grief.

Gautami: Good men are always intent on virtue. The death of my son was pre-destined. Therefore I cannot agree to the killing of this serpent. Brahmanas do not harbour thoughts of revenge, as such thoughts bring pain. Release this serpent out of compassion.

The fowler: O lady! Merit is obtained by killing an enemy. You will acquire great and true merit by killing this serpent.

Gautami: There is no good in tormenting and killing an enemy. Why should we not forgive this serpent and try to acquire merit by releasing it?

The fowler: A great number of creatures will be protected by killing this serpent. Therefore kill this wretched serpent.

Gautami: O fowler! My son will not be restored to life. Further, no other benefit will be attained by its death.

The fowler: Indra got the best portion of sacrificial offerings by killing Vritra. Mahadeva obtained his share of sacrificial offerings by destroying in a sacrifice. Therefore kill this serpent at once without any misgivings in your mind.

The high-souled Gautami did not yield to the wishes of the fowler although she was repeatedly incited by the latter for the destruction of the serpent.

Then the serpent began to speak in a human voice, "O foolish fowler, it is not my fault. I am not independent. I have no will of my own. Mrityu sent me on this errand. I have bitten this child by his command and not out of any anger or choice on my part. Therefore, if there be any sin in this, the sin is Mrityu's only."

The fowler: If you have done this evil act impelled by another, the sin is yours also as you are responsible for the act. The potter's wheel and rod are all considered as causes in the creation of an earthen vessel. Even so, you are the cause in the production of this effect. O serpent, you are indeed guilty. You yourself admit this. Therefore you deserve death at my hands.

The serpent: Just as the potter's wheel, rod and other things are not independent causes, so also, I am not an independent cause. Therefore this is not my fault. If you think otherwise then all these must be regarded as causes working with one another. For, thus working with one another, a doubt springs up about their relationship as between cause and effect. Therefore this is not my fault. I am not guilty of any sin and I do not deserve death on this score. If you think that there is sin in even such causation, the sin lies in the aggregate of causes.

The fowler: If you are neither the principal cause nor the agent in this matter, you are still the cause of the death of this child. Therefore I think you must be killed. If, O serpent, you think that, when an evil act is done, the doer is not implicated therein, then there can be no cause at all in this matter, but as there must be a cause and you having done this, you should surely be put to death.

The serpent: Whether any prime cause exists or not, no effect is produced without an intermediate act. Therefore, causation, being of no importance in either case, my agency only as the cause in this matter, ought to be considered in its proper bearings. If, O fowler, you consider me truly to be the cause, then the guilt or sin of killing a living being rests on the shoulders of another who led me to do this.

The fowler: You do not deserve life. Why do you then exchange so many words, O wretched serpent! You deserve death at my hands. You have done an atrocious crime by killing this infant.

The serpent: O fowler! As the priests officiating in a sacrifice do not acquire the merit of the act by offering oblations of clarified butter to the fire, but the person only, who undertakes the sacrifice and engages the priests acquires the merit, even so should I be considered with respect to the result in this matter.

The serpent having said this, Mrityu (God of Death) himself appeared there and addressing the serpent said, "Guided by Kala, I, O serpent, sent you on this mission. Neither are you nor am I the cause of this infant's death. As the clouds are driven hither and thither by wind, I am, O serpent, directed by Kala. All influences of Sattva, or Rajas, or Tamas, originate from Kala as they operate in all creatures. All creatures in heaven or earth are pervaded by the influence of Kala. The whole universe is permeated by this same influence of Kala. All acts in this world and all abstentions and also all their modifications or changes are influenced by Kala. The Sun, Moon, Vishnu, Water, Wind, the God of a hundred sacrifices, Fire, Sky, Earth, Mitra and Parjanya, Aditi and the Vasus, Rivers and Oceans and all objects, are created and destroyed by Kala. Knowing this, why do you, O serpent, consider me blameworthy? If I am to be blamed for this, you are also equally responsible."

The serpent: I do not, O Mrityu blame you nor do I set you free from all blame. I only say that I am directed and influenced in my actions by you. Whether Kala is to be blamed or not, it is not for me to find fault with it. We have no right to do so. As it is my duty to free myself from this blame, so it is my duty to see that you are not to be blamed.

Then addressing the fowler, the serpent said, "O' fowler Arjunaka! You have heard what Mrityu has said. Therefore it is not proper for you to torment me, who am guiltless, by tying me with this rope."

The fowler: I have heard you, O serpent, as well as the words of Mrityu, but these do not set you free from blame. Mrityu and you are the causes of this infant's death. I consider both of you to be the cause which is not truly so. Accursed be the wicked and vengeful Mrityu who causes misery and affliction to the good. I shall kill you, who are sinful and engaged in sinful deeds.

Mrityu: We both are not free agents but are dependent on

Kala and are ordained to do our appointed work. You will not blame us if you consider this matter thoroughly.

The fowler: If you both, O serpent and Mrityu, be dependent on Kala, I am curious to know how pleasure and anger are caused.

Mrityu: Everything is done under the influence of Kala. I have told you before, O fowler, that Kala is the cause of all. Therefore we both act under the influence of Kala and do our appointed work. Therefore, O fowler, we two should not be blamed by you.

Then Kala arrived at the scene where ethics were being discussed and spoke thus to the serpent, Mrityu and the fowler Arjunaka assembled together.

Kala: "Neither Mrityu, nor this serpent nor I, O fowler, is guilty of the death of any creature. We are merely the immediate exciting causes of the event. O Arjunaka, the Karma of this child was the prime cause of our action in this matter. There was no other cause for our action. There was no other cause by which the child met its death. It was killed as the result of its own Karma in the past. We all are subject to the influence of our respective Karmas. Karma is a help to salvation even as sons are; Karma also expresses virtue and vice in man. We urge one another just as acts urge one another. Just as men make from a lump of clay whatever they wish to make, so also do men attain to various results determined by Karma. As light and shadow are related to each other, so are men related to Karma through their own deeds. Therefore neither you, nor I, nor Mrityu, nor the serpent, nor this old Brahmana lady, are the cause of this child's death. He himself is the cause here." Upon Kala explaining the matter thus, Gautami was convinced in her mind that men suffer according to their actions. She spoke thus to Arjunaka.

Gautami: Neither Kala, nor Mrityu, nor the serpent, is the cause in this matter. This child has met with its death as the result of its own Karma. Moreover, as the result of my past Karma, I have lost my son. Let now Kala and Mrityu retire from this place. O Arjunaka, you also release this serpent.

Then Kala, Mrityu and the serpent returned to their respective places. Gautami and the fowler became consoled in mind.

Bhishma said: Having heard all this, O king, do you abandon all grief and attain peace of mind. Men attain heaven or hell as the result of their own Karma. This evil has neither been of your own creation nor of Duryodhana's. That these kings of earth have all been killed in this war is the work of Kala.

Having heard all this, the powerful and virtuous Yudhishthira became consoled in mind.

(Anusasana Parva, Ch. 1)

UNGRATEFUL GAUTAMA AND THE CRANE

Yudhishthira said: O Venerable Lord Bhishma! Tell me who are called injurers of friends and ungrateful persons?

Bhishma said: In this connection I shall narrate to you an old story. The incidents of the story took place in the country of the Mlecchas that lies to the North. There was a Brahmin called Gautama. He had no Vedic learning. One day he went to a prosperous village in search of charity. A robber lived in that village. He was a very rich man. He was devoted to Brahmins. He was highly charitable and truthful. Gautama went to the house of the robber and begged for charity. He asked the robber: 'Give me a house to live in and also such necessities of life as would last for one year.' The robber gave Gautama clothes, articles of food and a young widow for wife. Gautama lived happily in that village for many years. He practised archery with interest and zeal. He daily went into the forests and killed cranes. Compassionate nature vanished from him. He became a veritable robber on account of his close connection with robbers.

One day another Brahmin who was virtuous came to that village. He was well versed in the Vedas. He was an ascetic and a celibate. He was once an intimate friend of Gautama. He belonged to the same country from which Gautama came. He would not accept food from any person other than a Brahmin. He came to the house of Gautama. Gautama was just returning from the forest with a load of slaughtered cranes on his shoulders. His body was besmeared with blood. The ascetic Brahmin met his old friend Gautama and said: 'You are a Brahmin. You were born in a respectable family. How is it that you have become a wretched hunter now? Your relatives are well-versed in the Vedas. You have brought disgrace on your family. Leave this place at once. Practise self-restraint and compassion. Open your eyes. Study Vedas. Become a virtuous man. Abandon this wretched life immediately.'

Gautama replied: 'O my dear friend! I am very poor. I have no Vedic learning. I remain here for the sake of wealth only. I am blessed today at thy sight. Spend the night with me.' The ascetic passed the night with his friend. He, however, refused to touch any food in that house. In the early morning the pious Brahmin left the house of Gautama.

Gautama proceeded towards the sea. On the way he came across a delightful forest that was abounding with mango trees, palmyras and sandal trees. There was a large and beautiful banian tree on a level spot. He sat underneath the tree. Gentle breeze blew. Gautama soon fell asleep. Evening twilight came. A bird returned to that spot which was its home from the regions of Brahma. He was a dear friend of the Creator. He was a prince of the cranes. He was the son of the sage Kasyapa. He was endowed with great wisdom. He was known by the name Rajadharman. He had great reputation. Gautama woke up and saw the beautiful bird. He was very hungry. He thought of killing the bird for his food.

Rajadharman said: 'O Brahmin! Welcome. Thou art my dear guest today. It is my good fortune that I have thee in my abode. I am the son of Kasyapa by one of the daughters of the sage Daksha. Thou art my venerable guest today. Thou art welcome.'

Rajadharman offered the Brahmin hospitality in accordance with the rites laid down in the scriptures. He made an excellent bed of Sala flowers. He gave him several large fishes and blazing fire. After the Brahmin had finished his meal, the bird began to fan him with his wings to remove fatigue.

Rajadharman asked: 'O Brahmin! May I know your pedigree?' The Brahmin replied: 'I am a Brahmin by the name

Gautama' and then kept silent. The bird asked: 'May I know the cause of your arrival here?' Gautama replied: 'I am very poor. I am proceeding towards the sea for earning wealth.' Rajadharman told him: 'Do not be troubled. You will return to your place with wealth. The sage Brihaspati has said that there are four means of acquiring wealth, viz., inheritance, sudden acquisition due to the luck or the favour of the gods, acquisition by one's own exertions and acquisition through the help or kindness of friends. I have become your friend. I shall show you the way to attain wealth.' The night passed away and morning came. In the morning Rajadharman said: 'O my friend! Go along this very route. There is a mighty king of the Rakshasas at a distance of about three Yojanas from this place. His name is Virupaksha. He is a great friend of mine. Go to him. Mention my name. He will give you as much wealth as you require.'

The Brahmin walked speedily and reached the city known by the name Meruvraja. The king of the Rakshasas came to know that a dear guest was sent to him by Rajadharman. He received Gautama with immense delight.

The king of the Rakshasas worshipped the Brahmin with the usual offerings and asked: 'O Brahmin! May I know something about your birth, study of Vedas, penance and vow of Brahmacharya?' The Brahmin only stated his name and race. The king found out that the Brahmin was devoid of Brahmanic merits and the study of Vedas.

The king of the Rakshasas said: 'Where is your residence? To what race does your wife belong? Tell me truly. Do not be afraid.'

Gautama said: 'I belong to the middle country. I live in a village of hunters. I have married a Sudra woman, a widow. All that I tell you is the truth.'

The king reflected within himself thus: 'This man is by birth a Brahmin. He is a friend of Rajadharman who is a virtuous great soul of vast renown. He has been sent to me by that son of Kasyapa. I must do that which is pleasing to my friend. Rajadharman is my friend, my brother and a dear relative. A thousand Brahmins are entertained in my house. I shall entertain this Gautama and I shall give him wealth.'

He gave plenty of costly jewels, gems and gold to Gautama. Gautama received them with great joy and went away. He reached the same banian tree under which he had met the crane. He sat underneath the tree. He was very much fatigued and hungry. The best of the birds, Rajadharman, came there. He received Gautama with great hospitality. He fanned Gautama with his wings and relieved him of his fatigue. He gave him good food.

The wicked Gautama reflected within himself: 'The burden I carry is very heavy. There is no food on the way. I have to walk a long distance. This crane is full of flesh. I shall kill it and take the flesh with me for my food.'

Rajadharman, the prince of birds, kindled a fire under the banian tree for the protection of his guest Gautama. The ungrateful wretch Gautama determined to kill his sleeping host. He killed the bird with the help of the blazing fire and roasted the flesh on the fire. His heart was filled with intense delight. Then he fled quickly from the spot.

The Rakshasa king Virupaksha said to his son: 'O beloved son! Every morning Rajadharman goes to the realm of Brahma for worship and pays me a visit while returning. I do not see him these two days. I am very anxious about him. This Gautama who came to me might have killed him. He is not a learned man. He had lived with robbers. He seemed to be a wicked man. I read him through by the signs he showed. He is a robber. He had gone to the abode of my friend. O son, run to his place and find out whether he is still alive.'

The prince ran with great speed and arrived at the foot of the banian tree. He saw the remains of Rajadharman. He ran and succeeded in catching Gautama. He discovered the body of Rajadharman without wings, bone and feet. He took the ungrateful Gautama to Meruvraja and showed the king the mutilated body of the bird. The king of the Rakshasas, his counsellors and the priest wept loudly.

The king then said: 'Let this sinful wretch be slain. Let these Rakshasas here eat his flesh, joyfully.' The Rakshasas expressed their unwillingness to eat the flesh of that sinner. They said to the king: 'O venerable lord! Let the flesh be given to the robbers.' The king said: 'Let it be so.' The Rakshasas killed Gautama and cut his body into pieces and gave them to the robbers. The robbers refused to eat the flesh of that vile wretch. Though they were cannibals, they would not eat the flesh of an ungrateful person. The Rakshasas said to the king: 'O king! For one who slays a Brahmin, for one who drinks alcohol, for one who steals, for one who has fallen away from a vow, there is expiation. But there is no expiation for an ungrateful person. The flesh of that cruel, wicked and ungrateful man, who injures a friend, is neither eaten by the cannibals nor by worms that feed on the flesh of dead bodies.'

The king of the Rakshasas arranged a funeral pyre for that king of birds and adorned it with valuable clothes, jewels, gems and perfumes. The obsequial rites were performed according to the Sastras. At that time the goddess Surabhi, the daughter of Daksha, appeared in the sky above the place where the pyre had been set up. Her breasts were full of milk. Milk fell upon the funeral pyre of Rajadharman. The prince of cranes came to life. He rose up and approached his friend Virupaksha. Indra himself came to the city of Virupaksha. He said to the king: "O king, this prince of cranes once absented himself from the region of Brahma where his presence was necessary. So Brahma said to the prince of birds: 'As this vile crane has not come today in my assembly, he shall not die soon so as to be able to leave the earth.' Therefore though the prince of crane was killed by Gautama he has come back to life on account of the nectar which fell on his body."

Rajadharman bowed unto Indra and said: 'Let my friend Gautama be brought back to life through thy grace.' Then Indra sprinkled nectar on Gautama and restored him to life. Rajadharman embraced Gautama and became exceedingly happy. He took leave of Gautama and returned to his own abode. Next day he went to the region of Brahma. Brahma paid due honour to the prince of birds.

Gautama returned to the village of the hunters with much wealth and begot many children by his Sudra wife. the gods pronounced a curse. 'Let this ungrateful sinner be sent to a terrible hell for many years after his death.'

Bhishma continued: O Yudhishthira! All this was recited to me formerly by Narada. An ungrateful person does not deserve to be trusted. An ungrateful person can have neither happiness nor fame. No one should injure a friend. He who is ungrateful and injures his friend is thrown into a terrible hell. Everyone should be grateful. Everyone should try to serve his friends. Honours can be obtained from friends. One can enjoy various objects of enjoyments through friends. One may escape from various kinds of danger, distress through the influence of friends. A wise man should honour his friends with great attention and reverence. One should shun scrupulously an ungrateful and sinful wretch. He who injures his friends is a miserable wretch. He is the vilest of men. I have told you, O best of all virtuous men, all about the characteristics of a sinful wretch who is tainted by ingratitude and who injures his friend."

Yudhishthira felt great joy on hearing the wise words spoken by the high-souled Bhishma.

Man is beyond dispute the most excellent of created beings and the vilest animal is a dog; but all sages agree that a grateful dog is better than an ungrateful man.

(Santi Parva, Sec. CLXVIII-CLXXIII)

PRARABDHA AND PURUSHARTHA

Yudhishthira said, "Tell me O learned sire, who is versed in all scriptures, of 'exertion' (*Purushartha*) and 'destiny' (*Prarabdha*), which is the more powerful?"

Bhishma said, "The following conversation of Vasishtha and Brahma explains this matter. In days of yore, Vasishtha enquired of Brahma as to which among these two, viz., the Karma of a person acquired in this life or that acquired in previous lives (called destiny) is the more powerful in shaping this life. Then Brahma, who had sprung from the primeval lotus, answered him in these sweet and well-reasoned pregnant words."

"Nothing comes into existence without seed. Fruits do not grow without seed. From seeds originate other seeds. According as the seed is good or bad, which the peasant sows in his field, he reaps good or bad fruits. As the soil, unsown with seed, though tilled, does not give fruit so without individual exertion, 'destiny' is helpless. One's own acts are like the soil and 'destiny' (the sum total of one's deeds in previous births) is compared to the seed. The harvest grows from the union of the soil and the seed. It is seen everyday in this world that the doer reaps the fruit of his good and evil acts. Happiness results from good acts, pain from the evil ones. Acts must always bear fruit, without action no fruit arises.

"A man of good acts acquires merits and good fortune, whereas an evil-doer loses his estate and reaps evil. One acquires fortune and riches of various kinds by steady application. Everything can be obtained by 'exertion'; but nothing can be attained through 'destiny' alone by a man who is wanting in personal 'exertion'. One attains heaven, all the objects of enjoyment and also the fulfilment of one's heart's desires by well-directed individual 'exertion'. All the luminaries in the firmament, all the gods and also the Sun and the Moon and the Wind have attained their high status by evolution through dint of their own 'exertion' or action. Riches, friends, prosperity coming down from generation to generation and also the graces of life, are difficult of attainment by those who lack personal 'exertion'.

"The idler does not acquire riches and other objects of enjoyment. Nor are these ever acquired by a man who is not active or diligent in his pursuit. Even the adorable Vishnu who created the three worlds is engaged in austere penances in the bosom of the deep. If one's Karma bore no fruit, then all actions would become fruitless and depending upon 'destiny', men would become idlers. He who, without action follows 'destiny' alone, achieves nothing.

"If 'destiny' be unfavourable, there need not be much to worry in this world; whereas if one is lacking in 'exertion', he will entertain great fear with respect to the next world, because happiness can never be obtained in the other unless one exerts and acts righteously in this world. Man's powers, if properly applied, follow his 'destiny', but 'destiny' alone cannot produce any good where 'exertion' is lacking.

"How does Karma originate, if 'destiny' is the principal motive power of human action? By one's actions many virtues accumulate. It is well known that one's own Self is one's friend or one's enemy and also the witness of one's good and evil actions. Good and evil manifest themselves through Karma. Good and evil acts do not always produce immediate results. Righteousness is the refuge to attain to the feet of God. Everything can be attained by righteousness. 'Destiny' does not frustrate the man who has acquired virtue and righteousness. It merely creates situations for a man and it is his acts alone which count.

"In days of yore, Yayati fell down from his high position in heaven and descended to the Earth. But he was again restored to the celestial regions by the good deeds of his pious and virtuous grandsons. 'Destiny' does not help the man who is steeped in ignorance. Just as a small fire, when fanned by the wind becomes highly powerful, so also does 'destiny' when helped by individual 'exertion' develop to the ordained aim.

"Just as the light goes out with the oil in the lamp, so also does the influence of 'destiny' by the abandonment of one's duties. Having obtained immense wealth and all the means of enjoyment in this world, the man is not diligent in action, who is not hard-working, is not able to enjoy them long.

"The man who does not exert himself is never contented in this world. 'Destiny' cannot change the course of a man who has gone wrong. There is no power inherent in 'destiny'. Just as the pupil follows the preceptor, so does one's action, guided by 'destiny', follows one's own individual exertion. Where one's own 'exertion' is put forth, then only 'destiny' shows its hand."

Men attain heaven or not by one's individual actions influenced by 'destiny'. This combination becomes efficacious and fruitful, if the actions are good and righteous.

(Anusasana Parva, Ch. VI)

SAGE ALARKA AND THE SENSES

There was a royal sage named Alarka. He was a great

Tapasvin. He did many rigorous penances. He had full knowledge of duty and morality. He was truthful. He was very firm in his vows. This is how he attained Self-realisation.

One day he was sitting at the foot of a tree. He began to reflect on subtle things. He reflected within himself thus: "My mind has become unsteady and turbulent. The real victory is when the mind is conquered. The result of this conquest becomes permanent only if one gains victory over one's mind. It always wanders. It goads me to do acts for the gratification of my desires. I shall henceforth shoot very sharp-pointed arrows at the mind."

The mind said, "O Alarka! These arrows can never cut me through. They will pierce only your own vital parts and you will die. Try to find out other arrows to kill me."

Alarka heard these words and reflected thus: "The nose troubles me. It always hankers after scents. I shall discharge sharp arrows at the nose."

The nose said, "O Alarka! These arrows can never pass through me. They will pierce only your own vital parts and you will die. Look for other arrows to kill me."

Alarka heard these words and reflected thus: "My tongue is very mischievous. It troubles me much. It always craves to taste palatable things and savoury dishes. I shall discharge sharp arrows at the tongue."

The tongue said, "O Alarka! These arrows will not cut me through. They will only pierce your own vital parts and you will die. Find out other arrows to kill me."

Alarka reflected thus: "The skin troubles me. It runs after soft things. It always hankers after objects which are delightful to the touch. I shall discharge sharp arrows at the skin and tear off the skin."

The skin said, "O my beloved Alarka! These arrows can never pass through me. They will pierce your own vital parts only and you will die. Look for other arrows to kill me."

Alarka heard these words and reflected thus: "The ear troubles me much. It wants to hear melodious music. It hears various sounds and hankers after them only. I shall discharge sharp arrows at the ear."

The ear said, "My dear Alarka! These arrows will not pierce me. They will pierce your own vital parts only and you will die. Find out other arrows to kill me."

Alarka reflected: "The eye is very troublesome. It longs to see colours and beautiful forms. I shall destroy this eye with sharp arrows."

The eye said, "These arrows will not, O Alarka, pass through me at all. They will pierce your own vital parts only and you will die. Find out other arrows in order to kill me."

Alarka reflected thus: "This intellect only troubles me much. It forms many determinations with the help of reasoning. Therefore I shall discharge sharp arrows at the intellect."

The intellect said, "O Alarka! These arrows will not pass through me at all. They will pierce your vital parts only and you will die. Search for other arrows to annihilate me."

Alarka underwent rigorous penance to overcome the seven faculties, viz., mind, nose, tongue, skin, ears, eyes and intellect. But in vain! He then began to reflect for a long time on this one subject. At last he found out the real powerful arrows, viz., control of mind which would kill all the seven. He could not obtain anything better than this. He engaged himself in Yoga, fixed his mind on one object and remained perfectly still and calm. He quickly killed all the senses and the intellect with one arrow and even the mind. He entered into his innermost all-blissful soul or Brahman and thereby acquired the highest success.

He was struck with wonder and said, "Alas! It is a pity I wasted my life trying to acquire domain over earthly possessions which are transitory. I wasted my energy in sensual enjoyments. I did not know upto this time how to control the mind and the senses. I performed acts that are external. I courted power, wealth and sovereignty till now. I had no right understanding and discrimination. I had no idea of the Immortal Soul or Atman. I had no idea of the efficiency of Yoga. There is no happiness higher than control of mind by Yoga practices.

There is no wealth higher than the spiritual wealth. There is no bliss higher than the bliss of the Soul. This is the supreme state! I have learnt this truth at last! I have realised this only now."

Arrows cannot really destroy the senses. The senses are located in the astral body or subtle Linga Sarira (Sukshma Deha). Even if the external ears, eyes, nose, etc., are destroyed, the senses still retain their life, strength and vitality. What you see outside are external instruments only. The Indriyas or the senses should be withdrawn and absorbed in the mind itself, through dispassion, discrimination, practice of Dama (self-restraint) and Pratyahara (abstraction). Then only can the senses be destroyed.

All the Vasanas (desires) and Trishnas (cravings) should be destroyed and the mind should be absorbed in its source, i.e., Brahman. Then only the mind can be annihilated. You will have to kill these senses and the mind with the help of the spiritual arrows, viz., Dama, Pratyahara, dispassion, eradication of Vasanas and cravings and the practice of Yoga or meditation. That is the reason why the senses and the mind said to Alarka, "You cannot kill us with these ordinary arrows. Do look for other arrows with which to kill us."

As Alarka was a Tapasvin and firm in his vows, he found out the one true arrow of Yogic concentration and killed the seven faculties with this invincible and powerful arrow.

May you all take recourse to this spiritual arrow of Yoga and enjoy the eternal bliss like Alarka!

A BRAHMIN AND HIS WISE SON

Yudhishthira said: Time is running its course with great speed. People are afraid of time. Time is Lord Yama or God of Death. How should one spend his time in order to obtain the highest good? Please tell me this, O Grand Sire!

Bhishma said: Please listen to the story of a Brahmin and his son. It is very interesting and instructive. Once upon a time there was a Brahmin who was devoted only to the study of the

Vedas. He had a very intelligent son named Medhavin, who was well-versed in the religion of salvation. One day he asked his father who had no knowledge of this religion: "Time runs very fast. Man's span of life passes away very quickly. In these circumstances, what should a man of intelligence do, O revered father?"

The father replied: "One should study the Vedas, observing the vow of Brahmacharya. Then he should desire for offspring, for the sake of saving his sires. He should perform *Agnihotra* and other sacrifices that are ordained in the scriptures. Afterwards he should retire into the forests and become a *Vanaprastha* (forest-recluse or hermit). Then he should become a *Muni* by abandoning everything and calmly wait for dissolution."

The son Medhavin said: "When the world is thus assailed and thus besieged on all sides and when bolts of destruction are falling in every direction, how can you speak so calmly?"

The father said: "May I know, my beloved son, how is the world assailed? By what is it besieged? What are the bolts that are falling on every side? Why do you confuse me with your words?"

The son replied: "This world is assailed by 'death'. It is besieged by 'decrepitude'. Days and nights are falling incessantly like bolts. My beloved father, do you not think about this seriously? 'Death' snatches all away suddenly without any notice. It does not wait for any one. When such is the case how can I wait? Should I not diligently apply myself to conquer 'death' and attain that immortal abode of Eternal Bliss and Supreme Peace. It is foolishness if I attend merely to the mundane affairs of eating, procreating, etc. When one day passes away, remember that the period of one's life wears away with it.

"When one is engaged in very important work, 'death' takes him away. Therefore that which is kept for being done tomorrow should be done today; and that which one thinks of doing in the afternoon should be done in the forenoon. 'Death' does not wait. One should, therefore, practise Japa, meditation, Tapas and Yoga, while still young, because life is uncertain. He should not wait till he attains old age. There is no guarantee of life. 'Death' may come at any moment. If one is virtuous and pious, he will surely attain happiness, both here and hereafter.

"The ignorant man forgets all about his goal of life and engages himself to the end of his life in earning money by hook or crook to please his wife and sons. He gets attached to them. He has no time to do virtuous acts and practise devotion unto God. He engages himself in obtaining objects of enjoyment. While he is thus engaged he is carried away by 'death' suddenly. The friends and relatives may say: 'He has not completed this work. This remains to be done. That work is half done. His son is not fixed in life. He has not saved any money for his children. Only last month a baby was born to him.' But 'death' unmindful of all these things, snatches him away mercilessly. 'Death' seizes the brave, the learned and the young; he snatches away even the best doctor or the mighty potentate.

"Death, decrepitude, pain, disease, sorrow, fear and innumerable calamities besiege a man. How then, O beloved father, can you so sit at your ease? 'Decrepitude' and 'death' are ever waiting to devour a child as soon as it is born; when soldiers of the army of 'death' approach a man, nothing can resist save the power of 'Truth', because Immortality dwells in 'Truth' alone. Virtuous persons cut the cord of attachment and escape from the bond of death, but the sinful are caught in the net of Samsara or the wheel of birth and death.

"If any one does not injure other creatures in thought, word and deed, if he does not harm others by taking away their means of subsistence, he will never be injured by any creature.

"Truth alone triumphs. God is 'Truth'. One should realise 'Truth' by observing truth in thought, word and deed. He who longs for attaining the final emancipation should practise the vow of 'Truth'. He should be firmly devoted to 'Truth'. He should desire nothing but 'Truth'. One should control all one's senses and look upon all beings with an equal eye. He should have conquest over 'death' with the help of 'Truth'.

"O dear father! 'Immortality' and 'death' are planted in this body. One becomes a victim to 'death' through ignorance. Immortality is attained by the knowledge of 'Truth'. I shall free myself from desire and anger, practise non-injury and truth in thought, word and deed and observe celibacy in order to attain 'Immortality'. I will not perform animal sacrifice which is extremely cruel. If sacrifice is necessary, let it be the sacrifice of this ego. This is the highest sacrifice. This is the real sacrifice. I will practise serenity and restrain the senses and concentrate my thoughts constantly on Brahman. O beloved father, I should rest in my own Inner Self which is Immortal and All-blissful. Procreation is not the sole aim in life. I shall perform the sacrifice of self. I do not want any progeny to deliver me.

"If a man is truthful, if he keeps his mind and senses under his control, if he practises austerities, renunciation and Yoga, he is sure to attain everything through these. There is no bliss equal to the bliss of Self-realisation. There is no eye equal to the sight attained by knowledge. There is no wealth equal to the wealth of the knowledge of Brahman. There is no happiness equal to the happiness gained by renunciation. There is no sorrow equal to attachment. There is no misery equal to selfishness. There is no grief equal to that attached to worldly life. For a Brahmin, there can be no wealth like solitude, truthfulness of speech, simple living, humility, an equal regard for all beings, right conduct, Bhakti, penance and meditation. What will you gain through progeny, wealth, house and property? Will your wife, sons, relatives and friends help you in freeing yourself from the clutches of 'death'? Will they assist you in any way in attaining 'Immortality'? This is a world of self-interest and selfish motives. Do not trust them any more. They are your real enemies. They are dacoits inasmuch as by making you a slave to this worldly life, they deprive you of your legitimate right of achieving immortality. They are vultures because they feed on you. They squeeze you. What need hast thou of wealth, relatives, friends, wife and sons? You are a Brahmin. You must conquer 'death' and attain 'Immortality' and 'Eternal Bliss'. This is your real aim and duty. Search your own Atman that is hidden in the cave of your heart and attain that imperishable seat of ineffable splendour and glory.

"Time sweeps away everybody. Bodies of kings, emperors, poets, learned men—all turn into dust in no time. Whither have thy great-grandfather gone and whither thy grandfather and grandmother too? Become dispassionate. Learn to discriminate. Know thyself and be free from attachment, my beloved father!"

Bhishma said: Hearing these wise words of his son Medhavin, the father acted in the way indicated by him. O Yudhishthira, do thou also act in the same way, devoted to the religion of 'Truth'. You will attain the highest bliss. You will go beyond 'Time' and 'Death'.

(Santi Parva, Sec. CCLXXVII)

THE POWER OF AUSTERITIES

Once upon a time a handsome and energetic young prince of the Haihaya race went out hunting. He roamed about in the forest. He saw a Muni wrapped in a deer's skin. The prince mistook the Muni for a deer and killed him. He was very much grieved at heart for what he had done. He went to the Haihaya chiefs and informed them of the incident.

The chiefs saw the dead body of the Muni. They were very much afflicted at heart. They at once made enquiries as to whose son the Muni was and arrived at the hermitage of Arishtanemi, the son of Kasyapa. They bowed down to that great sage and stood there with folded hands. The sage welcomed them. They said to the sage, "O venerable sage! We are not at all worthy of your reception as we have unfortunately killed a Muni."

The sage said to the chief, "How have you killed a Muni? Please tell me where he is."

The chiefs gave a truthful account to the sage of all that had happened and came to the place where the dead body of the Muni was. They did not find it there! They returned to the hermitage of the sage.

The sage, the son of Kasyapa said, "O kings! Is this the Muni who was killed by you? He is my son. He does severe austerities." The chiefs saw the Muni and were struck with wonder. They all exclaimed: "This is really amazing! How has the dead Muni come back to life? Is it by the power of asceticism? O sage! We are all very curious to know about this."

The sage replied, "O kings! Death cannot exercise its power over us. I will tell you the reason briefly and argumentatively. We strictly adhere to our own Dharmas. We always respect the Brahmanas and praise them. We do not censure them. We are very hospitable. We always entertain our guests with food and drink. We first serve our guests with plenty of food and then eat what is left. Therefore, we have no fear of death.

"We are peaceful, charitable, forgiving, generous and benevolent. We dwelve in sacred places. We visit holy temples. We keep company with sages, devotees, Yogis and saints. So we entertain no fear of death.

"I have told you only a bit of our power of devotion. O kings! Abandon pride and vanity. Return to your homes and practise what I told you."

The princes said, "We shall follow your valuable instructions." They all prostrated before the sage and returned to their country with a merry heart.

(Vana Parva, Ch. 185)

NICETIES OF DHARMA

There was once a hunter by name Valaka. He used to kill animals in order to support his children, wife, aged mother, father and other dependants. He never killed the animals wilfully. He always spoke the truth. He was free from malice.

Valaka searched in the forest one day diligently for some animal or other, but he could not find any. At last, he found a beast of prey which was drinking water. He had not seen up to that time an animal of that kind. The animal was blind but it had a very keen sense of smell. The hunter killed the animal. The moment he killed the beast a shower of flowers fell from the skies. A celestial car wherein the Apsaras were singing melodiously came down from heaven to take the hunter.

That animal had performed severe austerities in order to acquire the power to kill all animals. Brahma granted the boon;

but made him blind. Valaka went to heaven because he killed the beast which had the cruel intention of killing all beings. A man by doing even cruel act may acquire the merit of a righteous deed as Valaka did by killing the blind beast.

Morality is, therefore, very difficult to understand. The killing of the animal was a good act in this particular instance. It was not considered as Himsa (inflicting cruelty), because much good resulted by the killing of the animal. Himsa and Ahimsa are relative terms only. To an ordinary man, Ahimsa should be the aim; but he will not fall from this principle if, out of sheer necessity and with no selfish aim, he has recourse to Himsa occasionally. But the aim should always be Ahimsa. One should not give leniency to the mind in this respect. If you are lenient, the mind will always take advantage of this and will goad you to do acts of violence. "Give a rogue an inch, he will take an ell." The mind will at once adopt this policy if you give a long rope for its movement.

This, however, does not apply to a Sannyasin. He should observe Ahimsa in the strictest sense of the term. Even if his life is at stake he should not have recourse to violence or Himsa even to defend his life. A Sannyasin is one who always asserts "I am not this body. I am Siva." If he is firmly fixed in Atma Bhava, if he feels that everybody is his own Self, the mind of a dacoit who proceeds to kill a Sannyasin will at once be changed through the power of Ahimsa or soul-force. Or in some mysterious manner the dacoit will be killed by somebody else, or diverted from or thwarted in his purpose, through divine interference or influence. Even if the body of a Sannyasin is killed, what is it for him who has no identification with the body, and who identifies himself with the All-pervading Immortal Soul?

A Sannyasin and a pious householder, who are striving after Self-realisation, should not kill even snakes or scorpions. A Bhakta who witnesses the Lila of the Lord everywhere worships even a cobra with Arati and Prasad and takes it as a form of Lord Krishna. His ideal should be to practise Ahimsa in the strict sense of the word at all times, in all conditions.

There was a Brahmin named Kaushika in a village which was situated at the confluence of two rivers. He was very strict in the observance of his vows. One of his vows was "I will ever speak the Truth." Therefore he became famous as a truthful man.

Once, the people of the village were afraid of robbers. They went into the forest. The robbers tried to find them out even in the forest. The robbers approached Kaushika and said, "O truthful man! Please tell us which way these persons have passed a little while ego? Tell us if you have seen them, in the name of 'Truth'." Kaushika told them the truth. The robbers seized those persons and killed them. Kaushika, who had no knowledge of the subtleties of religion, fell into horrible hell for the grave sin of uttering the truth which should not have been uttered. Even 'Truth' divorced from the principle of Ahimsa can be a source of sin—as in this case!

A foolish man who is not conversant with the principles and full meaning of morality is apt to fall into a horrible hell for not seeking the counsels of wise men to clear his doubts. All that is free from any motive of injury to any being is surely morality, because the moral precepts have been made to free creatures from all injuries. Dharma (morality) is so called because it protects all.

If a man takes a vow for some definite purpose, and if he cannot redeem the same by actions, he will not obtain the rewards of that vow.

If one's life is in danger, at marriages, or on occasions of risk to the life of one's Guru or father or relatives, anything spoken, which is far from the truth, will not be considered as falsehood. When falsehood is spoken in the cause of Ahimsa, it does not amount to a falsehood. That falsehood is permitted. One must be well-versed in the real secrets of Dharma.

When one's life is at stake, or when one's entire fortunes are about to be lost or in the cause of a Brahmin, untruth may be uttered. There is no sin in uttering falsehood on these occasions. On these occasions untruth is permitted as an exception to the rule. He alone who can distinguish between the niceties of truth and untruth can be said to be conversant with Dharma.

Because it is said one may utter falsehood on such occasions, you should not give leniency to the mind. Your ideal should be to speak the truth at all costs and not to speak falsehood even in jest. The above are exceptions when higher things are at stake, viz., the welfare of others.

(Karna Parva, Ch. 69)

GURU BHAKTI

Veda achieved the good fortune of the knowledge of the Universe as the result of the grace of his preceptor. He had a disciple named Uttanka. Uttanka served his preceptor to his entire satisfaction for several years and attained full knowledge of the Vedas.

The preceptor said, "I am much pleased with your faithful services. I grant you permission to go to your house. Let your wishes be fulfilled."

Uttanka said, "I wish to offer some Dakshina (token of homage) for you."

The preceptor said, "My beloved Uttanka, go to my wife and ask her what she would like for Dakshina."

Uttanka went to his preceptor's wife and said: "Mother! My preceptor has permitted me to go home. I wish to present you with something that would be pleasing as my Dakshina for the instruction I have received from preceptor. Command me, Mother, what will please you to receive as Dakshina."

The preceptor's wife said, "Go to king Paushya and beg from him the ear-rings that are worn by his queen and bring them here. I wish to wear those ear-rings on a sacred day which falls four days hence and appear before the Brahmanas for serving food to them."

Uttanka at once started on a journey to the city of king Paushya. When he was passing along the road he came across a very huge bull and a man of large stature who said, "O Uttanka! Eat the dung of this bull." Uttanka declined to eat it. The man again said, "O Uttanka, eat it without any hesitation. Your teacher also ate it before." Uttanka ate it, washed his hands and marched on his way. He arrived at the palace of Paushya. He went to the king and saluted him. The king returned his salutations and said, "Sir, what shall I do for you?"

Uttanka replied, "I have come to beg of you your queen's ear-rings as a Dakshina to be given to my preceptor. Please give me those ear-rings."

King Paushya said, "Go into the inner chamber and ask for them from the queen."

Uttanka went there but could not see her. He said to the king, "Please do not deceive me. The queen is not in the room. I could not see her."

Paushya said, "Sir, carefully recollect whether you are polluted with the impurities of a meal. The queen is a chaste woman. Therefore she cannot be seen by one who is tainted by the impurities of food."

Uttanka thought for a while and then replied: "Yes, it is so. I was in a hurry. So I did my ablutions when I was walking."

Paushya said, "This is a violation of the law. Ablutions cannot be properly performed standing or walking in a hurry."

Uttanka sat with his face turned towards the East. He washed his hands and feet thoroughly. He sipped the water thrice without any sound. He then washed his face twice and touched his eyes, ears, etc., with water. He again went to the inner chamber of the queen and saw the queen this time.

The queen saluted Uttanka with reverence and said, "Welcome Sir, command me, what shall I do for you?"

Uttanka said to her, "Kindly give me your ear-rings. I beg them from you as I wish to present them to my preceptor."

The queen was very much pleased with the conduct of Uttanka. She took off her ear-rings and gave them to Uttanka. She said, "Takshaka, the king of the Nagas (serpents) has an eye on these ear-rings. Therefore take them with great care."

Uttanka replied, "Do not be anxious, O queen! Takshaka cannot overcome me." Uttanka took leave of the king and queen after receiving the ear-rings.

On his way he saw a naked beggar coming towards him. He

was sometimes coming into his view and sometimes disappearing. Uttanka wanted to have some water. He placed the ear-rings on the ground and went for getting water. In the meantime the beggar came quickly to the place, took the ear-rings and ran away. Uttanka finished his ablutions and prayer, ran after the thief as fast as possible and caught hold of him. Takshaka, who was in the disguise of the beggar, assumed his own real form and quickly entered into a large hole in the ground. He entered the region of the Nagas and went to his own abode.

Uttanka pursued Takshaka. He began to dig open the hole with a stick but he did not make any progress. Indra thought that Uttanka was in great distress. He sent his thunderbolt to his assistance. The thunderbolt entered into the stick and widened the hole. Uttanka entered into the hole after the thunderbolt and saw the land of the Nagas with palaces, gateways, turrets and domes.

Uttanka worshipped the Nagas and made salutations to Takshaka and yet he did not get his ear-rings. He looked around him and saw two maidens working at a loom with a fine shuttle and weaving a piece of cloth. There were black and white threads in the loom. He also saw a wheel with twelve spokes which was turned round by six boys. He also saw a man with a horse.

Uttanka worshipped them. Then the man with the horse said, "I have been much pleased with your adoration. What good can I do to you?"

Uttanka replied, "Let the Nagas be brought under my control."

The man said, "Blow into this horse."

Uttanka blew into the horse. Thousands of flames and fires with smoke issued forth from every opening of the horse. The land of the Nagas was at the point of being burnt down. Takshaka produced the ear-rings and said, "Pray, Sir, take this back." Uttanka got back his ear-rings.

Uttanka thought within himself, "Today is the sacred day mentioned by my preceptress. I am far away from her. How can

I reach her the ear-rings?" When he was thus reflecting, the man said, "Uttanka, get on this horse. He will take you in a moment to the house of your preceptor."

Uttanka mounted the horse and reached his preceptor's house in a moment. By this time, the preceptress had taken her bath and dressed her hair. She was anxiously waiting for Uttanka. At this very time Uttanka entered the house of his preceptor, saluted the mistress and presented her with the ear-rings.

The mistress said, "O Uttanka! You have come just at the proper time. Welcome my child. Good fortune will come to you. May your wishes be fulfilled!"

Then Uttanka made prostrations to his preceptor. His preceptor said, "Uttanka, my child! What made you to be away so long?"

Uttanka replied, "Takshaka ran away with the ear-rings. I had to go to the land of the Nagas. There I saw two maidens working at a loom and weaving a cloth with black and white threads. What may it be? I then saw a wheel with twelve spokes, which was being continually turned by six boys. What does it mean? I also saw a man with a horse. Who is he? The horse was extraordinary in size. What is that horse?

"On my way I saw on the road a man mounted on a bull. He said to me, 'Eat the dung of this bull. Your teacher ate it before.' I ate the dung. Who is this man? What is that bull? I wish to hear all about them, my venerable Guru."

His preceptor said, "The two maidens you saw are Dhata and Vidhata. The black and white threads represent night and day. The wheel with twelve spokes turned by six boys is the year of twelve months having six seasons.

"The man with the horse in Parjanya (the God of Rain). The horse is Agni (the God of Fire). The bull which you saw on the road is Airavata (the king of the elephants). The man who rode on the bull is Indra himself. The dung of the bull which you ate is Ambrosia (nectar). You were not slain in the land of the Nagas, because you ate that dung. Indra is my friend. He did you a great favour by sending his thunderbolt to assist you. Therefore you have been able to return safely with the ear-rings.

"Now my beloved Uttanka, I give you my permission to go. You will obtain good fortune."

Uttanka returned to his home cheerfully with the blessings of his preceptor. He led a happy and virtuous life.

Mark! How Uttanka was devoted to his preceptor. He obtained the grace of his Guru through service and sincere devotion. A disciple cannot prosper in the spiritual path without the grace of his Guru.

(Adi Parva, Ch. III)

ASHTAVAKRA AND VANDI

Uddalaka had a disciple named Kohada. Kohada was devoted himself to the service of his preceptor and studied under him for a very long time. He was self-controlled and diligent. Uddalaka was very much pleased with Kohada. He gave his disciple his own daughter Sujata in marriage. Sujata became pregrant. The child who was dwelling in the womb of Sujata said, "O father! You have been reading for the whole night but your reading does not seem to me correct. I am learned in all the Sastras, the Vedas and the Vedangas."

The father took this as a great insult. So he cursed in anger the child in the womb: "As you speak from the womb, so you will be crooked in eight parts of your body." Thus the child was born crooked and was ever afterwards known by the name Ashtavakra. He had an uncle named Svetaketu who was of the same age as himself.

Sujata one day said to her husband, "I am very anxious about the child. We are not rich. What shall I do now as the time of his birth is very near." Kohada went to the king for getting some wealth. He was defeated in controversy by Vandi who was learned in the science of logic. The result was that Kohada was drowned in the sea by the orders of the king.

Uddalaka came to know that his son-in-law was drowned in the sea. He spoke to Sujata, "You must keep it a secret from Ashtavakra." Sujata accordingly kept it a secret from

Ashtavakra. Ashtavakra regarded Uddalaka as his father and Svetaketu as his brother.

Svetaketu one day saw Ashtavakra on Uddalaka's knee. He dragged Ashtavakra by his hand and exclaimed, "This is not your father's knee!" Ashtavakra began to cry.

Ashtavakra was very much afflicted at heart when he heard these words. He went to his mother, and asked "O mother! Where is my father?" She told all that had happened. Ashtavakra said to Svetaketu, "Let us go to the sacrifice of the king Janaka. We hear of many wonderful things in that sacrifice. We shall hear controversies there among the Brahmanas. We shall also eat good food. We shall also gain experience. It is very delightful to hear the recitation of the Vedas. Man is blessed by hearing the recitation of the Vedas."

Thereupon Ashtavakra and Svetaketu went to the splendid sacrifice of the king Janaka. They were prevented by the gate-keeper.

Ashtavakra: When no Brahmana passes along a path, it then belongs first to the blind, then to the deaf, then to the women, then to the carriers of burden and then last of all to the king. But when a Brahmana comes to it, it solely belongs to him.

A Brahmin: I leave the path. Go in whichever path you like. Even the smallest fire should not be slighted. Indra himself bows down to a Brahmana.

Ashtavakra: O Brahmin, we have come to see the sacrifice. Our curiosity is very intense. We have come as guests. We wish to see and speak with king Janaka. The gate-keeper does not allow us to enter inside. Kindly ask him to allow us inside.

The gate-keeper: We carry out the orders of Vandi. Boys are not allowed to enter here. Only old and learned Brahmanas can enter.

Ashtavakra: O gate-keeper! If this be the order that only old men can enter here, then we can also enter. We also are old in wisdom. We have observed rigid vows. We are endowed with the knowledge of the Vedas and have practised self-restraint. We have served our preceptor. We have also obtained proficiency in knowledge. Even boys who possess knowledge must not be slighted, for even the smallest fire burns.

The gate-keeper: Do not brag too much. Learned men are extremely rare. O boy, if you know, recite the verse which speaks of the existence of the Supreme Being, who is adored by the sages, which is composed of one letter.

Ashtavakra: True growth cannot be judged from the mere development of the body, as the growth of the knots of Salmali tree cannot tell its age. That tree which, though slender and short, bears fruits is called a full-grown tree.

The gate-keeper: Boys receive instructions from the old. They grew old in due course of time. Surely knowledge cannot be obtained in a short time. You are only a child. Why do you talk like an old man?

Ashtavakra: One is not old, simply because his hair has turned grey. Even boys who are endowed with true knowledge are regarded as old by the celestials, Rishis and sages. The *Rishis* have not said that one's merit depends upon age or grey hair or riches. One who is versed in the Vedas, who has knowledge of the Self, is truly great.

O gate-keeper, I have come with the desire of seeing Vandi. Go and inform the king Janaka. I will enter into controversy today with all the learned men and also with Vandi. I will defeat Vandi. When all the learned men and Vandi are defeated by me, the king with his chief priests will recognise my superiority.

The gate-keeper: You are a boy of ten years of age. How can you hope to enter into the premises of the sacrifices into which only learned men are admitted? I shall, however, admit you as you seem to be learned.

When he entered the sacrificial hall, Ashtavakra said, "O king Janaka, we have heard that the learned Vandi enters into controversy with learned men, defeats them and then causes them to be drowned in the sea by servants employed by you. I have come to expound the doctrine of the Supreme Self. Where is that Vandi? I will defeat him."

The king: O boy, you have no idea of the merits and powers of Vandi. He had been tested by the Brahmanas who were experts in arguments and discussion. Just as the stars do not shine before the sun, so also, many learned Brahmanas did not shine before him. Many learned persons who were desirous of defeating Vandi lost their glory on simply appearing before him. They have retired from his presence without even venturing to speak with him. You hope to defeat Vandi, only because you do not know his powers.

Ashtavakra: Vandi has never had an occasion to enter into controversy with one like me. That is the reason why he regards himself as a lion and goes about roaring like a lion. I will baffle him today when he enters into discussion with me. I will extract his teeth today. He will fall down like a dead man, O king! You will witness this today. He cannot stand before me, just as the stars cannot shine before the sun.

The king: He alone who knows the thing that has thirty divisions, twelve parts, twenty-four joints and three hundred and sixty spokes is a real learned man.

Ashtavakra: May that ever-revolving wheel (time) that has twenty-four joints, six naves, twelve peripheries and sixty spokes protect you!

The king: Who amongst the celestials gives birth to those two, which go together like two yoked mares and take with a sweep like hawks, and to what also do they give birth?

Ashtavakra: O king, may the Omnipotent Lord keep away from your mansion those two (thunder and lightning), nay, even from the house of your enemies. He who appears with the wind as his charioteer (cloud) gives birth to them and they also produce him.

The king: What is it that does not close its eyes even when it is asleep? What is it that does not move when born? What is it that has no heart? And what is it that increases in its speed?

Ashtavakra: A fish does not close its eyes when asleep. An egg does not move even when born. A stone has no heart. A river increases in its speed.

The king: O learned sage! You are not a human being. You are not a boy. You are indeed a grown-up man. You are endowed with great erudition. No one can be compared with you in learning. Therefore you can enter the sacrificial place. Just see! There is Vandi.

Ashtavakra: O Vandi, you are puffed with the pride of your learning. You consider that you are the best of all controversialists. I am like a flaming fire. Be silent before me.

Ashtavakra began to roar in the assembly. He said, "O Vandi! Answer my questions. I shall answer yours."

Vandi: Fire is only one which blazes in various forms. One is the Sun that illumines the Universe. One is the hero, Indra, the Lord of the Celestials. One is Yama, the sole Lord of the Pitris (ancestors).

Ashtavakra: The two friends, Agni and Indra move together. The celestial sages are two, Narada and Parvata. The Aswins are two. The wheels of a car are two. Two are the husband and wife, who live together as ordained by the deity.

Vandi: Three kinds of beings are born as the results of their acts. Three are the Vedas that perform the Vajapeya sacrifice. At three different times the Adhvaryus commence sacrifice. Three also are the divine lights.

Ashtavakra: Four are the Ashramas of the Brahmanas; four orders perform sacrifices; four are the cardinal points; four is the number of letters; and four also are the legs of a cow.

Vandi: Five is the number of fires; five are the feet of Punki (a metre); five are the sacrifices; five locks are on the heads of the Apsaras; and five are the sacred rivers in the world.

Ashtavakra: Six cows are given as Dakshina on establishing the sacred fire; six are the seasons that belong to the wheel of time; six stars form the constellation Krittika; and the Vedas say six is the number of Sadyasaka sacrifice.

Vandi: Seven is the number of domestic animals; seven also is the number of wild animals; seven metres are used in completing a sacrifice; seven are the Rishis; seven are the forms of paying homage; and seven are the strings of the Vina.

Ashtavakra: Eight are the bags that hold hundredfold; eight is the number of the Sarabha, which preys upon lions; eight are the Vasus amongst the celestials; and eight are the angles of a Yupa (stake) in a sacrifice.

Vandi: Nine is the number of the Mantras used in kindling the fire in a sacrifice to the Pitris; nine are the fixed functions in the progress of creation; nine letters compose the foot of Vrihati (a metre); and nine also are numbers in calculation.

Ashtavakra: Ten is the number of the cardinal points; ten times hundred makes a thousand; ten is the number of months of woman's conception; ten are the teachers of true knowledge; ten are the haters of knowledge; and ten are capable of attaining it.

Vandi: Eleven are the objects of enjoyment; eleven is the number of Yupas (sacrificial stake); eleven are the natural states of all living creatures; eleven are the Rudras among the celestials in heaven.

Ashtavakra: Twelve are the months in a year; twelve letters compose a foot of Fajati (a metre); twelve are the sacrifices; and twelve is the number of the Adityas.

Vandi: Thirteen lunar days are most auspicious; and thirteen islands exist on earth.

Having said this Vandi stopped. Thereupon Ashtavakra completed the other half of the Sloka.

Ashtavakra: Thirteen sacrifices are presided over by Keshi and thirteen are devoured by Atichandas of the Vedas.

Vandi was sitting silent with head downcast. Ashtavakra was roaring in the assembly. All men rose in great uproar. The Brahmanas became highly delighted. They all came to Ashtavakra with joined hands and paid him due respects.

The Brahmanas: Vandi defeated the Brahmanas in controversy and threw them into the sea. Let Vandi meet with the same fate today. Catch him and drown him in the sea.

Vandi: I am the son of King Varuna, O Janaka! Simultaneously with your sacrifice Varuna has commenced a sacrifice underneath the sea extending over twelve years. I have sent there those Brahmanas. They had all gone there to see Varuna's sacrifice. Just see, they are all coming. I pay due respects to the revered Ashtavakra. I shall today join my father through the favour of Ashtavakra.

Ashtavakra: Vandi defeated the Brahmanas by words and

threw them in the sea. I have today rescued them. O Janaka! It seems you are not listening to my words though you are pierced by them.

Janaka: I am listening to your words which are excellent and superhuman. You are also a superhuman being, though you appear to be a boy. You have today defeated Vandi in controversy. I place even him at your disposal.

Ashtavakra: O king, if Vandi remains alive he is of no use to me. If his father is really Varuna, let him be drowned in the sea.

Vandi: O Ashtavakra! I am verily the son of the king Varuna. Therefore, I have no fear in being drowned. Even at this very moment you will see your long lost father Kohada.

Then rose before Janaka all the Brahmanas after they had been duly worshipped by Varuna.

Kohada: O king Janaka! It is for this reason men desire for virtuous sons. My son has done that in which I failed.

When all the Brahmanas rose from the waters of the sea, they shone with increased splendour and effulgence. Vandi, with the permission of king Janaka, entered the ocean.

Ashtavakra then worshipped his father. He himself was adored by all the Brahmanas. Ashtavakra then returned with his uncle and father to his hermitage.

Kohada said, "O my beloved son Ashtavakra! quickly enter into the water of this river Samanga." Ashtavakra immediately entered the river. All his crooked limbs assumed natural form at once. From that day that river came to be known by the name of 'Samanga' and it became capable of cleaning sins. Those who take bath in this river are cleansed of all sins.

An illustrious learned son like Ashtavakra, brings great glory to his family and the world at large. A man's merit does not depend upon years or on grey hair. He who is well-versed in the Vedas, he who has knowledge of Brahman, is really a great man. He is adored by all Devatas and Brahmanas. Ashtavakra was a boy of ten years. How marvellous was his intellect! How wonderful was his knowledge! The whole assembly of learned Brahmanas was stunned at his thrilling controversy. His conversation was indeed amazing. Ashtavakra spoke when he was dwelling in his mother's womb: "O father! I tell you, what proceeds from your lips is not correct." What a great marvel! Ashtavakra was a *Yoga Bhrashtha* like Vamadeva who also delivered discourses on Atma Jnana, when he was dwelling in his mother's womb.

Mere remembrance of these high souls destroys atheistic tendencies of materialistic people, inspires people and goads them to strive for the final emancipation or Brahma Jnana.

The lives of Ashtavakra and Vamadeva also prove conclusively that there is rebirth. In one birth alone one cannot attain perfection and mastery over the Vedas. The accumulated good fruits (Samskaras of virtuous acts), study of religious books, practice of Tapas, Yoga and meditation in several births, produce a spiritual prodigy and a Yogic adept like Ashtavakra or Vamadeva in the last birth. Man gains experience in every birth. He becomes gradually moulded and attains perfection after several births. To attain excellence in all virtues and become a full blown Yogi or a perfect master is hardly possible in one birth.

Glory to Ashtavakra, the renowned boy-sage, who delivered all the learned Brahmanas and his father through his knowledge and who still lives in our hearts because of his supreme wisdom and divine effulgence!

(Vana Parva, Ch. 132-134)

KING JANAKA AND OWNERSHIP

King Janaka wanted to punish a Brahmin who had become guilty of some offence. He said to the Brahmin, "O Brahmin! Do not live within my dominion."

The Brahmin replied, "O king! May I know the limits of your dominion? I shall then leave your boundaries and go to the dominion of another king. I wish to obey your command."

The king did not speak a word in reply. At first his mind became clouded; then it cleared and he began to reflect seriously. The king said to the Brahmin, "Although I have inherited a large dominion which is under my subjection, yet I am not able to find, after deep enquiry and reflection, my dominion in the whole world. When I could not find in the whole world, I searched for it in Mithila. When I could not find it in Mithila, I searched for it among my own children. When I could not find it even there, my understanding became confused for a time. Then I regained clearness of understanding. Then I concluded that I have no dominion, or that everything is my dominion. This body is not mine, or the whole world is mine.

"O Brahmin, I think that that is as much mine as it is yours. Therefore live here as long as you like."

The Brahmin said, "O king! Kindly tell me how you eradicated the idea of 'mine-ness'. How have you come to the conclusion that you have no dominion, or everything is your dominion?"

Janaka said, "Everything is impermanent here. Everything perishes. Therefore, I could not find anything which should be called 'mine'. I thought of the Vedic text about the ownership of property. I could not find what should be called 'mine'. Therefore, I eradicated the idea of 'mine-ness'.

"Just listen to me how I arrived at the conclusion that I have dominion everywhere or that everything is my dominion.

"I do not wish for my own self those smells which are even in my nose. Therefore the earth is conquered by me. It is always under me. I do not wish for my own self those tastes which exist in contact with even my tongue. Therefore, I have subjugated water. It is always under me. I do not wish for my own self the colour or light which belongs to my eye. Therefore, the light is subjugated by me. It is always under me. I do not wish for my own self those sensations of touch which are in contact with even my skin. Therefore, I have controlled the wind. The wind is always under me. I do not wish for my own self those sounds which are in contact with even my ear. Therefore, sounds are always under my control. I do not wish for my own self the mind. I have neither Sankalpa nor Vasanas nor likes and dislikes. Therefore, the mind is always under my control. I perform acts for the sake of the Devatas, the Pitrus, the Bhutas and guests."

The Brahmin smiled and said to Janaka, "O king! Know that I am Dharma. I came here today for testing you. You are indeed the one person for setting this wheel in motion—this marvellous wheel which has the quality of goodness for its circumference, Brahma for its nave and the understanding or intellect for its spokes and which never turns back."

(Asvamedha Parva, Ch. 32)

SAGE JANAKA AND RENUNCIATION

Yudhishthira said, Tell me, O venerable grandsire! If anyone has attained emancipation without giving up the domestic mode of life. What is the supreme form of salvation or Moksha?

Bhishma said, O king! Listen to this discourse between Janaka and Sulabha.

In olden times there was a king of Mithila, named Janaka. He was well-versed in the Vedas and in the scriptures that treat on emancipation and the duties of a king. He was devoted to the practices of the religion of renunciation. He had all his senses under perfect control.

Sulabha, a woman, belonging to the mendicant order, practised Yoga and wandered over the whole world. In the course of her wanderings she heard from many Dandi Sannyasins that Janaka, the ruler of Mithila, was highly devoted to the religion of emancipation. She wished to have an interview with Janaka. She went to the capital of Mithila, abandoned her original form and assuming the form of a young beautiful girl through her power of Yoga, appeared in the guise of a mendicant before Janaka. Raja Janaka enquired, who she was, whose she was and whence she came? He paid her due respects. He offered her seat and water to wash her feet and gave her good food also.

Sulabha doubted whether Janaka was really emancipated or not. She entered the mind of the king through her power of Yoga.

Janaka said, "O pious lady! I am the beloved disciple of the reputed person Panchasikha, belonging to the mendicant order of Parasara's race. I am well-versed in the Sankhya and the Yoga systems, the ordinances regarding sacrifices and other rites. My preceptor gave me discourses on the various means for attaining salvation. He did not command me to give up my kingdom. Renunciation of all kinds of attachments is the highest means prescribed for salvation. Through Yoga one attains the knowledge of Brahman. One attains immortality through knowledge of the Self. I have acquired this knowledge. I have transcended all pairs of opposites. I have no attachment for anything. I have neither love for my wife nor hatred for my enemies. I have developed the faculty of regarding everything with the same equanimity. I regard him, that smears my right hand with sandal paste, and him that injures my left hand, with the same indifference.

"I am always happy. In my view, a clod of earth, a piece of stone and a lump of gold, are of equal value. Though I rule a kingdom, I have no attachment of any kind. Some say that emancipation has a triple path, viz., knowledge, Yoga and sacrifices. Some are of opinion that complete renunciation of acts is the means of attaining emancipation. Some say that knowledge is the only means. Yatis hold that acts constitute the means to attain emancipation. If men who lead the domestic mode of life, diligently and sincerely practise Yama and Niyama, they are equal to Sannyasins. If Sannyasins are subject to desires, hatred and pride, they are none better than men who lead the domestic mode of life.

"Both the king and the Sannyasin can acquire knowledge and therefore attain the final emancipation. If a person abandons the domestic mode of life and takes to Sannyasa, he cannot necessarily be considered as one who is at once freed from all attachments. The wearing of orange-coloured robes, shaving of the head, bearing of the trident or Danda and the Kamandalu, are the outward signs of one's mode of life. Emancipation is not confined to poverty, nor is freedom from bondage to be found in prosperous condition. One attains emancipation through knowledge of Brahman alone, whether he is poor or rich. I have cut off all attachments with the sword of renunciation, whetted on the stone of knowledge derived from the scriptures, which treat of emancipation.

"O Sulabha! I have great regard for you. But your behaviour does not correspond with the practices of the mode of life to which you have taken yourself. You are young and beautiful. I doubt very much whether you have controlled your senses or not. You have entered into me through your power of Yoga and caused my body to cease functioning for ascertaining whether I am really emancipated or not. This is a wrong action. You do not adhere to your Danda. For one who is not free from desires the trident (triple stick) is unfit.

"You are a Brahmin woman. I am a Kshatriya. You are a Sannyasini. I am a householder. There has been an unnatural union between persons who do not lead the same mode of life. You have caused intermixture of castes. You have done a sinful act. Have you done this act from ignorance or from perverted intelligence? On account of your evil nature, you have become thoroughly callous and unrestrained in your behaviour. You have tried to show your superiority. You wanted to defeat not only me but also all the learned persons of my court and to glorify yourself. You are proud of your Yogic powers. You have caused a union of your knowledge with mine and thereby you have mixed together poison with nectar. Do not continue to touch me. Know that I am righteous. Do not act according to your own mind. Do not conceal from me your secret motives. One should not appear deceitful before a king. What is your object in coming to me? To what order do you belong?"

Though Raja Janaka rebuked Sulabha in these unpleasant and improper words, she was not at all abashed. She gave the following apt answer to the king.

Sulabha said, "You have asked me, who I am, whose I am and whence I am coming? Listen to me with close attention. Just as lac and wood, grains of dust and drops of water exist, commingled when brought together, so also are the existences of all creatures. Sound, touch, taste, form, smell and the senses, exist in a state of assimilation like dust and drops of water. Nobody asks any of these, who art thou? Each of them also has no knowledge either of itself or of the others. The 'eye' cannot see itself. The 'ear' cannot hear itself. The 'eye' cannot perform the functions of any of the other organs. It can carry out its own function of seeing. Similar is the case with the other organs. If all of them even join together, they cannot know their own selves, just as dust and water brought together cannot know each other though existing in a state of union. They await the contact of objects that are external to them in order to perform their respective functions. Three things, viz., the eye, object and light are necessary for the function of seeing. Similar is the case with the functioning of other senses. Even then, the senses cannot function without the help of the mind. They simply transmute the sensations or vibrations to the mind. It is the 'mind' that really sees, hears, tastes, smells and feels. Mind is called the eleventh sense. Intellect is the twelfth principle. When doubt arises in the mind, intellect comes forward and settles all doubts. Sattva is the thirteenth principle. Consciousness is the fourteenth principle. It helps one to distinguish the 'Self' from what is 'not-Self'. Desire is the fifteenth principle. The entire world functions on this principle. On account of desire only, man is born again and again in this Universe.

"Avidya is the sixteenth principle. Happiness and sorrow, gain and loss, heat and cold, honour and dishonour, censure and praise, are called the pairs of opposites. Time is another principle. Births and deaths of all creatures are due to the actions of this principle. The five great primal elements are five other principles. Some regard the unmanifest Prakriti to be the source or cause of these principles. Kanadas regard the atoms to be their cause. The constituent elements of the body undergo change every moment. This body is composed of five elements. When the Prana departs, the body decomposes and disintegrates. When such is the state of the bodies of all creatures the questions 'who are you', 'whose are you' and 'where do you come from' have no meaning. What connection does there exist between creatures and their own bodies? When two sticks of wood are rubbed against each other, fire is generated. Even so, creatures are produced from the combination of the above principles. Why do you not see your own body and your own soul in the bodies and souls of others? If you see your identity with others, why then did you ask me 'who I am' and 'whose'? If you are really freed from the erroneous idea of duality, what use is there with such questions as 'who art thou', 'whose art thou' and 'whence dost thou come'? When you have so many faults, how can it be said that you have attained emancipation? The idea of duality is still in you. You can have, therefore, no equal vision. You claim that you are emancipated, but you still have attachment. You are not free. The king is always dependent on others. The king entertains fear of those who wait upon him. If a number of wise heroic and wealthy men come together, the king's mind is filled with distrust. The king is drowned in sorrow when his country is ruined, when his dear relatives perish, when the city is consumed by fire. The king is not free from desire, hatred, fear and the pairs of opposites, such as pleasure and pain. He is afraid of his enemies. A king is forced to remain attached to his possessions or responsibilities. He has no independence. He cannot have his own time for sleeping. Ministers and others will disturb him, even while he is sleeping, to attend to some urgent work. There is no happiness for a king. O ruler of Mithila! I can mention hundreds and thousands of faults like these that attach to kings.

"The real 'I' has no real connection with my body. How then can I be said to have any contact with the bodies of others? You cannot charge me that I have caused an intermixture of castes. It seems that you possess only worldly knowledge. You are bound by the bonds of touch, wife, palace, etc., like an ordinary man of the world. If you have really attained emancipation, if you are really freed from all bonds, what harm have I done by entering your person with only my soul-force? I have not touched you, O king, with my hands or feet or thighs or with any part of my body. What harm have I done to you by entering into your intellect from which alone comes the real knowledge? My entering into your body is in spirit only and was not known to others. It concerns us two only. Was it not improper for you to publish that private act before your court? You are born in a high and noble family. You have foresight. But you are not really acquainted with the rules of propriety with regard to speech. I am staying in you without touching you at all through my Yogic power like a drop of water on a lotus leaf that reamins in it without drenching it in the least. In spite of this you still feel my touch. You have not understood the instructions of your Guru. You have not practised any spiritual Sadhana. You have no abstraction of the senses from the objects. You have not attained emancipation. All your talk of being emancipated is mere empty or tall talk only. You have not grasped the truths of Vedanta. You are only a lip Vedantin. You have no direct knowledge of the Self. You have not yet experienced the light of true knowledge. You pretend that you have reached the goal of life. You have still a long way to go to reach it. You are neither a householder nor a sage who has realised Atman. The contact of a liberated soul with a Yogi, cannot lead to an intermingling of the kind you are afraid of. He who regards the soul to be identical with the body and thinks that the several orders or modes of life to be really different from one another has the erroneous idea of intermingling.

"My body is different from your body; but my soul is not different from your soul. I realise this. Therefore, I am quite sure that the real 'I' or my soul is really not staying in thine, though I have entered into your body by Yoga. There is a pot in the hand. There is milk in the pot. There is a fly in the milk. The pot is not certainly a part of the milk. Nor has the milk been converted to the nature of the fly. The condition of each can never be changed by the condition of that kind of thing with or in which it may exist temporarily. Similarly colour and practices do not really affect a liberated person. Intermingling of orders cannot occur on account of our union.

"I am not superior to you in colour. I am neither a Vaisya nor a Sudra. I am of the same order with you. I am born of a pure race. You might have heard of the royal sage Pradhana. I am born in his race. My name is Sulabha. Indra accompanied by Drona, Chakradwara and Satasringa used to attend the sacrifices performed by my ancestors. No suitable husband could be obtained for me. Thereupon I was instructed in the religion of emancipation and practised rigid austerities in order to attain it. Having done so, I now wander over the world alone.

"I am not a religious hypocrite. I strictly adhere to the

principles of the mode of life to which I belong. I am firm and steady in my vows. I never utter any useless word. I reflect well and then speak very cautiously. I heard that you are a liberated sage. I thought I would be profited spiritually by your Satsanga and discourses on emancipation. I do not want to glorify myself. I do not wish to humiliate my opponents. I am very sincere. I do not want to enter into intellectual discussion for attaining victory. I want to devote myself to meditation on Brahman, the sole seat of Eternal Peace. Just as a Sannyasi resides for only one night in an empty house and leaves it the next morning, so also I shall reside this one night in thy person which, as I have already said, is like an empty chamber, being devoid of true knowledge of Self. Tomorrow I shall leave this place. You have honoured me with speech, seat, refreshments and other offers. Thou art my venerable host. I am grateful to thee, indeed."

Janaka heard these words of wisdom. He was much benefited by the philosophy preached to him by Sulabha.

PART III

SAKUNTALA

Dushyanta was the founder of the Paurava dynasty. He was a powerful king. He was the protector of the Earth. He was an expert in riding elephants and horses. In strength he was like Vishnu. In splendour he was like the Sun.

Once Dushyanta, accompanied by a big army and many chariots, went into the deep forest for hunting. He wandered in the forest and killed many animals. Fatigued with hunger and thirst, he entered a most lovely grove. Therein he saw the auspicious and sacred hermitage of Kanva, son of Kashyapa, beautified by the Malini river. He left behind all his attendants and entered the hermitage alone but he did not find there the Rishi of 'rigid vows' (Kanva). Not finding the Rishi and seeing the hermitage empty, he called aloud "Who is here?" His voice echoed in the forest.

Then, on hearing his voice, a maiden in the garb of an ascetic, as beautiful as the Goddess Lakshmi, came out of the hermitage. As soon as she saw the king (Dushyanta), she bade him welcome and paid him due reverence. She offered him a seat with due respect. She gave him water to wash his feet and then offered him the Arghya. She then enquired after his welfare and asked, "What is it you desire?" The king replied, "My name is Dushyanta. I have come to worship the blessed Rishi Kanva. Tell me where he has gone."

Sakuntala: My noble father has gone out of the hermitage to collect fruits. If you kindly wait a moment, you can see him on return.

The king: Who are you, O maiden? Whose daughter are you? Why have you come into this forest? Whence have you come here? You have stolen my heart at the very first glance. I wish to know all about you. Please tell me everything.

Sakuntala: I am regarded, O Dushyanta, as the daughter of the illustrious, virtuous, wise and high-souled ascetic Kanva.

The king: The illustrious Rishi is adored by the whole world. He is a life-long celibate. How can you be his daughter? Kindly remove this great doubt of mine.

Sakuntala: O king! Hear what I have learnt from the Rishi, regarding all that happened to me and how I came to be regarded as his daughter. Once a Rishi came here and asked about my birth. Hear what the Rishi Kanva told him.

Kanva said, "Visvamitra was engaged in the practice of severe austerities. He alarmed Indra. Indra thought that the Rishi would hurl him from his high seat in heaven by his penances. Being thus alarmed, he called Menaka and told her, 'O Menaka! Visvamitra is engaged in severe penances. Go and tempt him. Turn him away from his austerities.'

"Saying 'be it so', Menaka proceeded to the hermitage of the great Rishi Visvamitra and appeared before him. She saluted the Rishi and began to spread her charms over him. Seeing her grace, beauty and accomplishments, Visvamitra was overpowerd by the desire to possess her. After some time, Menaka gave birth to a daughter, born of Visvamitra on the banks of the river Malini. She then left the child on the banks of the river and returned to the court of Indra.

"I went there to bathe and saw this child lying on the ground. I brought her to my hermitage and adopted her as my daughter. The child is Sakuntala. According to the scriptures, the maker of the body, the protector of life and the giver of food—these three—are in their order regarded to be fathers. As she was tended by young birds (Sakuntas) in the forest, the name Sakuntala (protected by birds) was given to her by me." Thus Rishi Kanva spoke of my birth to that great sage. Thus, O king, know me to be the daughter of Rishi Kanva.

The king: O blessed lady, be my wife. Let the whole of my kingdom be yours. I shall present you, this very day, pearls, gems and ear-rings. Let us wed according to the Gandharva form of marriage, because this form of marriage is said to be the best.

Sakuntala: O king! My father has gone out to gather fruits. Kindly wait for a moment. My father is my master and supreme deity. He on whom my father bestows me shall be my husband. The father protects one during infancy, the husband when one is in the prime of life, and the son when one has become old. A woman can have no independence. How can I, contrary to Dharma, marry without obtaining the previous consent of my saintly father?

The king: I desire that you yourself should accept me. I exist for you. My heart is completely in you. One is certainly one's own friend. One's self only is the refuge of oneself. Therefore, according to the ordinance, according to Dharma, you can make a gift of yourself by yourself.

Sakuntala: O best of the Puru race! If this is the dictate of the scriptures, if this is verily the path of Dharma, if I am really my own disposer, know then my terms. Promise to give me what I ask. The son that will be hereafter born of me must become the heir-apparent to your throne. If you agree, we can marry now.

The king: O blessed lady! Let it be so.

Sakuntala: Righteous people say that the observance of the marriage rites is highly conducive to the welfare of the progeny. Therefore, I desire, the rites may be performed duly.

Dushyanta brought the priest and performed the wedding ceremony according to the due rites. He took Sakuntala by the hand and she accepted him as her husband and stayed with him. He repeatedly told her, "I shall send my army and band to escort you to my kingdom. I shall receive you with all honour." Having thus promised her, the king returned to his city.

Kanva returned to the hermitage. Sakuntala did not go near her father on account of shyness. The great ascetic Kanva, who was endowed with divine sight, understood everything. Having thus seen everything with his divine sight, the illustrious Rishi said, "My beloved child! The act that you have committed today in secret, without having waited to get my sanction, is not a breach of Dharma. There is no cause for fear. Do not grieve. The marriage according to the Gandharva form between a willing woman and a willing man, is said to be the best for

Kshatriyas. Dushyanta, the best of men, is a high-souled and virtuous person. The son, whom you will give birth to, will be mighty and illustrious in this world. From today you are the queen of the great Dushyanta. Be devoted to your husband and lead a chaste life. I give the boon that the Paurava kings shall be ever virtuous and shall never be deprived of their thrones."

Sakuntala gave birth to a son. When he was born, a shower of flowers fell from the sky. Kanva performed all the holy rites, beginning with Jatakarma, ordained by the scriptures. When the child grew only three years old, he became in splendour as the blazing Sun. He was extremely handsome and magnanimous. He was endowed with all accomplishments. When he was six years old, he was able to catch tigers, lions and wolves and tie them to the trees of the hermitage. He played with them in sport. Sometimes he rode on some of these wild animals.

Sage Kanva and all the residents of the hermitage, who witnessed the superhuman deeds of the boy, exclaimed, "May this boy be called Sarvadamana, as he subjugates all beasts and as he is able to control everything." Thus the prince came to be called "Sarvadamana" as he was endowed with great strength, energy and valour.

Dushyanta did not send for Sakuntala on account of fear of the sage. Thus a long period elapsed and Dushyanta forgot all about Sakuntala. As Dushyanta did not send for Sakuntala, Kanva spoke to his disciples thus: "Take Sakuntala with her son from this hermitage to the house of her husband. It is not proper for women to live for ever in the house of their paternal or maternal relations. Such residence destroys their good name and affects their conduct and virtues. Therefore take her to her husband's house without delay."

The obedient disciples started with Sakuntala and her son towards the city of Dushyanta and soon reached it. She entered the palace with her son. The disciples of Rishi narrated everything to the king and returned to the hermitage.

Sakuntala duly worshipped the king. She said to her son, "Bow down to the king, your father." She stood there with her face bent down in modesty and told the king, "Be gracious to me." The son also bowed to the king with folded palms in adoration.

Dushyanta: Tell me, O lady, the object of your coming here.

Sakuntala: This is verily your son, born of me. Let him be installed as your heir-apparent. Fulfil now the promise you made me. O illustrious king! Please recollect the agreement you made with me on the occasion of our marriage at the hermitage of Kanva.

Having heard these words, the king understood everything, but he said, "I do not remember anything."

Sakuntala was abashed. She was overwhelmed with grief. She said to the king, "Knowing everything, how can you, like an ordinary man in the street, say that you know nothing? Your heart is the witness to the truth or falsehood of my words. Therefore speak the truth. Do not degrade yourself. He who has one thing in his mind but represents another thing to others is a thief and a robber of his own self. He deceives his own self or all-witnessing soul. You think, while committing a sin, 'Nobody knows.' But the great Omniscient One who dwells in your heart knows all your sins and thoughts. You sin in His presence.

"The Sun, the Moon, the Air, the Fire, the Earth, the Sky, the Water, the Heart, Yama, the Day, the Night, the Twilight, the Celestials and Dharma, see every act of man. He who tells lies, who falsely represents his self and thus degrades himself, is never blessed by the celestials. Even his own soul does not bless him.

"I am a devoted wife to my husband. I am your wife. I deserve to be treated respectfully. Do not disrespect me. Why do you treat me like an ordinary woman before these men?

"The wise sages say that the husband himself enters into the womb of his wife and comes out as the son. Therefore the wife is called Jaya. The son rescues the deceased forefathers. As the son delivers his ancestors from the hell called Puth, he has been called by the self-created Brahma himself as Putra. The husband divides his body into two parts and is born in the womb of his wife as the son.

"She is a true wife who is a good house-wife. She is a true

wife whose heart is devoted to her husband. She is a true wife who is faithful to her husband. A man's half is his wife. The wife is her husband's best friend. The wife is the source of Dharma, Artha and Kama. The wife is the source of salvation. He who has a wife can perform religious rites. He who has a wife can achieve good fortune. He who has a wife can lead the domestic life. The wife who converses sweetly is the friend of the husband on the occasion of joy. She is like a father on occasions of religious acts. She is like a mother in times of illness and woe. Even in the deep forest, the wife is the consoler and solace to her roaming husband. He who has a wife is trusted by all. Therefore the wife is man's great means of salvation.

"When the husband goes to the region of Yama, only the devoted wife accompanies him there. The chaste wife waits for her husband and follows him.

"The wise men have said that a man himself is born as his son. Therefore, a man, whose wife has given birth to a son should consider his wife as his mother.

"No man, even in anger, should do anything that is disagreeable to his wife; because happiness, joy, virtue and everything depend on the wife.

"Even ants support their offspring and do not destroy their eggs. Why then should you not, learned in the rules of Dharma, support your own child?

"The following Vedic Mantras are recited by the father at the birthday ceremony of the child: 'You are born of my body. You have sprung from my heart. You are myself in the form of my son. Live for one hundred years. My life depends on you. The continuation of my race depends on you. Therefore live happily for one hundred years.

"This boy has sprung of your body. See your own self in your own son, as you see your image in the clear waters of the lake.

"Gait, appearance, gesture, movement of limbs, curls and marks—these characteristics that are seen in the father are found in the sons. Why do you ignore your son, who has come to you, who is full of affection for you, who is noble-minded, brave and energetic and who is looking at you with joy?

"O king! When I was a virgin in my father's hermitage, I was approached by you in your hunting expedition. You clasped my hand according to the prescribed rites in the Gandharva form of marriage. I have now taken shelter under you. I fully rely on the nobility of your family, good conduct, truthfulness and your adhering to your own Dharma. You should not abandon me after making a promise. If you abandon me, I may go back to the hermitage. But you should not cast off this child who is your own flesh and blood."

Dushyanta: O Sakuntala! I do not know that I begot this child on you. Women generally utter untruth. Who will believe your words? Your mother is the lewd Menaka, devoid of affection. She cast you off in the forest. Your father is the lustful Visvamitra. Your son is very bonny and strong. How has he, within so short a time, grown up like a Sala sprout? You are born very low. I do not know you. Go away wherever you please.

Sakuntala: My birth is indeed superior to your birth. You walk on the earth. But I move about in the sky. Know that the difference between you and me is like that of a mustard seed and the Meru mountain. The ugly man considers himself more handsome than others, till he sees his face in a mirror.

If the fruit of one-hundred horse-sacrifices and 'truth' were weighed, 'truth' would be found heavier than all those sacrifices. Studying all the Vedas or bathing in all the holy rivers is not worth even a sixteenth part of the merit of uttering the 'truth'. There is no virtue equal to 'truth'. There is nothing in this world superior to 'truth'. There is nothing more sinful than falsehood. 'Truth' is the great Brahman. 'Truth' is the highest Dharma. 'Truth' is the highest vow. Therefore, O king, do not violate your pledge. Let 'truth' and yourself be ever united.

If you are associated with falsehood, if you do not believe me, I am without witness, I am very unfortunate and I will go back to my hermitage.

Having said all this to the king, Sakuntala turned her back. Then a voice from heaven addressed Dushyanta who was sitting surrounded by his ministers and priests: "Support your son.

Sakuntala spoke the truth. Do not insult Sakuntala. As you will support this child at your word, your son will be known by the name of 'Bharata'. He will earn great fame. He will rule the whole earth surrounded by the seven Seas. From him will spread the fame of a Bharata family." So saying the gods rained flowers on him.

Dushyanta told his ministers and priests, "I myself know that this boy is my son. If I had accepted him as my son at Sakuntala's words, my people would have been suspicious and my son also would not have been considered to be of pure birth."

The king was immensely pleased because the purity of the birth of his son was established by the messengers of heaven. He accepted him as his son and embraced him with affection. He received his wife with all honour and affection. He spoke to her thus, "O blessed Sakuntala! My union with you took place in private. None knew of it. Consequently it is natural that people should have thought that our union was only out of lust and that we were not husband and wife. This son would have been regarded as one of impure birth. Therefore I was trying my best to establish your purity. I have forgiven you all the harsh words you have spoken in anger. You are my darling. Forgive me also for uttering cruel words to you."

The king Dushyanta thereupon installed the son of Sakuntala as his heir-apparent and gave him the name of 'Bharata'. He accepted Sakuntala as his chief queen. Dushyanta thereafter led a happy and peaceful life for many years and in his old age handed over the kingdom to Bharata.

Bharata brought under his sway all the kings of the world. He ruled his subjects virtuously and earned great fame. He performed many sacrifices. He was known by the name of 'Chakravarti' and 'Sarvabhauma'. This land of ours 'India' is called 'Bharatavarsha' after this king Bharata. So great was his fame and all peolple loved him like their father. He protected the people in all respects.

If a promise or pledge is solemnly made, it must be kept up at all costs. Truth alone triumphs but not falsehood in the long end. It is the duty of man to speak truth. Sakuntala had no witnesses. She was in a helpless condition; but she was supported by the Asariri voice from heaven. A truthful man gets help from various quarters, though he is troubled in the beginning by the worldly-minded persons who utter falsehood. God is ever ready to help a truthful man. People say that they cannot pull on in this world and in business by speaking the truth. It is a serious misapprehension indeed. The prosperity of a man who earns money by speaking falsehood is transitory. It is a false glittering. He will reap a bad harvest in his next birth. He will be punished in the other world. A truthful man only really prospers herein and hereafter.

(Adi Parva, Ch. 74)

SAVITRI AND SATYAVAN

The story of Savitri, the ideal wife, is told by sage Markandeya to Yudhishthira.

There lived in the Madra country, a pious, exceedingly virtuous and high-souled king, called Asvapati. He was firm in promise and truthful. He was ever engaged in sacrifices. He had subdued his senses and devoted himself to the welfare of all living beings.

He had no offspring and so became sorrowful. In order to be blessed with a child, he observed rigid vows and austerities. He offered daily ten thousand oblations to the Goddess Savitri and partook of moderate food only at midnight. He observed all the penances for eighteen years and at the end of the period, the Goddess Savitri was pleased with him. She said, "O Asvapati, king of the Madra country, choose a boon whatever you desire."

Asvapati: O Goddess! May many sons worthy of my race be born to me. I choose this as my boon.

Goddess Savitri: O king! I know your desires before hand. I spoke to Brahma. You will soon have a glorious daughter through His grace. I tell you this at His command. You need not, therefore, make any reply.

After conferring this boon, the Goddess vanished. In due course of time, Asvapati's wife, princes Malavi, gave birth to a lotus-eyed daughter. As the goddess Savitri gave the king this daughter, on account of his daily offering her oblations, both the father and the Brahmins named her 'Savitri'. In course of time the girl attained maidenhood.

Savitri was exceedingly beautiful. She was shining with divine splendour. People thought that she was a divine being who had come down to the Earth. Therefore none thought himself equal enough to marry her. The king became anxious.

The king: Beloved Savitri! This is the proper time for giving you in marriage but none asks me for your hand. Go and choose yourself a worthy husband.

Thereupon Savitri made prostrations to her father and carried out his command. She visited all the holy places and the hermitages with the ministers and returned to her father's place. Savitri saw her father seated along with sage Narada. She bowed down with her head at the feet of both.

Narada: O king! Where has your daughter been? Where does she come from? Why have you not given her in marriage?

Asvapati: She was sent abroad for this very purpose and she has just returned. Listen to her, O divine sage, and hear who has been chosen by her as her husband.

Urged by her father to relate everything in detail, she said thus, "There was in Salva a pious Kshatriya king, Dyumatsena by name, who lost his eyes. When that wise monarch, whose son was yet a boy, became blind, his kingdom was seized by his old enemy who lived in the vicinity. Dyumatsena accompanied by his wife and the boy went to the forest. He began to practise asceticism. His son, Satyavan, born in the city and brought up in the hermitage has been chosen by me, with all my heart, as my worthy husband."

Narada: The son of Dyumatsena is brilliant like the Sun, wise as Brihaspati, heroic as Indra, forgiving as the Earth. He is equal to Rantideva in charity. He is devoted to the Brahmanas and truthful as king Sibi. He is equal to Yayati in generosity. He is as lovely to look at as the full moon. He is as beautiful as either of the twin Asvins.

Asvapati: O adorable Rishi! You have described his noble qualities. Now tell me of his defects, if there be any.

Narada: He had only one defect and no other. Satyavan, who has only a short span of life in store for him, will, within a year from this day, breathe his last.

The king: O beautiful Savitri, go and seek another for your husband. The divine Narada tells me that within a year Satyavan will pass away.

Savitri: Whether his life be long or short, whether he be gifted with good qualities or destitute of them, I have once for all chosen him for my husband. I will not certainly select any other a second time.

Narada: O king! Your daughter is firm in her resolve. She cannot be made, in any way, to swerve from her righteous path. The noble qualities that are present in Satyavan are lacking in any other person. Therefore, I wish that your daughter be given in marriage now to Satyavan only. May you all be happy!

The king: The words of your pious self are wise, true and should never be dishonoured. You are my preceptor. I will act as directed by you.

Then Narada ascended the sky and reached heaven. The king began to make preparations for the marriage of his daughter. He went to the Medhya forest with his daughter and the priests on an auspicious day and reached the hermitage of Dyumatsena. There he saw that highly wise and old king seated on a mat of Kusha grass under a Sala tree.

The king Asvapati paid his respects to that royal sage and introduced himself to him. The king Dyumatsena offered the monarch Asvapati a seat and Arghya, etc., and asked what brought him there.

Asvapati: O royal sage! This fair damsel Savitri is my daughter. Please accept her as your daughter-in-law.

Dyumatsena: Exiled from our kingdom, we have taken to forest life. We live the life of ascetics and practise virtue with subdued senses and passions. Therefore, how will your delicate daughter endure the hardships of forest life in a hermitage?

Asvapati: Neither happiness nor misery has any permanence. My daughter and myself are aware of this. I have come to you, O king, with a firm resolve. Do not say 'nay' to me. You are my equal.

Dyumatsena: Long ago, I entertained a desire of forming an alliance with you. But I am now destitute. Therefore I hesitate. Let what I then desired be accomplished this very day. You are a welcome guest to me.

Then the two monarchs invited all the Brahmanas dwelling in the hermitages and celebrated marriage with the prescribed rites. Having given away his daughter in marriage with suitable presents, Asvapati left for his own place with contentment.

Satyavan was extremely delighted as he had for wife a woman endowed with all noble qualities. Savitri also was equally glad as she had Satyavan for her husband whom she had desired in her heart.

She removed all her ornaments and put on bark-dress and red-coloured cloth. She pleased everyone by her good services—her mother-in-law by ministering to her physical comforts, helping her in her age and all other acts of service; her father-in-law by worshipping him as a god, serving him with reverence and also by restraint of speech in his presence. She delighted her husband by agreeable words, sweet disposition and attending to his wants.

Savitri counted each day as it passed away because the words of Narada were always present in her mind. On a particular day, she ascertained by calculation that her husband's death would take place on the fourth day thereafter. She observed the Triratra (three-night) fast and remained without food both day and night. The father-in-law of Savitri came to know of her vow and became very anxious.

Dyumatsena: Princess! It is very difficult to observe the vow you have taken, because it is extremely hard to fast continuously for three nights.

Savitri: O venerable sire! You need not be sorry. I will be able to complete the vow. I have undertaken this vow with a very firm resolve. Determination is the sole cause of success in every undertaking.

Dyumatsena: O Savitri! I cannot ask you to break your vow. Men, like us, should rather encourage you to complete it. May you fulfil your vow!

On the fourth day Savitri said to herself, "Today is that day." In the early morning she performed her worship and offered oblations to the blazing fire. She then bowed down to all the Brahmanas, elders, her mother-in-law and father-in-law, one after the other and stood humbly before them with folded hands.

All the ascetics pronounced for the welfare of Savitri and the benediction that she might never be a widow. Then her mother-in-law and father-in-law said: "You have fulfilled the vow. The time for breaking the fast has come. Do what you think proper." Savitri said, "I will take food only when the Sun sets."

While Savitri was thus talking about the breaking of her fast, Satyavan was starting for the forest with an axe on his shoulder. Thereupon Savitri said to her husband, "You should not go alone. I will go with you. I dare not let you go alone today."

Satyavan: My dear, you have never visited the forest before. The path is very rugged. You must be exhausted and weak by the observance of the fast. How will you be able to walk?

Savitri: I do not at all feel exhausted on account of the fast. There is no exertion in this. Moreover, I am very eager to go with you today. Pray, do not therefore prevent me.

Satyavan: As you are eager to go with me, I will fulfil your desire. But take the permission of my parents first.

Savitri who had fulfilled a great vow made obeisance to her mother-in-law and father-in-law and said, "My husband is going into the forest for gathering fruits and fuel. It is my fervent desire that your worshipful self and my father-in-law will kindly permit me to accompany him. I cannot bear to be separated from him this day. Almost a full year is past and I have not gone out of our hermitage. My desire to see the forest in bloom is indeed very great."

Dyumatsena: Up to this time Savitri had never made a request to me. So let her desire be fulfilled.

Savitri thus obtained permission from her mother-in-law and

father-in-law and accompanied her husband to the forest with a smiling face though with a heavy heart. She saw the charming forest.

Satyavan gathered fruits and filled his bag. He then began to cut down a tree for fuel. As he was cutting the branches he felt severe headache. He came to Savitri and said to her thus, "I have a severe headache on account of exertion. I feel unwell. It seems to me that my head is being pierced by arrows. I am unable to stand."

Then Savitri sat down on the ground with his head on her lap. While thus sitting she saw the dark and dreadful form of a man with blood-red eyes and clad in red garments. He was standing near Satyavan with a noose in his hands and gazing at him. Beholding him, Savitri gently placed her husband's head on the ground. She was stricken with grief. She arose quickly and folding the palms of her hands in reverence said these words with a trembling heart in great sorrow, "I know you to be a divine being from your superhuman appearance. Kindly tell me, O great god! Who you are and what is your desire?"

The figure: O Savitri, you are devoted to your husband. You have acquired merit by your austerities. It is for this reason that I address you. Know me, good lady, to be Yama. The life of this prince Satyavan, your husband, is finished. I will bind him with my noose and take him away with me. Know this to be my intention.

Savitri: We have heard that your messengers come to take human beings away. Then how is it, O Lord, that you have come in person?

Yama: My messengers are not fit to bring to my abode such a pure and holy person as Satyavan, who is an ocean of good qualities. Therefore, I have come in person.

Then Yama forcibly drew out of the body of Satyavan his subtle body (*linga sarira*) or astral body, which is of the size of a thumb and bound it with the noose. The body being deprived of Prana or the vital life element lost its lustre and remained there like a log of wood. It was a sad sight. Yama, holding the subtle body of Satyavan bound with the noose, proceeded towards the South. Savitri arranged for the safety of the body of her husband and followed Yama with an afflicted heart.

Yama: Go back, Savitri, and perform the last rites of your husband. Your duties to your husband have been discharged by you. This far only you can come, no further.

Savitri: Whither my husband is carried or goes of his own accord, thither I must go. This is the ancient path of duty. There shall be no obstacle to my course on account of my asceticism, my devotion to superiors, my affection for my husband, my observance of vows and also because of your grace. It is said by the wise, versed in true knowledge, that one contracts friendship with another by going only seven paces with him. I will tell you something, keeping this friendship in view. Pray, listen to it. Men who lack in self-control do not observe the proper rites and sacrifices even in the forest; not do they discharge the necessary duties of the three modes of life, viz., married life, life of celibate in the preceptor's hermitage or the life of renunciation (Sannyasa). A householder's life leads to true religious merit. That is the reason why the wise assert that the life of a householder which leads to righteousness is the best of all modes of life. All of us follow the householders' path because of the virtues of married life. I do not wish to follow either the second or the third path above mentioned, because wise people say that married life is the most important.

Yama: Go back. I am delighted with your speech. Choose a boon now, with the exception of your husband's life.

Savitri: My father-in-law has been driven away from his kingdom. He has lost his eyesight. He now leads a pious life in a hermitage in the forest. Let that king, through your grace, regain his sight and become powerful.

Yama: O Savitri! I give you this boon; that which you have asked of me will take place. I see you are fatigued now by your journey. Do not proceed further. Go back.

Savitri: I do not feel fatigue as I am with my husband. I must surely follow the same path as my husband. I must surely go to that place where you are taking my lord. Listen again to what I say. It is said by the wise that even a single interview with the virtuous is highly desirable. Friendship with them is much more so. The company of the righteous persons is never without fruit. Therefore one should always live in the company of virtuous persons.

Yama: The words spoken by you are pregnant with great significance. They are delightful to the mind also. They are thought-provoking. They augment the wisdom of even the learned. Choose a second boon with the exception of Satyavan's life.

Savitri: May my father-in-law regain his kingdom which he has lost.

Yama: The king will be soon restored to his kingdom. He will be ever firm in his own duties as a king. Princess! I have now gratified your wish. Go back to your abode so that you may not have to undergo any further fatigue.

Savitri: O Lord! You have controlled all the creatures by rules of Dharma. You carry them away, not according to your caprice, but according to Dharma. Hence you are called, Yama, i.e., one who governs by ordinances. Hear again my words. The eternal duty of the righteous is mercy, charity, benevolence and absence of malice towards all living beings in thought, word and deed. The righteous show mercy even to their enemies who attack them.

Yama: The words uttered by you are as delicious to me as water to a thirsty person. Choose any other boon that you like but not the life of Satyavan.

Savitri: My father, the king, has no son. Let him have one hundred sons who will perpetuate his family. This is the third boon that I ask you.

Yama: O good girl! Your father will have one hundred brave sons, the perpetuators of his race. Princess! your desire is now gratified. Go back. You have come a very long way with me.

Savitri: I do not feel that I have travelled any distance when I am in the presence of my husband. It is my mind that travels a great distance. Now, listen, as you proceed on, to these words.

You are the powerful son of Vivasvan (the Sun God). You are therefore called by the wise as Vaivasvata. You judge all creatures impartially and rightly and for this reason, O Lord, you are styled as the Lord of Justice (Dharma Raja). People do not place so much confidence on their own selves as on the virtuous. Therefore everybody wishes particularly to be in the company of the virtuous.

Yama: O auspicious damsel! I never before heard such words as have been just spoken from any other person than you. I am pleased with them. Ask for a fourth boon with the exception of Satyavan's life and then go away.

Savitri: Let me have one hundred strong and powerful sons who will perpetuate our line. This is the fourth boon I pray for.

Yama: Gentle lady! You shall have one hundred strong and powerful sons who will make you happy. Princess! You have come very far. You must be very tired. Therefore go back to your abode.

Savitri: The virtuous people are ever unceasingly devoted to religion. The company of the virtuous is ever productive of good. Virtuous people are not afraid of other virtuous people. The virtuous people by their merits make the Sun move. It is the virtuous who support the Earth by their practice of austerities. Good acts done to the virtuous are never fruitless. As the righteous are characterised by noble qualities, they become protectors of all creatures.

Yama: The more you give expression to words pregnant with meaning, which deal with righteous conduct and which are delightful to the mind, the more I am inclined to respect you. Ask for an incomparable boon, O chaste lady!

Savitri: You have granted me the boon that I shall have one hundred sons and yet you are carrying away my husband. The boon that you have just given me cannot bear fruit without my husband. I choose my incomparable boon: 'Let Satyavan live' and may your words then prove true.

Yama, saying 'be it so,' loosened the noose that bound Satyavan and said, "O chaste lady! I release your husband. He will be free from disease. He will achieve his object in life. He will be ever successful in his undertakings. He as well as you will live four hundred years. He will become very famous in the world. He will certainly have a hundred sons by you."

Then the Lord of Justice (Yama) returned to his abode. Savitri returned to the place where her husband's dead body lay. Beholding her husband on the ground she sat down placing his head on her lap.

Soon after, Satyavan regained his consciousness and said to Savitri, "O, I have slept for a very long time. Why did you not wake me up? Where is that dark-complexioned person who was dragging me away?"

Savitri: You have been in deep sleep for a long time. You are very tired. Look, it is now late in the night.

Satyavan got up like one who was refreshed after an undisturbed sleep. He looked round in all directions of the forest regions and said, "I set out with you for gathering fruits. When I was cutting wood I had a shooting pain in my head. I could not stand up long and I fell asleep in your lap. I remember all this, my good Savitri. Then I saw the dreadful dark form of a highly effulgent being. Please tell me whether what I saw was a dream or a reality."

Savitri: Prince, the night is deepening. Tomorrow I will disclose to you faithfully all that occurred. I see you are unwell. You will not be able to discern the path to our abode as it is very dark now. We will go at the break of dawn when the forest paths are visible.

Satyavan: I have recovered from the headache. I am quite refreshed. I am eager to see my parents now. Surely my parents will be sorely afflicted on account of my absence. My father, with an afflicted heart, will be at this time enquiring of the residents of the hermitages, one by one, about me. My father is old; so also my mother. Surely I am their only stay. I live because it is my duty to make them happy. I am impatient to see my parents. Therefore, O Savitri, let us start immediately.

Thereupon Savitri rose up. She took her husband by his arms and made him rise. She placed her husband's left hand on her left shoulder, supported him with her right hand passed round him and thus walked slowly.

In the meantime, Dyumatsena regained his sight. He could behold everything with a clear vision. Accompanied by his wife Saivya, he visited all the hermitages in search of his son and daughter-in-law, being anxious for their safety. The hermits comforted them by saying: "Satyavan is certainly alive, because his wife Savitri is a virtuous girl. She has great powers acquired by austerities and self-control."

Then in a short time Savitri accompanied by her husband Satyavan reached the hermitage and entered cheerfully. All the residents of that grove were eager to know what had happened. They questioned Satyavan: "O renowned prince! Why did you not return earlier with your wife? What obstacle stood in your way? We were all anxious. You must relate all about it."

Satyavan: Taking leave of my father I went out with Savitri. While cutting down firewood in the forest my head began to ache. Afflicted with pain, I rested for a long time. Hence my return so late in the night. There is no other reason for my late arrival.

The Sages: You do not know how your father Dyumatsena has suddenly recovered his eyesight. Therefore let Savitri relate it. O Savitri! We are desirous of learning all this from you. You are surely acquainted with the mysteries of good and evil. Know that you are like the goddess Savitri in glory. You know the cause of this. Therefore speak truly. If it is fit to be related, please tell us.

Savitri: It is as you know it to be. Your desire can never prove fruitless. I have nothing to conceal from you. Now hear the true cause of this. The high-souled Narada had foretold the death of my husband. Today was that fatal day. Therefore I did not leave my husband's side. When my husband fell asleep, Yama, in person, approached him, bound and led him away in the southern direction where the manes or the Pitrus reside. I then began to praise that Lord. He conferred on me five boons. Hear from me what they are. I have obtained two boons for my father-in-law, i.e., recovery of his sight and of the kingdom which he had lost. I have further obtained for my father a hundred sons and an equal number of sons for myself. Again my husband Satyavan has been blessed with a life of four hundred years. I observed the vow three-nights; fast for the sake of my husband's life. I have now faithfully given you a full account of the happenings.

The Sages: O chaste girl! You are endowed with virtuous qualities and asceticism. It is by you that the family which was drowned in troubles and miseries has been rescued.

The assembled sages then eulogised Savitri and paid their adorations to her. They took leave of the king and his son and returned to their hermitages with merry hearts.

The night passed. The Sun's disc appeared on the horizon. All the sages performed their morning rites and assembled at the hermitage of Dyumatsena. They were not tired of telling Dyumatsena all about the great fortune and achievement of Savitri.

Then all the ministers came from the country of the Salvas to see their king. They informed Dyumatsena of the death of his enemy at the hands of his own minister. They further added that all the subjects had declared him as their legitimate king even though he was blind and that they were sent on the strength of this determination on that part of the subjects to reinstall him as their king.

When they saw him with eyesight restored, they were extremely delighted. They bowed down their heads to him.

Then Dyumatsena made his obeisance to the old Brahmins in the hermitage. He was in turn honoured by them. He set out for his capital surrounded by his army and with his queen Saivya, Satyavan and Savitri.

Then the Brahmins joyfully installed Dyumatsena as king and his high-souled son as crown prince (Yuvaraja).

Then, after a long time, a hundred sons were born to Savitri. They were heroic and attained great renown. She had also one hundred highly powerful brothers (sons of her father Asvapati).

Thus Savitri rescued from misfortune her own self, her father, mother-in-law, father-in-law and her hunsband's line. The glory of chastity or Pativrata Dharma is indescribable. A chaste woman can do and undo things. She can have victory over fate.

He who listens with devotion to this excellent story of Savitri will attain happiness and achieve all that he desires. He will never have any cause for sorrow.

(Pativrata Mahatmya—Vana Parva, Ch. 298)

NALA AND DAMAYANTI

Yudhishthira was in great despair when he staked his kingdom on the result of dice-playing and lost. He was afflicted with great sorrow. He thought that he was the most unfortunate person on the surface of this Earth. Thereupon, the sage Brihadasva consoled Yudhishthira. He then gave him words of encouragement and then narrated the story of Nala who also had lost his kingdom in a game of dice and had to roam alone in the forest, leaving his wife, children and relations, who was more miserable and in a worse plight than Yudhishthira. Yudhishthira gained great moral strength and courage. This is the story of Nala.

There lived a famous king in the Nishada country known as Virasena. He had a son named Nala. He was well-versed in religion and moral sciences. He was very handsome and was endowed with many virtuous qualities. He was particularly skilled in horsemanship.

At this time, there was also a king in the Vidarbha country, named Bhima, who was brave and powerful. He also possessed good qualities. But he was without an issue. He made great endeavours for the blessing of a child. One day, the Brahma-Rishi Damana came to see him. The king and his wife satisfied that revered Rishi with the most respectful offerings and served him with intense devotion. Damana was exceedingly pleased with the king. He conferred upon the king and his wife a boon. Damayanti, a gem among girls, and three sons, Dama, Danta and Damana were born. Damayanti was famous for her beauty.

Nala also, that foremost of men, was matchless in the world for his beauty and valour. He resembled in beauty Kandarpa, the god of Love himself.

Nala's fame spread far and wide and soon reached the ears of

Damayanti, in the same way as Damayanti's beauty and good attributes reached the ears of Nala. People were praising Nala again and again in Damayanti's presence and likewise praised Damayanti in the presence of Nala. Thus, although Nala and Damayanti had not seen each other, they developed a love for each other on account of repeatedly hearing each other's accomplishments. That mutual attachment and love began to grow very strong. It developed into a passion.

Nala was not able to keep his feelings of love within himself. One day, when he was alone in a garden near the palace, he saw a lot of swans with golden wings. He caught one of those birds with his hands. The bird spoke to Nala, "O king! Do not kill me. I will render some good service to you. I shall speak of you to Damayanti in such a manner that she will become your wife." The king, thereupon, set the swan free.

Thereafter the swans flew away to the country of the Vidarbhas and alighted near the palace of Damayanti. Damayanti and her playmates saw those birds. The girls and Damayanti desired to catch those rovers of the skies. They chased those swans, running after one of them.

The swan which Damayanti pursued addressed her thus: "O Damayanti! There is in the Nishada country, a king named Nala, who is extremely handsome. We have never seen the like of him. He has not his equal amongst men. If you become his wife, your birth and your beauty would find the most suitable place. As you are a gem amongst the maidens, so Nala is a jewel amongst men. He is the best amongst men. It is good that the best woman marries the best man!"

Damayanti in return said to the swan, "Please speak likewise to Nala also." The bird flew back and informed Nala of all that happened.

Thereafter Damayanti was uneasy. She was always thinking of Nala. She became pale and slender. The companions of Damayanti informed king Bhima of the conditions of his daughter. King Bhima thought and understood what the matter was and what he should do. So he made arrangements for Damayanti's *Svayamvara*, where she could choose her husband herself.

The king notified all the neighbouring kings and princes of the Svayamvara ceremony of Damayanti. Having learnt of Damayanti's Svayamvara (marriage), all the kings, the rulers of the earth, in response to the invitation, came to the court of Bhima.

As king Nala was also proceeding to that place, the gods Indra, Agni, Varuna and Yama met and spoke to him thus: "O Nala! You are always truthful and obliging. You must do us a favour. Be our messenger." Nala promised them that he would and asked them: "Who are you, sirs? To whom should I be a messenger? What should I do, when I go there? Please tell me precisely."

Indra said, "We are gods who have come for the Svayamvara of Damayanti. Please inform Damayanti that we have come here as her suitors and request her to choose one of us as her husband."

Nala said, "I shall act accordingly." He went to the palace of Damayanti. There he saw the daughter of the ruler of Vidarbha.

Damayanti asked him, "I wish to know who you are. Why have you come here? You look like a god."

Nala replied, "Know me as Nala. I have come here as the messenger of the gods. The gods Indra, Agni, Varuna and Yama have come here as your suitors. Choose one of these gods as your husband. I was able to enter this place unnoticed by anybody on account of their power."

Damayanti said to Nala, "O prince! The speeches of the swans are burning me out. It is for you indeed, O lord, I have caused the kings to assemble here."

Nala said to her, "Why do you choose an ordinary human being for your husband when the guardians of the world await you? Fix your heart upon one of those illustrious celestials who protect the world. I am not equal to the dust of the feet of these gods. What lady will not accept him as her husband, by the terror of whose power all the creatures are moved to walk in the path of virtue? What lady will not accept as her husband 'Mahendra' who is the lord of the heavens?"

Damayanti said, "I offer my salutations to all the gods. To tell you the truth, I can choose only you as my husband. But let all the gods and you, too, attend my *Svayamvara*. There I shall choose my husband."

Nala returned to the place where the gods were waiting. The gods asked Nala, "Did you, O prince, see Damayanti? What did she say?" Nala replied, "I entered the chamber of Damayanti. I related to her everything about you. But she has made up her mind to choose me for her husband. She said, 'Let all those gods come along with you to the place of my Svayamvara where I shall choose my husband'."

When the auspicious hour approached king Bhima summoned all those present to the Svayamvara. The kings and the gods entered the assembly hall and took their seats. They were all eager to obtain the hand of Damayanti in marriage.

Thereupon Damayanti entered the hall and attracted the eyes and hearts of the assembled princes. When the names of the several kings were being announced one by one Damayanti saw five persons all like Nala in face and form. She could not make out which one was prince Nala. As she looked at each of them she thought that every one was prince Nala. She pondered in her mind, "How am I to know who the gods are and how am I to know who Nala is? The marks that belong to the gods are not seen in any one of these assembled here." She resolved upon obtaining the assistance of the gods themselves. She saluted the celestials with folded hands. Trembling with agitation she spoke to them thus, "O gods! On hearing the words of the swans I have chosen Nala as my husband. For the sake of that vow of mine, O celestials, point him out to me. As I have firmly devoted myself to him both in body and thought, so for the sake of Truth, it behoves the gods to point him out to me. I pray that the gods assume their respective forms to enable me to identify that virtuous prince Nala."

The celestials heard the earnest appeal—full of anxiety— of Damayanti. They found out that she was firmly devoted to Nala only and that she had determined to marry him alone. They appreciated her purity of heart, fixity of mind and love for Nala. They perceived that her love for the prince was most fervent. They took compassion on her and assumed their own respective forms and showed their several distinguishing characteristics as requested by Damayanti.

She then saw all the gods, their eyes fixed, spotless garlands round their neck and seated without touching the Earth. On the other hand, she beheld Nala with his own shadow and with flower garland stained with dust. He was seated on the ground with quivering eyes. Damayanti saw now who the gods were and who Nala was.

She placed the most beautiful garland round Nala's neck. All the celestials were highly pleased. They granted eight boons to Nala and departed to their abodes. The assembled kings also left the place. Then Bhima celebrated the marriage ceremony of Damayanti and Nala.

Nala stayed in Vidarbha for sometime in obedience to the wishes of king Bhima. Then he came back to his own city with the consent of the king. He ruled over his subjects most righteously. He passed his days happily in the company of Damayanti. He had a son Indrasen and a daughter Indrasena, born of Damayanti.

✿ ✿ ✿

When the guardians of the world were returning to Heaven after the Svayamvara, they met Dvapara accompanied by Kali. Indra asked Kali, "O Kali, tell me where you are going with Dvapara as your companion." Kali replied, "I am going to Damayanti's Svayamvara. I will choose her as my wife, because my heart has been captivated by her."

Then Indra smilingly said to him, "That Svayamvara is now over. King Nala has been accepted by her as her husband even in our presence." The gods then proceeded their way.

Kali said to Dvapara, "O Dvapara! I cannot restrain my anger. I will enter into Nala and expel him from his kingdom. He shall not be happy with Damayanti. You must enter the dice and help me in this enterprise."

Having fixed this arrangement with Dvapara, Kali went to Pushkara and said, "Come and play a game of dice with Nala. With my help you will certainly defeat Nala and you will win his kingdom."

Then Kali entered into Nala. Pushkara came to Nala and pressed him again and again saying, "Let us play a game of dice." The high-souled Nala could not refuse the invitation. Being influenced by Kali, Nala lost at dice his gold, his jewels, his cars, and also his valuable garments. None of his frineds was able to restrain him from the play at dice. He was deprived of all his possessions. Damayanti and his subjects also intervened and implored Nala to desist. Nala did not hear Damayanti's sweet words. He persisted in the game and was always defeated.

Then Damayanti sent for the charioteer Varshneya and said, "Yoke to the chariot the favourite horses of Nala. Place Indrasen and Indrasena in the chariot and proceed to Kundinapura." The charioteer carried out the behests of Damayanti. He delivered his charges and took leave of king Bhima. Varshneya was very much distressed at the misfortunes of Nala. He then went to king Rituparna and entered into the service of that king as a charioteer.

Nala lost all his kingdom and wealth. He staked and lost even his garments and ornaments. Then he went away wearing a single piece of cloth. Damayanti also accompanied him almost in the same state.

In the meantime Pushkara had it proclaimed within the city that anybody who would treat Nala with respect and hospitality would be punished. On account of the proclamation of Pushkara and of his hatred towards Nala, the people were afraid to treat Nala with kindness and respect. Nala stayed three nights outside the precincts of the city subsisting only on water. He was very much afflicted with hunger. He started from the vicinity of the city with the object of gathering some fruits and roots in the forest. Damayanti also accompanied him.

Nala saw some young birds whose wings shone like gold. Nala thought within himself, "These birds will be my repast today and their plumage shall be my wealth." He threw over those birds the single piece of cloth he was wearing round his waist but they flew away with the cloth and told Nala, "O silly fool! We are the dice. We had come here to snatch away your cloth. For, surely, we would feel no pleasure if you go with your cloth on."

Nala said to Damayanti, "Those very dice have assumed the form of birds and are now flying away with my cloth. I have been deprived of my royal throne. I am oppressed with hunger. I have met with a great catastrophe. I am afflicted with sorrow. I have reached extreme adversity. I am confused and unable to think clearly. I am your husband. Please listen to my words which are for your good. This is the way to the Vidarbha country."

Thereupon choked with tears, Damayanti spoke to Nala these piteous words in a tremulous voice, "My heart trembles and all my limbs are sinking, when I think again and again of your intention. How can I go away leaving you in this lonely forest? You are deprived of your kingdom and wealth. You wander in the forest. You are naked, hungry and weary. When you are fatigued and oppressed with hunger in this dreary forest I can give you solace and comfort and remove your fatigue. There is nowhere a medicine or a slave similar to a wife in curing one who is afflicted with any kind of misery or sorrow. This is the plain truth. This is the opinion of all the physicians. You always refer to the path of Vidarbha. If you approve we shall go together."

Nala said, "O Damayanti! What you have said is indeed true. To a man who is afflicted with sorrow, there is no friend comparable to a devoted wife. I went to Vidarbha with great joy when I was a ruler and gave you much happiness. How can I go there now in this destitute and miserable condition? Why are you afraid? I do not wish to forsake you. I can part with myself but not with you."

Damayanti said, "O venerable lord! If you do not wish to abandon me, why do you again and again point out to me the road that leads to the dominion of the Vidarbhas? I know well you yourself will not desert me. But you might forsake me as you are influenced by Kali."

Wrapped in a single piece of cloth they wandered here and there and arrived at a resting house, worn out with hunger and thirst. With his body covered with dust, Nala laid himself down by the side of Damayanti on the ground in sheer fatigue and fell asleep. Damayanti also was overcome with sleep.

Nala got up after some time with an afflicted heart and moved here and there in the Dharmasala. There he found a knife. He cut with that knife a part of Damayanti's garment and wrapped himself with it. He lost his senses through the influence of Kali and ran away leaving his sleeping wife all alone and lamenting intensely for her.

❁ ❁ ❁

Damayanti woke up from her sleep and was much frightened in that wilderness. She did not find her hunsband. She was very much oppressed with grief. She said, "O my beloved husband! Why hast thou forsaken me? O lord! Show thyself. I lament neither for myself nor for anything else. But, O king, I only grieve in the thought, 'How will you live alone?' Who will remove your fatigue, my lord?"

When she was thus crying aloud, a big hungry serpent caught her in its coils. But a hunter who was passing that way killed that serpent and released her.

The hunter was overpowered by lust. Damayanti cursed him. She said, "If, even in my mind, I have ever thought of any other person than the king of Nishada, then let this hunter fall down devoid of life." The hunter fell dead on the ground, like a tree consumed by fire.

She roamed about in the forest for three days and then saw the hermitages of ascetics. She saluted the Rishis and stood in an attitude of reverence and humility. The ascetics offered due respects to Damayanti and said, "O blessed lady! Sit down. What shall we do for you? Who are you? Why have you come here?"

Damayanti said, "I am Damayanti, wife of Nala. My husband is roaming about in this forest. Shall I be able to meet him?"

The ascetics said, "O venerable lady! We see, by our power of asceticism, that you will soon meet Nala. You will soon attain happiness." After saying this, they disappeared from sight. Damayanti became greatly amazed at this phenomenon.

She walked a long distance and in the evening reached the big city of Subahu, the king of the province of Chedi. She came to the palace. The king's mother saw her surrounded by a large number of men and boys. She caused the crowd to disperse and asked the maiden servant to take Damayanti inside the palace. She asked Damayanti, "Tell me, who are you and to whom do you belong?"

Damayanti said, "Know me to be an ordinary mortal. I am devoted to my husband. He was defeated in a game of dice. He retired into the forest with me. Then he left me alone and entered into the interior. I have been searching for him. I am unable to find out my lord, who is the delight of my heart, who is like the celestials in appearance."

The king's mother told Damayanti, "O blessed lady! Stay with us. You will find your husband soon. My men will search for him in the forest." She told her daughter Sunada, thus: "This lady is of your age. Take her as your companion." Thereupon Sunada received Damayanti with immense delight. She took her into her own apartments. Damayanti lived there for some time.

❁ ❁ ❁

After separating himself from Damayanti, Nala beheld a great fire breaking out in that dreadful forest. There, in the midst of the great fire, he heard the loud voice of some living thing which cried over and over again unto the righteous Nala, "Come hither quickly."

Nala answered, "Do not fear," rushed into the fire and saw there the king of serpents lying in coils. Then that serpent in a trembling voice addressed Nala, "O king! Know me as the serpent Karkotaka. The great sage Narada, who was practising very rigid penances was once deceived by me. He cursed me in his wrath saying, 'Remain in this place like some immovable thing till Nala comes here. Wherever he shall take you, there you shall be released from my curse.' On account of this curse I am unable to move even a step further. Kindly release me. I will do you good. I will surely help you." The serpent assumed the size of the thumb and became very light.

Nala lifted the serpent and ran to a place which was free from the forest fire. He was about to let the serpent go. The serpent said "O king! Proceed counting your own steps by speech. I will render great service to you." Thereupon the king started counting his own steps. When Nala reached the tenth step, he uttered the word 'Dasa' which means either 'ten' or 'bite'. The serpent bit him at the tenth step and assumed his original form.

As soon as Nala was bitten, he was disfigured and lost his handsome appearance. Beholding the change of form, Nala was horrified and became miserable. Then the serpent Karkotaka consoled Nala and spoke to him thus: "Do not be afraid. I have done you good only. I have wrought this change in your appearance for the reason that the people will not be able to recognise you. Go to the city of Ayodhya, appear before king Rituparna, who is highly skilled in the game of dice, and say that you are a charioteer, Bahuka by name. Impart to him the knowledge about horses. He will teach you in return all the secrets of dice-play. When you became an expert at dice-play you will become prosperous. You will find your wife, son and daughter. You will also get back your kingdom. I tell you the truth. When you wish to assume your own handsome form, remember me and put on these pieces of cloth. You shall recover your original form." Having said thus, the king of the snakes gave him two pieces of superior divine garments and disappeared from view.

After the disappearance of the serpent, Nala went towards the Rituparna's city and reached it on the tenth day. He approached the king and said, "I am Bahuka. I am skilled in the management of horses. There is no one in this world who can equal me in the science of managing horses. I am also proficient in the art of cooking in which I am unsurpassed by any other. I shall try my best to learn any other art or science and also other matters which are difficult of accomplishment. Therefore support me, O noble Rituparna!"

Rituparna said, "O Bahuka! Stay with me. Adopt some such means that my horses may run very fast. Devote yourself to the work of chariot driving. I am very fond of rapid motion of the chariot. Be also the superintendent of my stables on a salary of ten thousand coins. Varshneya and Jivala shall always be guided by you." Bahuka (Nala) accepted and spent his time discharging his duties and thinking always about Damayanti.

When Nala and Damayanti disappeared, king Bhima was struck with sorrow. He gave immense wealth to Brahmanas and asked them to go in quest of his daughter and Nala. The Brahmanas went out in all directions searching in the various cities and provinces. But they did neither find Nala nor the daughter of Bhima anywhere. At last, a Brahmana, Sudeva by name while continuing his search in the city of the king of Chedis, saw Damayanti in the royal palace. He recognised her by observing various marks of identification and addressed her thus, "I am Sudeva, O daughter of Bhima, an intimate friend of your brother. Commanded by king Bhima, I have come here searching for you. O princess, your father, mother and brother are in good health; so also your son and daughter. Hundreds of Brahmanas are wandering all over the world in search of you."

Then the king's mother called Sudeva by her side and asked him: "Whose wife is this lady? Whose daughter is she? How has she been separated from her husband as well as her relatives? How do you come to know her? I wish to know from you all about her in detail."

Sudeva sat at ease and gave a true account of Damayanti. He said: "There is a virtuous and illustrious king of the Vidarbha country named Bhima. This lady is his daughter. Her name is Damayanti. There is the king of Nishadas named Nala, the son of Virasena. This lady is Nala's wife. He was defeated at dices by his brother and deprived of his kingdom. He went away with Damayanti without the knowledge of anybody. Hundreds of Brahmanas are roaming about all over the world in search of him and Damayanti. Damayanti is at last discovered in your palace. She has an auspicious mole in the middle of her eyebrows, by which I recognise her."

On hearing these words, the king's mother said, "O Damayanti! You are indeed my sister's daughter. Myself and your mother are the daughters of that illustrious king Sudaman who is the ruler of the Dasharnas. As is your father's house, so is mine to you. My wealth is to you even as your own."

Damayanti bowed down unto her aunt with a grateful heart and said, "Although I stayed here unrecognised, still I lived with you happily. I wish to go to Vidarbha. You will do me a great favour by allowing me to go to my father in a chariot." The aunt gave Damayanti valuable presents and sent her in a palanquin with a strong escort to guard her.

❁ ❁ ❁

Damayanti reached Vidarbha. Her father, mother, brothers, children and all her relations were highly delighted. They gave her a hearty welcome and offered grace to the Almighty for her arrival.

Damayanti said to her mother, "O mother, if you wish me to be alive, try to bring here that hero among men, Nala." The queen spoke to king Bhima, "Damayanti is lamenting for her husband. She herself said that our men should try to find out the whereabouts of that virtuous Nala." The king sent out several Brahmanas in all directions and ordered them to trace king Nala.

Damayanti set them on their mission with the following injunction: "Repeat these words again and again in every country and wherever people meet together. 'O gambler, O beloved one! Why did you go, cutting your wife's garment in two, leaving alone your dear and devoted wife sleeping in the forest? In obedience to your commands that lady, covered with the half piece of cloth and greatly burning with woe, is eagerly expecting your return. Be merciful, O lord! Give her a reply.' If any person makes any reply when you say these words, you must, O great Brahmanas, convey that reply to me and inform me how he is and where he lives. Take care that nobody knows that these words are uttered by you at my instigation."

Thereupon the Brahmanas departed in all directions in search of Nala who had fallen into such great calamity. They repeated the words which Damayanti had ordered them to do, wherever they wandered.

After a very long time, a Brahmana, Parnada by name, came back to the city of the king of Vidarbha and spoke to Damayanti these words, "I searched for Nala in various places. At last I went to the city of Ayodhya and presented myself before Rituparna (Bhangasvari). I recited the very words of yours before that illustrious Rituparna. The charioteer of that great king is an ugly man with stunted arms. He is known by the name 'Bahuka.' He is skilled in driving the horses with great speed. He is also skilled in the culinary art. Sighing heavily and frequently, shedding tears profusely, he asked about my welfare and then spoke to me these words: 'Although fallen into great distress and adversity a chaste woman is protected by her power of chastity. She lives by the force of her purity. She guards herself by her own efforts. Heaven and heavenly blessings are ultimately her dues. Even if a chaste woman is forsaken by her husband, she should never become angry with him. She was forsaken by him when he was out of his senses, when he was in great distress and difficult circumstances; she should not therefore lose her temper. She should not be angry with a person who was deprived of his cloth by the birds when he attempted to seize them for food.' On hearing these words of the charioteer Bahuka, I returned quickly to this place."

On hearing these words of Parnada, Damayanti shed copious tears. She then called Sudeva and told him, "O Sudeva, like a bird which darts straight to its object, you do at once depart to the city of Ayodhya. Tell the king Rituparna that Damayanti, the daughter of king Bhima, will again hold a Svayamvara, to which all the kings and princes are rushing from all directions, that it would be held at the next sunrise and that she would accept a second husband as it was not known whether the heroic Nala was alive or dead." Sudeva, the Brahmana, started at once and spoke to king Rituparna exactly as Damayanti had asked him to say.

Hearing the words of Sudeva, king Rituparna said to Bahuka, "O Bahuka, I desire to go, in the course of this day, to the country of the Vidarbhas where the Svayamvara of Damayanti is going to be held. Get the chariot ready immediately. Secure good horses."

When Bahuka (Nala) heard the news of the second Svayamvara of Damayanti his heart burst with grief. He thought within himself, "It may be that Damayanti, afflicted with sorrow, does this; or perhaps by doing this she has contrived a plan for my sake. Obviously she has conceived this idea in order to get me. I will go there and know for certain the truth or the falsehood of this. I will surely fulfil the desire of Rituparna. In doing this I will serve my own purpose."

Bahuka said. "O king Rituparna! I will drive the chariot in a day to Vidarbha. You need not be anxious at all." Bahuka went to the stables and there he examined the horses and selected good ones which were lean, swift as the wind, strong, energetic and capable of bearing the hardships of a long jouney. He yoked the horses to the chariot. The monarch most speedily mounted the car. The horses ran with the velocity of the wind. Rituparna was struck with wonder.

When the chariot was thus coursing, the king Rituparna saw his cloth drop down upon the ground. The king said to Bahuka, "Restrain the horses and stop the chariot. My garment has dropped down. Let me pick it up."

Thereupon Bahuka said to him in reply, "Your garment has dropped down far away. We have advanced about eight miles from that place. Therefore it is difficult to get it back."

Then they came near a tree called Vibhitaka full with fruits. Rituparna said, "O Bahuka! See my wonderful powers of calculation. All men do not know all things. In fact there is none who is acquainted with all the branches of knowledge. These two branches of the tree contain five million leaves. Examine the two main branches and all other boughs. Their fruits will number two thousand and ninetyfive."

Then Bahuka counted the fruits and satisfied himself of the truth of what the king had said. They were exactly as many as Rituparna stated. He told the king, "This is most wonderful. I wish to learn this science by which you knew this." Rituparna said, "I am conversant with the secrets of dice-play as well."

Bahuka said, "Kindly impart to me the knowledge of both these sciences and take from me the knowledge ragarding the management of horses." Rituparna imparted to Bahuka the great secrets of dice-playing.

After Bahuka (Nala) acquired the knowledge of the art of playing at dice Kali came out of his body. King Nala became free from all afflictions brought on by Kali. He mounted the chariot and drove on to Kundinapura with tremendous speed.

Then the people informed the king Bhima that the king Rituparna had arrived in the evening. Damayanti heard the rattle of Nala's car. She was struck with great astonishment to hear that sound. She went to the terrace of the palace in order to see Nala. She saw king Rituparna and Bahuka in the car.

Thereupon king Rituparna got down from the chariot. King Bhima received Rituparna with respectful offerings. Rituparna saw no signs of the Svayamvara, though he looked about again and again. He repaired to his appointed quarters, accompanied by the servants of the royal household. Bahuka took the chariot away to the stables.

Damayanti thought within herself, "This loud sound is like that of Nala's chariot. But I do not find the prince of the Nishada. It may be then that this art of driving was learnt by Varshneya from Nala." Damayanti sent a female messenger Kesini in search of king Nala. She said to Kesini, "Go, Kesini, and find out who is this deformed chariot-driver with stunted arms. Ask him about his welfare. Enquire all the particulars about him. I suspect that this person might be king Nala. Tell him the words of Parnada and note what reply he gives."

The female messenger met Bahuka and told him, "O best of men! You are welcome. I wish you well. When did you start on your journey? Why have you come here? Tell me all the particulars. Damayanti the princess of Vidarbha wishes to hear all about these."

Bahuka said, "The king of Kosala learnt from a Brahmana that there would be held a second Svayamvara of Damayanti. Hearing this, the king set out with excellent horses which are capable of travelling one hundred Yojanas and which are as fleet as the wind itself. I am his charioteer."

Kesini said, "The Brahmana who had first gone to the city of Ayodhya uttered again and again some words. You heard the words and gave him a reply. Damayanti wishes to hear from you again the words uttered by you."

Hearing these words of Kesini, Nala's heart became afflicted with grief. His eyes too were filled with tears. He suppressed his grief and uttered those words again in a voice choked with tears. Then Kesini returned and reported everything to Damayanti.

Damayanti said, "Go Kesini, and scrutinise the conduct of Bahuka. Remain silent near him and watch his actions and behaviour well. Mark well whenever he performed any thing skilful. Whenever he may ask for fire or water do not be in a hurry to give it. Let me know what supernatural things are seen in him."

Kesini watched Bahuka's actions minutely. She informed Damayanti everything as it happened. She said, "I have never heard or seen before any person of his calibre. He has a great power over the elements. He never bends his head when he comes to a low doorway. The doorway becomes large and wide and he easily passes through it. Water pots get filled with water when he looks at them. Then again he grasps a handful of grass and holds it to the Sun when suddenly there is a flame of fire. I was struck with astonishment. Although he touched the fire, he was not scroched. I have marked another wonder. He took some flowers in his hands and pressed them slowly. Although these flowers were pressed by him, they did not lose their original forms. On the contrary they became more fragrant and beautiful than they were. Observing these miracles I hurried hither."

On hearing these words Damayanti suspected that Nala was in the disguise of Bahuka. She sent her two children with Kesini. Bahuka recognised Indrasena and Indrasen. He embraced them and shed tears. He said, "Good lady! These twins are exactly like my children. If you come to me very often, people may misconstrue. We are guests from another country. So, good lady! Go away hence if you please." Kesini came back and represented everything to Damayanti.

Damayanti obtained permission from her father and mother and caused Bahuka to enter her own apartments. Damayanti said, "Did you ever see any man who is known as virtuous, had gone away leaving his wife asleep in the forest? Formerly I had selected Nala as my lord, rejecting the very celestials. Therefore how did he desert his faithful wife whom he loved and who had borne him children? He had taken my hand; and before the fire and in the presence of all the gods, he had pledged that he would truly be mine. But where had that pledge gone?" While Damayanti was speaking thus, tears of grief flowed copiously from her eyes.

Nala also shed tears and said to Damayanti, "O blessed lady! The loss of my kingdom was not brought about by me. It was the work of Kali. I abandoned you in the forest on account of Kali only. He remained within my body, scorched and consumed by curse. He has been totally vanquished by my observances and devotion. King Rituparna heard that Bhima's daughter is choosing a second husband and so he came here in haste."

On hearing these words Damayanti shivered and said with folded hands, "O lord! Do not suspect my chastity and loyalty to you. I devised this plan in order to get you back. I can truly swear that even in thought I have not committed any sort of sin. Let the all-pervading Air, that always moves about the whole world, take away my life if I have committed any sin."

When Damayanti spoke thus, the Wind God spoke from the sky, "O Nala! I tell you the truth that she has not committed any sin." While the Wind God was thus speaking there was a shower of flowers from the sky. Thereupon king Nala put on the celestial garments given to him by Karkotaka and thought of the king of serpents. At once he assumed his original handsome form.

King Rituparna came to know that it was Nala who was in the disguise of Bahuka and that he was now united with Damayanti. He said, "O mighty Nala! Pray, pardon me. I am extremely happy to see that you are now in the company of Damayanti, your noble and chaste wife. May you both prosper gloriously." Then Rituparna engaged another man as his charioteer and gladly returned to his capital.

Nala stayed there for a month. He obtained the permission of Bhima and proceeded with a small number of attendants to the country of the Nishadas. Again Nala and Pushkara had a game of dice. Pushkara who had even staked his life was defeated by a single throw by Nala. Nala said, "O Pushkara, previously I was not defeated by you. It was Kali who defeated me. Live happily. I grant you your life. I give you your portion of the whole kingdom. The depth of my love for you is undoubtedly the same as before. You are my brother. May you live the full span of life!"

Nala entered his own palace which was most gorgeously decorated. He consoled all the citizens and the ministers and other officials.

King Nala brought Damayanti and his children back to his capital with a large army. He passed his days in great happiness. He began to rule the kingdom in a virtuous manner once again. He duly performed many sacrifices. He practised self-restraint and Tapas and attained great fame and glory.

Those who recite the great history or noble life of Nala and those who often hear it are never tainted by misfortune or calamity. They get all their desires fulfilled and obtain wealth, sons, grandsons, high position, health and joy. There is no doubt in this.

Whenever you are in great distress or in the midst of calamity think of Nala and Damayanti. You will get solace and comfort. Nala while living in the forest had neither brothers nor relations, nor friends, nor servants, nor chariots. He and Damayanti slept on the ground. They had no food to eat. They were oppressed by hunger and thirst. They had no second cloth to cover themselves. They, who enjoyed the royal comforts, led such a hard life.

The power of chastity protected Damayanti. The power of virtues protected Nala. Those who lead a virtuous life will never meet with destruction, though they may have to live in adverse conditions. Your sufferings are nothing when compared to the trials and tribulations undergone by Nala and Damayanti. Sufferings visit a man to strengthen his will and power of endurance and to instil mercy and godliness in him. They are blessings in disguise. Face them with a smiling countenance and march on boldly towards the goal.

Do not gamble. Nala lost his kingdom and underwent sufferings on account of his playing dice. Yudhishthira lost his dominion on account of gambling. Playing cards for stake is also a form of gambling. Betting on the result of horse races is also gambling. Many have been ruined by gambling. No one has really prospered. Maya and Kali dwell in gambling dens. Gambling is enticing, alluring and tempting. Earn money by honest means with the sweat of your brow. Lead a simple, virtuous and pious life. Pray. Sing the Lord's Lila. Meditate and attain Eternal Happiness.

Nala was tormented by Pushkara in a variety of ways. Pushkara even proclaimed to his people that Nala should not be treated with kindness and hospitality when he remained for three days on the outskirts of the city. But still Nala embraced Pushkara with love and gave him a portion of his kingdom. What a magnanimous soul Nala was! He had not a bit of the spirit of revenge or malice. He had a large heart.

You must learn from this story of Nala, the lesson of equal vision and unbounded love even for one who persecuted you.

(Nalopakhyana, Vana Parva, Ch. 53-79)

THE SUPREME VIRTUE OF WOMEN

Satyabhama, queen of Lord Krishna and the daughter of Satrajit, asked Draupadi, "O Draupadi! How do you manage to rule the sons of Pandu who are endowed with great strength? How is it that they are obedient to you and are never angry with you? They are all ever ready to carry out your wishes. Tell me the reason."

Draupadi replied, "O Satyabhama! Hear now of my conduct towards the high-souled Pandavas. I always serve them with intense devotion, giving up vanity and controlling my own desires and passions. I do not conduct myself with an air of superiority. I do not utter what is evil and false. My heart is never fascinated by anybody young or handsome, wealthy or attractive.

"I never bathe or eat or sleep till my husband has bathed or eaten or slept, till all our servants and followers have bathed, eaten and slept. Whenever my husband returns from the field, the forest or the town, I immediately rise up, welcome him and offer water and seat.

“I always keep the house and all the household articles and the food clean. I keep them in order also. I carefully cook the food and serve them at the proper time.

“I never utter harsh words. I never get angry. I never imitate wicked women. I always do what is pleasant and agreeable to them. I am never idle and lazy. I never laugh except at a joke. I do not dally at the gate of the house. I never stay long in the pleasure gardens of the house when my duties require my presence elsewhere. I always refrain from laughing loudly or getting emotional and from anything that may give offence. I am ever engaged in serving my husband.

“Separation from my husband is never agreeable to me. When my husband goes to other places leaving me behind, I do not use flowers and scented paste and I observe rigid austerities. I always like what my husband likes and dislike what he dislikes and adjust myself to his requirements. I always devotedly seek the welfare of my husband. I always do those duties which my mother-in-law formerly told me concerning the relatives, guests, alms-giving, worship of the gods and oblations to the ancestors. I always perform my duty night and day without the least idleness.

“I behave towards my husband with great reverence and humility. I never deviate even an inch from the approved rules of conduct while serving him.

“I am of opinion that to attend to one’s husband is the supreme virtue of women. The husband is wife’s God. He is her sole refuge. There is no other refuge for her. How then can a wife act in a way that is disagreeable to her husband?

“I am always guided by my husband. I never speak ill of my mother-in-law. I never, either in the matter of taking rest, or of eating, or of adorning my person, act against the wishes of my husband. I am diligent, brisk and prompt in my actions. I serve my Guru with extreme humility. Therefore my husband is highly pleased with me. Everyday I serve my revered mother-in-law with intense love and humility. I personally wait on her with food, drink and clothes.

“I never show any preference for myself over my

mother-in-law in matters of food, dress and ornaments. I treat her with reverence.

"I worship duly with food, drink and clothes all those Brahmanas who recite the Vedas in the palace of Yudhishthira.

"I listen to the complaints of all the maid-servants, remove their grievances and keep them contented. I framed rules for their observances. I attend on all guests with devotion. I rise up from my bed first and retire to bed last.

"O Satyabhama! This has been my conduct and habit. That is the reason why my husbands are obedient to me."

❁ ❁ ❁

Draupadi said, "O Satyabhama! I shall now tell you a way for attracting the heart of your husband. In all the three worlds, there is no God equal to the husband. If the husband is pleased with you, there is no limit to your achievements. If he is displeased with you, you will lose everything. From your husband you can obtain good garments, ornaments, great fame and heaven itself hereafter. To the woman who is chaste, loving and dutiful towards her husband, happiness is her birthright. She may have periods of difficulties and troubles, but they are temporary and sometimes illusory. Therefore always worship Krishna with love and devotion.

"Be prompt in service. Consider only his comforts. He will be devoted to you. He will think, 'I am truly loved by my wife. She is highly devoted to me. I should live for her. I should be devoted to her.'

"As soon as you hear the voice of your husband at the gate, rise from your seat and stand in readiness to serve him with a glad heart. As soon as he enters the room, worship him by offering him a seat and water to wash his feet.

"When he orders a maid-servant to do anything, get up at once and do it yourself. Let Krishna realise, by your actions and conduct, that you worship him with all your heart and soul.

"Whatever your husband speaks before you, do not speak it out to everybody, although it may not be a secret; because he will be annoyed with you if any of your co-wives refers it to him again.

"Always seek the good of your husband. Feed him with those things which he likes best. Do not mix with those who are inimical to your husband.

"Do not get excited in the presence of men. Conceal your mind by observing silence.

"Make friendship with only those ladies who are devoted to their husbands, who are high-born, who are sinless and who are endowed with virtues and good character. You should always avoid the company of women who are wrathful, addicted to drinks and who are wicked or bad-tempered or selfish.

"Such conduct is highly laudable. It produces prosperity, fame and happiness. It neutralises hostility and leads one to Heaven. Therefore worship your husband with love, faith and devotion."

Then Satyabhama embraced Draupadi and spoke thus, "O blessed lady! You will with your husband enjoy peace on this Earth. Your sons are all living in Dwaraka very happily. You are endowed with auspicious marks. You can never suffer misfortune for a long time. I am immensely benefited by your inspiring speech. It is pregnant with wisdom and high thoughts. My beloved Draupadi, may you be happy!"

Having said these words she entered the car and started for her own city along with Lord Krishna.

(Vana Parva, Ch. 232-233)

❁ ❁ ❁

India, the sacred land, has produced women sages like Sulabha, Gargi, Madalasa, Pativratas like Sita, Savitri, Anasuya and Nalayini, lady devotees like Mira and Yoginis like queen Chudala. These are only a few names of the thousands known and unknown in history.

Women of modern times should draw inspiration from them. They should try to lead the life they led. They should give up fashion and lead a humble and virtuous life. They should avoid the poisonous materialistic influences. These fashionabe materialistic women have no idea of real independence. To move freely here and there, neglecting one's duty, to do whatever one likes, to eat and drink anything, to drive a car and to imitate Westerners is not independence. Modesty is the most precious ornament of a woman. To go beyond the limits of modesty and to behave like a man, destroys the elegance, grandeur, grace and beauty of the fair sex.

The speech of Draupadi may not be appealing to the Western women and Westerners and even to many of our modern women of India, who have imbibed Western education and to those ladies who fight for equality with men.

Even in the West there are many persons who are not in favour of women claiming equality with men. Even those who are in favour of this movement are seriously repenting for their evil advice, because, they are actually witnessing before their eyes its pernicious effects.

The movement of women towards independence and equality—women's rights—will not lead to any beneficial results. To have a seat in the Assembly or the Council will not give real independence to women. India is a spiritual country. It is a country of sages, Rishis, Yogis, Yoginis and philosophers. It is a country without parallel in matters relating to the Soul or the Adhyatmic science. The ladies have a very important part in the religious field and in the shaping of their children.

Women are in no way inferior to men in any respect. They are sublime personages. They are by their nature, patient, enduring and devotional. They possess finer qualities than men. They have more self-restraint. They must be adored as Devis. Yet they cannot claim perfect independence and equality with men. They should be obedient to their husbands. They should be modest. They should restrain their speech before men. This will add to their grace, splendour and *Pativratadharma*.

Wife is *Ardhangini*, an equal partner with her husband. No sacrifice or religious rite will bear fruit without the wife. She is the life-partner of man. There are instances of wives becoming Gurus of their husbands on account of their devotion and purity. If a man treats his wife as a slave or as inferior and thinks that a woman is meant for cooking and procreation only, he commits a heinous or unpardonable crime indeed!

Women should be educated. Cultured ladies are doubtless a

blessing to the society. But too much liberty and too much freedom lead to disastrous results. This is significant in daily life. Golden medium is the best. Extremes of anything are always bad.

They should certainly have knowledge of the Gita, the Bhagavata, the Ramayana and other holy scriptures. They should know something of hygiene, domestic medicine, nursing of the sick, training of children, dietetics, gynaecology, etc. They should not be shut up within the four walls of the house. This will hinder their evolution.

Women are, by nature, good mothers. This is the function they have to perform in the grand plan of God. This was meant in the divine plan. This is the will of God. Women have their own psychological traits, temperaments, capacities, virtues, instincts and impulses. Women have got their own sphere of duty in society and men have their own. They cannot and should not compete with men. They should not do the work of men. They should certainly be educated. They should have knowledge of religious books. It is the duty of the parents to give their daughters sound education. This is indispensable. The position of good mothers in society is highly praiseworthy. Good mothers are revered and adored by all. Why do they strive for equality and voting, freedom and independence, when they already occupy an unique position and unprecedented status and rank in society? Is it not folly and ignorance?

At the present moment, a rich man or a big official engages three or more tutors for educating his daughter, one for Hindi, another for English, a third for dancing or music, a fourth for embroidery, etc. He thinks that his daughter has become an accomplished girl when she can play tennis and is efficient in playing bridge. This is not real culture. She cannot do any domestic work in the house. She always wants a cook and a maid-servant. Ladies of the house should not depend upon cooks and servants. They themselves should do all the household work. Then only they can keep the mind wholly occupied and will be strong and healthy. She is more like a painted doll of the house, instead of being the mistress of the house. By leaving the household work entirely to the care of servants, she has no control over the domestic management and if she is not properly trained in the usual domestic duties, she is neither in a position to control the servants nor guide them. In such a house there can never be peace or lasting happiness.

"Full many a gem of the purest ray serene, the dark, unfathomable caves of the ocean bear." Even so, India still abounds with Sulabhas, Draupadis, Madalasas, Miras, Chudalas and Gargis.

May this sacred soil of India abound with chaste and devoted women like Sulabha and Mira! May they train their children in the true and only path of Dharma and Truth!!

PART IV

HIGH-SOULED BHISHMA

Bhishma, the greatest and most heroic figure in the Mahabharata, was undoubtedly the noblest person of his time. He was the greatest hero amongst the Kshatriyas. This world has not as yet seen a brave and wise hero like Bhishma. Though he was a brave warrior, he was kind, mild, humble, just, righteous and truthful. He was true to his salt. He advised even his opponents how to encompass his own death. He was a prophet, a philosopher and a saintly warrior. All kings of his time recognised him as their adviser, teacher and statesman. The teachings given by him to Yudhishthira in Santi Parva are sublime, elevating, soul-stirring and practical. They are as instructive today as they were in those days.

Bhishma was very firm in his principles. He was absolutely free from the slightest tinge of selfishness. He was an embodiment of self-denial and self-sacrifice. His power of endurance and patience in all the difficult trials he met with, was marvellous and unprecedented. He was matchless in fortitude and courage. All men honoured him. All the Kshatriya chiefs paid their homage to him. He was a mighty Yogi and a sage. He was above body-consciousness. He rested in his own *Sat-Chit-Ananda Svaroopa.* That is the reason why he was peaceful and serene even though he was pierced by sharp arrows all over his body. Lying on the bed of sharp arrows which was as soft as the bed of roses for him he gave wonderful discourses on political, philosophical, religious, social and moral subjects to Yudhishthira. Have you ever heard of any one, save the great Bhishma, in the history of the world, who was able to give lofty and sublime discourses on his death-bed? He laid his life for others. He lived to serve and elevate others. The noble life led by the high-souled Bhishma of mighty will-force, still inspires sterling virtues in those who study his discourses in the Santi Parva. Bhishma died long, long ago but his voice in the Santi Parva and his ideal and exalted life awakens slumbering people to action, righteousness, duty and enquiry, rigorous Tapas and meditation, to this day.

Look at the extraordinary spirit of renunciation and self-denial of this marvellous saintly hero. He said when he was lying on the bed of arrows, "My head is hanging down very low. Please give me a pillow." Thereupon, Duryodhana brought an excellent, soft pillow. Bhishma declined to accept it. Then he told Arjuna, "Give me a pillow that will be suitable to me now." Arjuna supported his head with the three sharp arrows. Bhishma was very much pleased to have this sort of pillow.

Then again, Bhishma asked for some water to drink. Duryodhana brought some scented water in a costly golden jug. Bhishma said, "I cannot use any article of human enjoyment." He asked Arjuna to get him some water. Arjuna pierced the earth by the side of his grandsire with a sharp arrow. A jet of cold water gushed out from the Earth. Bhishma drank this water to his heart's content. Such was the simple nature of the grand and glorious Bhishma of heroism and bravery, unheard of in this world. He spurned luxury and embraced plain living and high thinking.

❁ ❁ ❁

There was once a king named Santanu, a descendent of king Dushyanta. He was the ruler of Hastinapura. He was a valiant and heroic king, brave and undaunted, wise and righteous, truthful and learned. One day he met a very handsome lady on the bank of the Ganga. He fell in love with her and asked her to accept him as her husband. The lady replied, "O king! I am quite willing to marry you on one condition. I will remain with you so long as you do not interfere with me in anything I do, be it agreeable or disagreeable to you. The moment you show the slightest unkindness or rudeness towards me, the moment you meddle with my affairs, I will leave you at once."

The king said, "O blessed lady! Let it be so."

The name of the lady was Ganga Devi. She was Ganga or Bhagirathi herself who had assumed the form of an ordinary woman. Santanu married Ganga with great pomp and eclat. They both lived very happily. Santanu was highly pleased with the conduct and noble qualities of Ganga.

Ganga Devi brought forth eight beautiful sons; but as regards the first seven, as soon as they were born, they were thrown into the river by herself. She said to her husband, "This is for your good." The king was inwardly afflicted by the strange conduct of Ganga but he could not speak a word to her, for fear that she would forsake him at any moment.

Once the Ashta Vasus visited the hermitage of Rishi Vasishtha. The Rishi was then away to the river for a bath. The Vasus saw Surabhi (Kamadhenu) in the hermitage. They wanted to possess this divine cow for themselves and were trying to take her with them without the Rishi's knowledge. In the meantime, the sage Vasishtha returned. He divined the evil intention of the Vasus and told them thus, "O Vasus! I know what you are attempting to do. For this improper act, every one of you shall take birth in the world of men and live there your full life's time, after which you will regain your original status."

The Vasus were much crest-fallen at this and prayed to the sage for mercy. They said, "Revered sire! Have pity on us. We cannot bear the pangs of birth." Then Vasishtha said, "The leader of your party who actually committed the offence shall have to live his full life's time there. The remaining seven who merely assisted him can return, the moment after taking birth in the Mrityuloka. Ganga Devi is incarnating in the world. Pray to her to accept your motherhood. She will surely help you."

The Vasus prayed to Ganga Devi who sanctioned their prayers. They were born as sons of Ganga Devi. Ganga Devi threw seven of her sons into the river in order to save them. That is the reason why Ganga did not like Santanu to interfere in her ways. Her eighth son was 'Bhishma'.

When Ganga wished to throw the eighth child in the river, Santanu said, "O Ganga! Do not kill this child. Love of mother for her child cannot be adequately described in words. It is sacred, pure and sublime but I am stunned when I see you killing your own sons. It is quite strange indeed! Save this child at least. Give up this horrible habit of killing your child. You have committed heinous sins. Why do you add one more to them?"

Ganga replied, "I will certainly save this child. I will act in accordance with your request. I will train him in the best possible manner to the best of my abilities and return him to you as soon as he gets sufficiently old. I must leave you now according to our agreement. So, good-bye!" Ganga left the king taking the child with her.

❁ ❁ ❁

Santanu was very much troubled at heart on account of the separation from Ganga. One day the king was walking along the bank of the Ganga in the evening. He noticed to his great astonishment, that the river had become suddenly shallow. He tried to find out the cause for this strange phenomenon. He found out that a handsome boy of strong physique had checked the flow of the river by his sharp celestial weapon. This boy was none other than his own son. Santanu was not, however, able to identify the infant with this grown-up boy, as he had seen him only once and that too for a few minutes. The boy suddenly dived under the water and disappeared. The king was astounded. He stood spellbound. After a short time a handsome lady came to him holding the same lad by the hand. She said, "Do you remember me? I am your wife Ganga. I have come here to fulfil my promise. Here is your eighth son! He has learnt the entire Vedas and the Vedangas under the great sage Vasishtha. He has been taught also the use of all weapons. He knows well the duties of kings. His name is Devavrata." She handed over to the king the illustrious boy and disappeared immediately.

Santanu returned to his capital with his son and installed him as his heir-apparent in his seventeenth year. Devavrata was firm, courageous and benevolent. Devavrata was endowed with high moral qualities. He had a sharp intellect. He won the hearts of the ministers, officials and his subjects by his amiable disposition and good behaviour. Santanu was highly pleased with the character and noble qualities of his son. Devavrata and Santanu lived happily together. Four years thus passed away. Devavrata learnt archery from Parasurama and became a perfect adept in this science.

❁ ❁ ❁

One day Santanu went into the forests, close to the bank of the Yamuna, for hunting. He came across a handsome maiden. He said to her, "Who are you? What are you doing here?" She replied, "I am the daughter of Dasaraj, the fisher-chief. My name is Satyavati. I am engaged at his command in rowing the boat for taking passengers across this river."

King Santanu wanted to marry her. He went to Dasaraj and asked his consent. The fisher-chief replied, "I am quite willing to give my daughter to you in marriage. But, first, I want to take a promise from you."

The king replied, "O Dasaraj, what is that? I will certainly do what lies in my power." The fisher-chief said, "The son born of my daughter should succeed you."

Santanu did not wish to give this pledge to the fisher-chief because his valiant and intelligent son Devavrata, whom he loved intensely, would have to abandon the throne. He would no longer be the heir-apparent. But the fire of love for the maiden burnt him. He was in a great dilemma. He grew pale and did not take any interest in the affairs of the state. He opened his heart to the chief minister whom he trusted; but the latter was not able to give any advice in the matter. Santanu tried to conceal his love for the maiden from his son Devavrata.

Devavrata was wise, though he was very young. He suspected something and thought that his father was unhappy. He said to his father, "O beloved father! You are prosperous. You have got everything. There should be no cause for any anxiety. Why are you cheerless now? You are losing your vigour and strength. Kindly let me know the reason for your grief. I am ever ready to do what lies in my power to relieve it."

The king replied, "O beloved Devavrata! You are my only son. If any calamity falls on you, I will become son-less. I will be deprived of Heaven. You are equal to hundred sons. Therefore, I do not want to marry again. But one son is no son according to the words of the Rishis. These thoughts are troubling me in my mind."

Thereupon, Devavrata went to the old minister, whom his father trusted, and asked him about the cause of his father's grief. The minister told him about the king's love for the daughter of the fisher-chief and the pledge demanded by the fisher-chief.

Thereupon, Devavrata, accompanied by the old minister and many respectable Kshatriya chiefs, went to Dasaraj and pleaded on behalf of his father. He asked him to give his daughter to his father in marriage.

The fisher-chief replied, "O amiable prince! I have already told your father about the condition on which I can give my daughter in marriage to him."

Devavrata said, "O fisher-chief! I make a solemn declaration now that the son that may be born of this girl shall succeed my father to the throne. I shall do all that you wish."

The fisher-chief said, "I highly appreciate your noble character and high ideal. But your sons may expel my daughter's son at any time at their sweet will. I entertain a grave doubt on this point."

Devavrata prayed, "O Truth! Dwell in me for ever! Come and pervade my whole being! Give me inner strength to stick to the vow of perfect celibacy, I am going to take now, in the presence of these people!" He, then, resolutely said to the fisher-chief, "O Dasaraj! Listen to what I say. From today, I shall lead a life of strict Naishthika Brahmachari till the end of my life. All the women of the world are my mothers. I am the most devoted and loyal subject of the king of Hastinapura. If I die son-less I shall yet attain the abode of Eternal Bliss and Immortality."

From heaven at that time, the celestial damsels, the gods and the assemblage of sages, showered flowers on him and said, "This is verily Bhishma—the terrible."

The fisher-chief said, "O prince! I am quite ready now to give my daughter in marriage to your father." Thereupon, the fisherman and his daughter accompanied Devavrata to the palace of Santanu. The old minister informed the king all that had happened. The monarchs and the chiefs who assembled in the hall greatly appreciated the extraordinary spirit of self-sacrifice and renunciation of Devavrata and said, "Devavrata is really Bhishma (the terrible)." Since then Devavrata bore the name of 'Bhishma'. King Santanu was immensely pleased with the noble conduct of his son and conferred upon him the boon of death at will. He said, "May the gods protect you! Death shall never come to you as long as you wish to live."

What an exalted soul! This noble example is unprecedented in the history of the world. No one, save Bhishma, on the surface of this earth, had made such a great sacrifice for the sake of filial duty at such an young age. Bhishma's filial duty and piety might be very well compared to that of Lord Rama. His words were as true in spirit and letter as his actions. He did what he said and said what he meant to do. He did not move an inch from what he uttered. He adhered to truth in thought, word and deed. He would sacrifice his life even, for the sake of truth.

He possessed dispassion, insight and discrimination at such an early age. He kicked away ruthlessly royal possessions and happiness arising therefrom, as mere straw, because, he knew that the objects of this world were illusory and pain-giving. He was able to distinguish between the substance and the shadow, the permanent and the impermanent, the real and the unreal. He scorned the pomps and vanities of this illusory world.

On an auspicious day, Satyavati was married to king Santanu with great pomp and eclat. In due course, two sons named Chitrangada and Vichitravirya were born to Satyavati.

After ruling the kingdom for several years righteously, Santanu passed away. Bhishma then installed Chitrangada on the throne and looked after the affairs of the State under the wise guidance of Satyavati, his step-mother. Chitrangada was proud of his valour. He fought against a powerful Gandharva king but was killed by him. As he was unmarried, he died without any issue. Therefore, Vichitravirya, who was a boy, ascended the throne. Satyavati was ruling the kingdom as regent. Bhishma was helping her and carrying out her orders.

When Vichitravirya grew sufficiently old, he took the reins of the administration of the State under the wise and able guidance of Bhishma.

❁ ❁ ❁

Bhishma wanted to arrange for the marriage of his brother. He went to Kasi, defeated all the kings who had assembled there to marry Amba, Ambika and Ambalika, the daughters of the king of Kasi and brought the girls to his capital.

Amba, the eldest daughter of the king of Kasi, said to Bhishma, "I have already chosen mentally Shalya, the king of Saubha, as my future lord. He too, in his heart, had accepted me as his partner. Therefore allow me to go back. You are just, learned and virtuous." Thereupon, Bhishma sent Amba to king Shalya in a chariot with great honour along with an old and virtuous Brahmin. He married Ambika and Ambalika to his brother Vichitravirya.

Amba reached the palace of king Shalya. King Shalya said, "I cannot marry you now as you have lived unprotected in the house of a stranger after being kidnapped. You can go wherever you like."

Amba wanted to take revenge on Bhishma and kill him, because, she lost her would-be husband on account of his kidnapping her. She got the assistance of Parasurama. There was a severe fight between Bhishma and Parasurama. Eventually Parasurama was defeated. Parasurama took a vow on the spot, "I will not in future teach the archery to any Kshatriya." Here is a supreme instance of devotion to duty. Parasurama was Bhishma's preceptor in archery and Bhishma revered him as a Guru. But when Parasurama challenged him in a duel, Bhishma as a Kshatriya accepted it regardless of consequences. It is given in the Sastras that all the while he was in a sort of Samadhi.

Amba did rigorous penance in order to destroy Bhishma. Lord Siva was very much pleased with her austerities. He appeared before Amba and said, "O Amba! Ask for a boon." Amba replied, "Let Bhishma die immediately! Grant me this boon now." Lord Siva replied, "You will kill Bhishma. You will remember all the incidents of this life in your next birth. You will be born in the royal family of king Drupada as a daughter but you will be changed into a male warrior after some time." Having said this, Lord vanished.

Thereupon Amba made a large funeral pyre on the bank of the Yamuna, set fire to it and entered the fire bravely with a heart burning with anger, saying, "I do this for the destruction of Bhishma." This Amba was born as Shikhandi, Drupada's son.

Vichitravirya lived happily with his two wives, Ambika and Ambalika, for a few years. He was very lustful and so he passed away quickly on account of consumption. Satyavati then pressed Bhishma to marry in order to perpetuate the line. But Bhishma declined to marry. He said to her, "O mother, you know that I took a vow to lead a life of celibacy till the end of life. I cannot move an inch from Truth. I would even renounce the happiness of the three worlds but I could never abandon Truth. Earth may give up its scent; Sun may abandon its lustre; Ice may renounce its coolness; Fire its heat; Ether its sound; Water its moisture; Jasmine its sweet fragrance; the God of Justice his impartiality; Tiger its ferocity; Indra his prowess; but I cannot abandon Truth from my heart."

What a soul-stirring speech! The person for whose welfare he took the vow is pressing him hard to give up the vow! Bhishma stands adamant in his resolve and determination. Nothing could dissuade him from the firm position he had taken up. He would not give up his determination even to the point of a bayonet. He would sacrifice his life for the sake of adhering to 'Truth' and his vow. What a mighty personality! He had a rigorous ethical training in his boyhood. He stuck to his vow and duties tenaciously. He practised the rigorous austerities of the life of Brahmacharya. He was heroic and courageous. Therefore, he had an iron will, fiery determination and a strong character.

But Satyavati still urged her plea. Bhishma, who could not be moved, said, "O queen! Take not thine eye from Virtue. Destroy us not. Breach of Truth in a Kshatriya is never applauded in our scriptures. I shall soon tell thee, O queen, what is the established Kshatriya usage to which recourse may be had to prevent Santanu's line from becoming extinct upon Earth. The practice of Niyoga is sanctioned by the scriptures at the times of necessity and distress, forgetting not at the same time what is the ordinary course of social conduct."

Bhishma then advised that some great Rishi be invited to be the father of children who, being borne by the two widows, would be regarded as the sons of the dead man. Satyavati told him that there was a Rishi, who had been born of her with Parasara as his father, and who, having been a mighty ascetic in the past life, had gone away with his father immediately after his birth. This was sage Vyasa. He had promised his mother that he would come to her if she thought of him when she was in difficulty. "I will now recollect him, if thou, O Bhishma of mighty arms, so desireth." She then thought of the Rishi, and, on his appearing, the difficulty was laid before him and his help was asked. Vyasa consented and said, "The two widows should dress themselves beautifully and put on rich ornaments. They should pass before me without any shame. I will once look upon them full in the face. They will conceive at once and in course of time bring forth brave sons."

Ambika and Ambalika put on gorgeous dresses and rich ornaments. As they were shy to appear before the Rishi, they took a maid-servant with them to the forest. They reached the place. They hesitated to pass before Vyasa. At last Ambika took courage and went before the Rishi. She saw the dark face of the Rishi, his matted hair, grim beard, and body smeared with ashes and closed her eyes. Then Ambalika followed her. When she saw the fearful and ascetic form of the Rishi, she turned pale and quickly passed before him. Lastly the maid-servant passed before Vyasa joyfully without any disgust or being shy.

Rishi Vyasa came to his mother Satyavati and said to her, "Your daughters-in-law would bring forth two sons equal in strength to ten thousand elephants. They will both be learned. But the daughters-in-law did not carry out my injunctions fully. Hence Ambika, who passed before me with closed eyes, will bring forth a blind child. Ambalika, who turned pale when she looked at me, will give birth to a son who will have a pale face and a pale body. The maid-servant, who was neither shy nor disgust and who was cheerful when she passed before me, will bring forth a fortunate, virtuous and most intelligent son."

In course of time, Ambika brought forth a son with a brilliant face but blind of both eyes. He was named 'Dhritarashtra'. Ambalika's son was very handsome and strong but had a pale face and pale body. Hence he was named 'Pandu'. The maid-servant brought forth a son who was an embodiment of Dharma. He was named 'Vidura'.

✿ ✿ ✿

Dhritarashtra, Pandu and Vidura were brought up by Bhishma, as if they were his own children. Pandu and Vidura learnt the Vedas and the Sastras, the science of morality, archery, etc. They were well versed in the duties of kings.

Dhritarashtra married Gandhari, the daughter of king Sirvala. Pandu married Kunti, the adopted daughter of Kuntibhoja and Madri, the daughter of Salya, the king of Madra. Dhritarashtra had one hundred sons. Duryodhana was the eldest. Pandu had five sons. Yudhishthira was the eldest. The former were called the 'Kauravas' and the latter the 'Pandavas'. Bhishma installed Pandu duly on the throne.

Pandu conquered many kings. He was virtuous and obtained great fame. After some time he relinquished his kingdom and retired into the forest with his wives and children to practise austerities. He died in the forest. Madri also died with him. The Rishis of the forest took Kunti and her children to Hastinapura and entrusted them to Bhishma and Dhritarashtra.

Bhishma gave the reins of administration to Dhritarashtra for some time as the princes were all minors. Bhishma kept the princes under Kripacharya and Dronacharya for their secular and religious training. The Pandavas were very smart, intelligent and powerful. They excelled the sons of Dhritarashtra in everything. When the Pandavas played with the sons of Dhritarashtra, they were superior in strength, valour, prowess and intelligence. Bhimasena beat the Kauravas in physical strength, Arjuna in the art of archery. Duryodhana became very jealous of them. He entertained hostility and deep hatred towards them. He wanted to kill Bhima. He gave him poisoned food and threw him in the Ganga; but Bhima was saved miraculously.

When Yudhishthira came of age, Dhritarashtra installed him as the heir-apparent. Yudhishthira became very famous within a short space of time, on account of his firmness, fortitude, benevolence and righteousness. Bhimasena obtained great renown in fighting with the sword and mace. Arjuna was matchless in the use of various weapons. This caused intense jealousy in the heart of Dhritarashtra. He consulted with Kanika his chief minister. Kanika told him to use proper diplomacy in dealing with the Pandavas.

Duryodhana said to his father, "Send these Pandavas to Varanavata by some contrivance. We are not at all safe here. If I get the throne, there will be no danger even if they return and live here."

One day some clever counsellors, instructed by Dhritarashtra, began to describe in court, the beauties and charms of the town Varanavata. Dhritarashtra also highly praised the grandeur of this place. This excited the curiosity of the Pandavas. They all proceeded to the town Varanavata.

Duryodhana already built a large palace, made of inflammable and combustible material (lac), for the residence of the Pandavas. This was constructed by Purochana without an outlet for the helpless Pandavas. Duryodhana wanted to burn the Pandavas alive in that palace.

Vidura came to know of this treacherous conspiracy. He informed Yudhishthira of this plan of Duryodhana, beforehand. He also asked a trustworthy miner to make a large subterranean passage. When fire was set to the building, the Pandavas escaped through this underground passage. The mighty Bhimasena, son of Vayu, walked fast, carrying Kunti and his brothers.

Thereafter the Pandavas roamed about in the forest in a destitute condition. They were homeless. They came to Panchala and dwelt in the house of a potter. The Pandavas married Draupadi during their wanderings. King Drupada became their ally. This excited the wrath of Kaurvas. They wanted to destroy the Pandavas and Drupada.

Bhishma said to Dhritashtra, "Do not entertain hatred towards the Pandavas. Do not attempt to annihilate them. They are as much dear to me as you are all to me. I must protect them. Make treaty of peace with them and give them half the kingdom."

He addressed Duryodhana, "Do not spoil your name. Follow the path of your ancestors. The Pandavas have not perished. Purochana was not able to accomplish his evil object. He himself perished. Virtuous persons will live for ever. Evil-minded persons will always meet with disaster and death. The whole world is blaming you for this horrible and merciless act done secretly. If you wish to do what is agreeable to me, if you act justly, if you wish to seek your welfare, give them half of the kingdom voluntarily."

At last Dhritarashtra called the Pandavas and Draupadi back to Hastinapura and gave them half the kingdom. The Pandavas began to rule in the new capital called Indraprastha. They soon conquered many kingdoms. Yudhishthira ruled the subjects in a righteous manner. All lived very happily.

Yudhishthira performed the Rajasuya Yajna. Bhishma, Dhritarashtra, the Kauravas and many great persons were invited. Duryodhana was lodged in the new palace which was built on a novel design for this auspicious occasion at an enormous cost.

One day while Duryodhana was moving about in the palace he saw a crystal surface. He mistook it for a sheet of water and drew up his clothes. At another place, he mistook a lake of crystal water for land and fell into it. The Pandavas, Draupadi and their servants laughed at him. Duryodhana took this as a great insult. He felt that he was greatly dishonoured. Further he became intensely jealous of the Pandavas when he witnessed the splendid palace and the Durbar hall of Yudhishthira and their prosperity. He opened his heart to his wicked uncle Sakuni.

Sakuni said to Duryodhana, "Invite Yudhishthira for a dice-play. I will contrive to have him defeated at every throw, by taking recourse to deception. I give you definite promise to win all his wealth. You will enjoy all his wealth and possessions."

Yudhishthira was invited for gambling by Duryodhana. Yudhishthira played with him and lost the stakes one after another. He at last staked his brothers, himself and Draupadi and lost everything. Draupadi was dragged to the court by the wicked Dussasana. Dussasana even attempted to strip off her clothing in the presence of the elders and Bhishma. Duryodhana showed his bare thighs to Draupadi.

Dhritarashtra was moved when he heard the heart-rending lamentations of Draupadi. He gave back the wealth and kingdom to the Pandavas and allowed them to return to Indraprastha.

Duryodhana, Karna and Sakuni again went to Dhritarashtra and said, "We should again gamble with the Pandavas. This is the only way to subdue them. The defeated party will have to go to the forests in exile for twelve years. They will have to spend the thirteenth year incognito, without being recognised by us. If they are identified during the thirteenth year, they will have to undergo exile for another period of twelve years." Dhritarashtra was forced to give his consent.

Yudhishthira was again invited for gambling. He was defeated and the Pandavas were exiled. Thereafter Duryodhana reigned over the kingdom without any fear from the Pandavas. They walked barefooted in the forest. Despite the cruel treatment they received from Duryodhana and other cousins, they had no hatred towards the Kauravas. This is the nature of great souls.

The period of exile was over. For one year the Pandavas remained incognito. They underwent severe hardships and sufferings during their exile. They made preparations now to regain their kingdom, which had been deceitfully usurped by the wicked Kauravas.

Bhishma said to Duryodhana, "The Pandavas underwent untold sufferings. Now, the period of exile is over. They have fulfilled to the very letter what you asked them to do. You will have to give them back their kingdom. Otherwise they will wage war with you."

Duryodhana replied, "O venerable grandsire! I will not give them back the kingdom. I will make every preparation for waging war."

Bhishma said, "Yudhishthira desires to have peace with his cousins. The Pandavas are surely entitled under the law to get all the property of their father. Arjuna is a mighty bow-man. He is dexterous in the use of weapons. No one can withstand him in battle. O Duryodhana! If you do not pay any attention to my words, you will all be killed in battle. Arjuna is supported by Lord Krishna who is Lord Narayana himself. Do not try to wage war with the Pandavas. Invite Yudhishthira to accept the kingdom."

Duryodhana replied, "I will not give even an inch of land to the Pandavas. I will sacrifice my kingdom, wealth, honour, even my life, but I would not live side by side with them. Let them kill me and take the kingdom or I will kill them. This is my firm resolve."

Bhishma said to Dhritarashtra, "Your wicked son will soon meet with destruction. He is not paying the least heed to the words of his well-wisher. He has chosen the path of evil and abandoned the virtuous path. You are also following in the wake of this wretch." Having said this, Bhishma left the Assembly Hall.

Yudhishthira sent Sri Krishna as an emissary to make peace with the Kauravas. Krishna gave good advice to Duryodhana and entreated him to come to peaceful terms. Bhishma again advised Duryodhana to follow the wise counsels of Krishna and said, "Do not destroy the name and fame of the Bharatas. Do not bring grief to your parents by entering into war with the Pandavas. If you do not act in accordance with the advice of Krishna, you will have neither prosperity nor happiness. Do not allow the Earth's population to be slaughtered by unnecessary war."

Duryodhana did not pay any attention to the words of

Krishna and Bhishma. War was declared. Both sides made grand preparations for the war.

❁ ❁ ❁

Dhrishtadyumna was the general of the army of the Pandavas consisting of seven Akshauhinis with seven car warriors. The supreme command was in the hands of Krishna. They all proceeded to Kurukshetra.

The army of the Kauravas consisted of eleven Akshauhinis. Duryodhana elected Bhishma as the general of his forces. Bhishma said, "O Duryodhana! The Pandavas are as dear to me as you are. Therefore I should certainly seek their good as well. I shall fight for you as I have given you a pledge before, and as I am your loyal subject. I will fight on the following conditions: I will not kill a woman or one who was a woman before or one whose form resembles that of a woman. Therefore, I will not slay Shikhandi. I will not fight with one who has surrendered his arms, who has fallen down, one who bears the name of a female, who is not able to take care of himself, who is an only son, or who is a vulgar fellow. I will kill ten thousand warriors of the Pandavas daily and then stop the battle for the day. I will make Krishna fight on behalf of the Pandavas, although he promised that he would remain neutral and act only as a charioteer of Arjuna."

This is justice or fair play in war. A brave soldier should fight with an opponent of equal strength. Then only he is noble and just. All the military virtues, rules, justice, fairness in everything should be carefully observed in war. An unjust war cannot bring glory to the fighting parties. Just warfare will open the gates of Heaven. The words of Bhishma are like nectar. You could never find a just warrior like Bhishma in the history of the world.

Duryodhana requested Bhishma to tell about the merits of the brave warriors on both sides. Bhishma replied, "Arjuna is the best on the side of the Pandavas. Karna is only an Ardharatha not above the average." Karna was very much infuriated when he heard the remarks of Bhishma. He took it as a great insult. He abused Bhishma in the presence of all warriors and took a pledge that he would not fight till Bhishma was overthrown.

Yudhishthira approached the grandsire Bhishma and said, "We have to fight with you. Kindly grant us permission and give us your usual blessings and benedictions."

Bhishma replied, "I am very much pleased to see you here. Do fight and win victory." Yudhishthira asked, "Can I ever win the war in which you are the general of the opposite party? Tell me the means by which I can attain victory." Bhishma said, "Time has not come to give a reply to your question. Come to me once again. Surely you will win victory."

Bhishma fought for Duryodhana. He gave up his physical body for him as he was a devoted and loyal subject; but he kept up the purity to his soul.

Bhishma gave an inspiring speech to his warriors: "O Kshatriyas! Be brave. Be chivalrous. Exhibit your manliness and heroism now. We are now standing on the very threshold of Heaven. The broad door of Heaven is open to you now. To die of disease at home on a cot is a shame, nay a sin, for a Kshatriya. To die in the battlefield is his supreme goal. If you die bravely, pierced every inch of your body with the sharp arrows, you will go direct to Heaven."

Bhishma fought for ten days. The war lasted for eighteen days. Many warriors on both sides were killed. Duryodhana accused Bhishma that he was showing favour to the Pandavas. There was a fierce battle between Bhishma and Dhananjaya. Arjuna cut the bow of Bhishma. Bhishma fought with great valour and prowess.

By the end of eight days, the Kauravas lost many elephants, horses and a large army; seventeen brothers of Duryodhana and the charioteer of Bhishma were also killed. Duryodhana was very much afflicted at heart. He held a council with Karna, Sakuni, Dussasana and others and said to them, "O wise counsellors! Bhishma is said to be invincible even to the gods. But he cannot destroy even a small army of the Pandavas. What is the cause of this? The Pandavas are gaining ground now. They have killed a major portion of our army. If this goes on for a few days more, we all will be destroyed. Please advise me what should be done at this critical juncture. How can we conquer Arjuna?"

Karna replied, "O Duryodhana! Do not grieve. I will attain victory over the Pandavas. I am ready to do whatever you wish me to do. Let Bhishma retire from the battlefield at once. Bhishma and Drona are not fighting in right earnest as they love the Pandavas. I would have killed the Pandavas by this time, had it not been for the pledge I have taken. Request your grandfather to retire from the battlefield. I will take up the command of the army in my hand and kill them in no time."

Duryodhana went to the grandsire and said, "If you do not want to kill the Pandavas yourself, kindly permit Karna to become the Commander. He gives a definite pledge that he will kill them."

Bhishma replied, "O Duryodhana! This is not the play of chess which you can win with the help of Sakuni and Karna. Arjuna cannot be conquered even by gods. Krishna is his charioteer. I cannot lay down my arms as long as I am alive. I cannot act against my pledge. I will fight very fiercely tomorrow and try to kill them all, except Shikhandi. Protect me from Shikhandi."

On the ninth day, the battle was very terrible. Bhishma killed a very large army of the Pandavas. Even Arjuna was so completely exhausted and could hardly sit in his chariot that Lord Krishna had to interfere and jump from the chariot to protect him and fight Bhishma with the discus. In the evening, Yudhishthira, despairing of victory, went to Bhishma and said, "O grandsire! You promised to give me advice. Tell me now how you could be defeated. This is a grave juncture."

Bhishma replied, "Ask Arjuna to keep Shikhandi in front of me and discharge sharp arrows all over my body. If you can kill me in this manner you can certainly vanquish me. When I am possessed with weapons in my hands, even gods cannot conquer me. If I lay down my arms in the presence of Shikhandi, your car warriors can easily kill me. I would never fight with Shikhandi, as he was a female before."

On the tenth day, Shikhandi was brought before Bhishma. Shikhandi fearlessly rushed at Bhishma. Bhishma laid down his arms according to his pledge. Arjuna and Shikhandi pierced Bhishma with sharp arrows all over his body. He fell down from his car. His body did not touch the ground, as it was full of arrows. He was lying on the bed of arrows with perfect calmness and great fortitude. The Sun was in the southern solstice when he fell down from the car. He wished to abandon his life in the northern solstice only. He could die at his will as he had this boon from his father. As he was a great Yogi, he kept Death in abeyance.

As soon as Bhishma fell down, all the heroic warriors of both the armies laid down their arms.

❁ ❁ ❁

After eighteen days' severe fighting, the great war ended in favour of the Pandavas. The Pandavas, Vidura and Dhritarashtra offered oblations of water to all their relatives. They dwelt on the bank of the Ganga. Yudhishthira was very much afflicted at heart on account of loss of several lives in the war. He wished to relinquish the whole kingdom and to retire to the forests to spend the remaining days peacefully in prayer and meditation. His brothers, Vyasa and other sages, dissuaded him from renunciation and highly eulogised the merits of sovereignty as the sure means of attaining Heaven. Krishna also exhorted Yudhishthira to abandon grief and resume his royal duties.

Krishna advised, "O Yudhishthira! Be brave and cheerful. You will gain nothing by repentance and giving vent to your feelings. Shake off your grief. Stand adamant. Be calm and serene. Control your emotions and sentiments. Draw courage from within. Develop fortitude and bear the calamity with a bold heart. You can conquer grief and sorrow but you cannot remove its causes. Generate the powerful Sattvic forces within. Increase your Sattva. Bring the spiritual forces into full play. Allow them to operate. Concentrate your spiritual energies instead of frittering them away. Practise concentration and meditation. You will draw strength and power from great souls who are fearless, strong and courageous."

Yudhishthira was strongly impressed by the short and stirring advice of Krishna. He proceeded to Hastinapura along with his brothers, Dhritarashtra and other kings.

Krishna took Yudhishthira and others to Bhishma to receive

instructions and advice. These teachings are embodied in the Santi Parva of the Mahabharata in the form of discourses. These learned discourses contain philosophical and ethical precepts. They form a treatise on secular duties and moral teachings, science of war, duties of kings, etc., which are highly useful for daily life in the world for kings and various sorts of people. There are many beautiful stories of absorbing interest with excellent morals.

TEACHINGS OF BHISHMA

Dharma (Righteousness): It is very difficult to define 'righteousness' accurately. Dharma is so called, because it upholds all creatures. All creatures are upheld by righteousness. Therefore that which leads to advancement and evolution is righteousness. That which prevents or restrains persons from doing injury to one another is righteousness.

Virtuous Persons: They are endowed with self-restraint and contentment. They do not take animal food. Truth is their soul refuge. They worship ancestors, gods, sages and guests. They are universal friends and benefactors. They always work for the good of others. They are fearless and courageous. They observe all the injunctions laid down in the scriptures. They can give up their lives for others. They will never deviate from the path of righteousness. They possess untainted character and good behaviour. They are calm, mild, compassionate and humble.

They are free from greed, egoism, pride, lust, anger and jealousy. They are not attracted to any worldly objects. Their minds are ever fixed at the lotus feet of the Lord. They spend their time in prayer, Japa, meditation, Kirtan and study of sacred scriptures.

They have a balanced mind in pleasure and pain, success and failure. They have no liking for what is pleasant and agreeable and no dislike for what is unpleasant and disagreeable. They always give but do not take. They observe vows and stick to their vows. They are devoted to Truth. They look upon all with an equal vision. Gain and loss, weal and woe, life and death, gold and stone, are equal in their eyes.

Truth: Truth is the eternal goal of man. Truth is the eternal Brahman. It is the highest refuge of all. Truth is penance. Truth is Yoga. Everything rests upon Truth. Truth is immutable, eternal and unchangeable. Truth is of thirteen kinds. Impartiality, good-will, self-control, forgiveness, modesty, endurance, goodness, renunciation, meditation, dignity, fortitude, mercy, refraining from injury, are all forms of Truth.

When desire, hatred, lust and anger are destroyed, one develops virtue through which he is able to look upon himself, his enemy and upon one's evil, with an equal eye. This virtue is called impartiality. Self-restraint consists in controlling the senses and in practising non-violence, truthfulness, non-stealing, celibacy and non-covetousness.

Observance of all duties and the practice of liberality constitute good-will. Constant devotion to Truth leads to the attainment of universal good-will.

That virtue through which one endures what is agreeable and disagreeable, without either feelings of pleasure or pain, is forgiveness. This can be acquired through the practice of truthfulness.

Modesty is the virtue of self-effacement. Such a man is neither elated by the success of any meritorious actions nor is depressed in mind by failure nor is annoyed by the censure of others. He is steadfast in his devotion to duty.

Renunciation is the abandonment of affections and all earthly possessions. He who is free from anger, hatred and malice can attain renunciation.

Goodness is that virtue which seeks to do good to others without any selfish motives. He who is free from all selfish attachments can do good to others.

Fortitude is that virtue through which one remains steadfast in pleasure and pain, happiness and misery, joy and sorrow. One should always practise forgiveness and devotion to Truth. He who succeeds in getting rid of anger, fear and joy can succeed in acquiring fortitude.

Refraining from injury to all creatures in thought, word and deed, kindness and charity, is the eternal duty of man.

Penance: Sages declare that everything has penance for its root. Brahma created this universe with the help of penances. Abstention from sensual pleasure is the best penance. Renunciation is the highest penance. Concentration of mind is the highest and the best penance. Abstention from food is also good penance. The senses are kept under control and the heart is purified. The acts of so keeping them under control are penances. The gods acquired their superiority and attained highest merits through penance. The status of God-head can be attained through penance.

Self-restraint: The rules of duty prescribed by the Sastras and the Rishis are many. The highest among them all is self-restraint. It bestows great benefits or highest merits. It is the eternal duty of a Brahmin. Self-restraint purifies the heart, destroys sins and leads to the attainment of happiness herein and hereafter.

Forgiveness, patience, refraining from violence, impartiality, truth, sincerity, control of the senses, mildness, steadiness, liberality, control of anger, contentment, sweetness of speech, benevolence, freedom from malice, conquest of lust, compassion—the combination of all these is self-restraint. A man of self-restraint avoids false speech, greed, pride, arrogance, boasting, jealousy, disgrace, depravity, fear and disrespect. A man of self-restraint is considered by the world as a weak man. But it is not actually so; it is the highest form of courage—for example to keep oneself under control in the face of provocation.

Ignorance: Ignorance is the root cause of all misery. One sinks into hell on account of ignorance. Attachment, dislike, hatred, prejudice, vanity, lust, anger, pride, idleness, procrastination, desire, jealousy, backbiting, talebearing, and all sinful acts are known as the fruit of ignorance. Ignorance and greed are the same substance. Greed grows with ignorance. When greed diminishes, ignorance also diminishes. Wherever there is greed, there exists ignorance also.

Greed: Greed or covetousness is the source of all troubles and sorrows. It is born of ignorance. Loss of discrimination is its inseparable attribute. It takes a manifold course. Sin proceeds from greed. Greed is the source of irreligiousness, crime and sin. Greed is the source for cunningness, deceit, falsehood and hypocrisy. Greed brings anxiety and disgrace. From greed proceed anger, lust, pride of learning, pride of beauty, arrogance, hatred, revenge, miserliness, mercilessness, treachery, ungratefulness, etc.

When the objects of covetousness are not obtained, ignorance appears. From ignorance proceeds greed and from greed proceeds ignorance. Therefore, greed is both the cause and effect of ignorance. Greed produces all faults.

A greedy man loses his understanding and power of discrimination. He is shameless and vicious. He will stoop to do any kind of improper and mean act. He never trusts another. He is insincere. He is ever ready to appropriate other people's wealth and property. He is rude and harsh in his speech. He speaks ill of others.

Boastfulness, perpetuation of wicked deeds, malicious propensity, insatiable craving for the indulgence of lust—all these proceed from greed. Therefore, this enemy—greed—should be destroyed after careful thought, practice of honesty, nobility and contentment.

Evil Qualities: There are eleven vices or evil qualities. These are powerful enemies to human beings. These are the real causes for grief or sorrow. All kinds of sin proceed from these. They are anger, lust, envy, loss of judgment, grief, greed, malice, pride, jealousy, slander and hatred.

Anger proceeds from greed. It is strengthened by the fault of others. It remains dormant through forgiveness and vanishes through forgiveness.

Lust springs from irresolution and want of self-restraint. Indulgence strengthens it. When man resolutely turns away from it, through discrimination and wisdom, it vanishes and dies.

Envy proceeds from anger, greed and seeing the well-being of other people. It vanishes when one develops compassion, dispassion and knowledge of Atman.

Loss of judgment springs from ignorance. When the man associates with wise men and takes their advice this vanishes.

Grief springs from false attachment which is cut by separation. When one knows that the dead do not return, it subsides. It disappears through enquiry and discrimination.

Greed has its origin in ignorance. If one understands clearly the impermanence of all objects of enjoyments, it dies.

Malice originates from the relinquishment of truth and indulgence in wickedness. If one serves the sages, this evil quality disappears.

Pride originates from birth, learning and prosperity. When one realises the true value of these three, this evil quality vanishes at once.

Jealousy originates from lust. It is destroyed through knowledge.

Slander takes its origin from lack of good behaviour and conduct and from evil thoughts towards others. It disappears when one develops good behaviour and right conduct through association with the sages.

Hatred manifests when the man who injures is powerful and the injured one is unable to avenge the injury. It vanishes through love and kindness.

Worship of Parents and Preceptor: He who worships his parents and the preceptor becomes illustrious here and attains eternal regions of happiness. Whatever they command should be done unhesitatingly. One should never do what they forbid. Their commands should always be carried out. They are as sacred as the sacred fires. The father is the Garhapatya fire. The mother is the Dakshina fire. The preceptor is that fire upon which oblations are poured. One may cross the ocean of Samsara by serving the father. One will attain the regions of happiness in the next by serving the mother. One can attain Brahmaloka by serving the preceptor regularly with faith and devotion. Never disobey these three. Never violate their biddings. Never eat before they eat, nor eat anything which is better than what they eat. Never attribute any fault to them. Serve them with humility.

One Acharya is superior to ten Brahmins learned in the Vedas. One Upadhyaya is superior to ten Acharyas. The father is again superior to the Upadhyayas. The mother is superior to the father or perhaps the whole world, in importance. There is no one who deserves so much reverence as the mother. The preceptor is worthy of greater reverence than the father or even the mother. The father and mother only create the physical body. But the preceptor helps the aspirant to attain Immortality and Eternal Bliss. He helps him to free himself from the round of births and deaths. The preceptor who imparts spiritual knowledge should be regarded as both father and mother. He who pleases his preceptor, pleases Brahma Himself. The preceptor is worthy of greater reverence than either the father or the mother. The father and mother, however much they may offend, should never be even disliked.

The father, the mother and the preceptor should never be insulted. One should not find fault with any act of theirs. He who injures in thought, word and deed his preceptor, father or mother, incurs the sin of killing a foetus. There is no sinner in the world equal to him. If the son does not protect his parents when he comes of age, he incurs the sin of killing a foetus. There is no sinner in the world like him.

He who injures a friend, he who is ungrateful and treacherous, he who slays a woman and he who kills a preceptor, never succeeds in purifying himself.

Ideal Kingship: If there is no king, there is no security for people. Wicked people and dacoits will plunder everywhere in broad daylight and carry away wealth, women and children by force. The strong will devour the weak. There will be anarchy and lawlessness everywhere. The strong will seize the property of the weak and will kill those who resist them. A king gives protection to his subjects, punishes the wicked and maintains law and order.

An ideal king should practise all duties. He should be kind, brave, generous, just and righteous. He should be free from cruelty. He should not indulge in sensual pleasures. He should not oppress his people with too high taxes. He should not punish anybody without enquiry. He should be free from jealousy. He should not be the slave of women. He should serve his preceptors and elders with respect and devotion. He should worship the gods with faith and sincerity. He should not be gentle towards wicked people.

A king should know the scriptures well. He should perform sacrifices. He should appoint as his ministers four Brahmins, eight Kshatriyas, twentyone Vaishyas and three Sudras. The king's seven qualities are that of father, mother, teacher, protector, the gods of fire and wealth and the judge of the dead.

The king who guards himself in every respect can be the guardian of a kingdom. The king should always find out what defect is there in him and from what quarter he is blamed. He should ascertain whether men praise him or blame him for his past actions.

Taxation: Taxation should be very moderate. Let a king extract revenue from his subjects, as bees do from flowers. Let him milk the cow having regard to the calf and not bruise the source of milk. Let him collect taxes without injuring people, as a bee gathers honey from flowers without hurting them. A man should collect the flowers but not uproot the plant. He should act like a gardener, but not like a charcoal burner.

The king should levy a just tax on his subjects according to expediency and necessity. He should promote the welfare of the country in all possible ways. The subjects are undoubtedly pleased with a king who is just, righteous, liberal, who is a protector, and who is free from desire and hatred. He should not try to accumulate wealth by injustice and covetousness. An unjust king who puts too much tax on his subjects cannot prosper. All the wealth which he has acquired by unjust means and by oppressing his subjects with heavy and unjust taxes will be lost. He does injury to himself.

He who cuts a cow's udder in order to get more milk, obtains none. Similarly, the king who oppresses his subjects with heavy tax does not enjoy prosperity. He should protect the people, make them prosper and obtain reverence by skillful and able management. People hate a king who is covetous and unjust.

How can he, who is disliked by his subjects, prosper? The king who protects his subjects and treats them with kindness and takes from them what they can spare, enjoys great merit and fame herein and hereafter.

❁ ❁ ❁

Bhishma instructed Yudhishthira as above till the fifty- eighth day after his fall from the war-chariot.

At the dawn of that day all gathered around him as usual. Yudhishthira addressed, "Beloved grandfather and true king of the whole land! Open your eyes. Dhritarashtra and Yudhishthira salute you. The holy sages are also present. Lord Krishna also is here."

Then Bhishma slowly opened his eyes and said, "The million-rayed Lord of Heaven has now turned to the North. For fiftyeight nights I am lying here over these sharp-pointed arrows. I must pass on now to the other world. Follow Dharma and be to the king Dhritashtra as a son, as I know thou wilt be."

Bhishma was the first man to realise that Sri Krishna was God Himself. Then he turned in adoring love of Krishna and said, "Give me permission, O Krishna, to cast off this mortal coil. Permitted by Thee, I shall attain to the highest end." Krishna said, "I give thee permission. Go unto the Vasus, thou stainless soul! Thou hast not been guilty of a single transgression in this world!"

Then Bhishma once again said to all, "Follow the Truth always. Strive for it ever in thought, word and deed. Practise self-denial. Be compassionate. Attain knowledge of Brahman. This is the Dharma of all Dharmas. Where Krishna, the Universal Self is, there Dharma ever is, and where Dharma is, there always is certainly victory."

He closed his eyes again and steadily gathered, by concentration, all his vital forces in the head and thence passed out as a great light. The light rose into the Heaven and vanished in the twinkling of an eye. Bhishma left his mortal coil at the age of 135.

Such is the short life sketch of Bhishma, son of Santaṇu and Ganga, the mighty saintly warrior of great purity, self-denial and valour, the philosopher of the terrible vow of celibacy, the grandfather of the heroes of the great Epic, who was called "Narendra" though he renounced the kingdom in favour of Satyavati's son, who was a man of knowledge and action, who was a great saint, who was a great Bhakta, a matchless warrior, an embodiment of resolute will and celibacy, who was truthful in thought, word and deed, who was a preceptor, friend, benefactor and guide to the Pandavas, the Kauravas and the world at large.

Glory to Bhishma, whose teachings in the Santi Parva thrill our hearts even today and elevate our minds to magnanimous heights of divine glory and splendour!

YUDHISHTHIRA THE RIGHTEOUS

Some five thousand years ago, there stood the magnificent city of Hastinapura (elephant city), on the banks of the Ganga, about sixty miles to the North-east of the modern Delhi. It was a city of beautiful palaces with pretty gardens. Even now its ruins may be traced. Raja Pandu lived in this city and ruled his subjects in a virtuous manner.

He was very fond of hunting. One day he went into the forest and saw a deer coupling with its mate. Pandu shot the deer with pointed arrows. This deer with its mate was the Kanva Rishi and his wife in transformed form. The two deers fell down on the ground. The Rishi assumed his human form and said to the Raja, "O virtuous king, you have today committed a great crime and sin. You shot us down when we were enjoying each other's company. You should have waited. You have done a cruel act. I now give you this curse. Since you killed me when I was in the company of my wife, you will also die in the same manner at the first opportunity. My heart was very much afflicted with grief when I was happy. You also will be drowned in sorrow when you are in happiness."

Pandu repented very much for his rash and cruel act. He told all that happened to his two wives. They lamented and wept bitterly.

One day, Pandu said to his wife, "O beloved Kunti! I am very unhappy. I have no son. All my austerities, sacrifices, vows and gifts to Brahmins and gods will not make me free from sin, as I am sonless. I have a strong desire to beget sons; but my power of procreation has been frustrated by the curse of the Rishi Kanva. If I die without a son, my ancestors will perish, as there will be none to perform their Sraaddha ceremony."

Kunti realised that her husband was very much troubled at heart as he was without a son. Then she remembered of an incident which took place when she was a virgin in the house of her parents. Rishi Durvasa had come to her house. Kunti's father, Raja Kuntibhoja, asked her to serve the Rishi. Kunti pleased the Rishi in all ways. The Rishi was very much delighted and gave Kunti a gift in the form of a Mantra by which she could call any of the gods in time of emergency and trouble. Now Kunti remembered this incident and informed her husband of this secret. Pandu asked Kunti to call the gods and thus beget sons through them.

Kunti recited the sacred Mantra and called the god Dharma (Yama). As soon as she recited the Mantra, god Dharma appeared before her and said, "O Kunti Devi! I am pleased with your devotion. What shall I do for you now?" Kunti said, "O god Dharma! Bless me with a son." Dharma looked at the eyes of Kunti and she conceived at once. In course of time, she gave birth to a truthful and righteous son who was an embodiment of Dharma.

As soon as the child was born, a mysterious heavenly voice spoke, "O Kunti! Your child will be matchless in truthfulness and righteousness. He will be the ruler of the Earth. He will earn undying fame. Let him be named 'Yudhishthira'." There was a shower of flowers from the gods above.

Another heavenly voice spoke thus to Pandu, "O king Pandu! You are the most fortunate person on the surface of this Earth, because you are blessed with a son of great merit. He will become very brilliant and illustrious. He will be an embodiment of patience, forbearance, truthfulness, justice and righteousness. He will bring immortal fame and glory to your clan. He will impart principles of Dharma to the people. He will be a spiritual guide. The whole world will revere him. This world has not seen as yet and will not ever see in future, an equal to your son in righteousness, prosperity, spiritual and moral strength. No man has ever gone to the Heaven with this physical body and no man in future also will have the grace of the Lord to do so, but your son will have that most unique honour. This is a rare privilege for him through the blessings of the Lord. You are indeed the most blessed man on this Earth in having such a son."

Pandu was immersed in happiness when he saw the resplendent face of his glorious son when he heard the heavenly voice.

Pandu asked Kunti to propitiate the god Vayu and beget a son of great strength through his blessings. Thereupon, Kunti recited the Mantra and invoked Vayu, the Wind god. The Wind god appeared before her immediately and said, "O Kunti! What shall I do for you? I am pleased with your devotion." Kunti said, "O Lord! Bless me with a son who should be strong and capable of destroying the pride of everyone." The Wind god looked at the eyes of Kunti. Kunti conceived at once and in due course gave birth to a son who was named 'Bhima'—the terrible—who became famous for his immense strength and skill in the art of wrestling and fighting with mace or clubs.

Again, according to the request of Pandu, Kunti invoked Indra and recited the Mantra. Indra blessed her with a son and in due course she gave birth to a third son who was named 'Arjuna' who became famous for his skill in archery.

King Pandu's second wife, Madri, had no son. She was also desirous of having a son. Kunti taught her the sacred Mantra. Madri recited the Mantra and invoked the twin Asvins. Through their blessings, she gave birth to the twins named 'Nakula' and 'Sahadeva'. Nakula became famous for his skill in horsemanship and swordsmanship. Sahadeva obtained renown for his knowledge of stars. He was also an expert in the rearing of cows.

Gandhari, wife of Dhritarashtra, served Vyasa with great faith and devotion and as the result of his blessings, she had one hundred sons and one daughter. 'Duryodhana' was the eldest and the most powerful of the sons and the youngest was the daughter. Her name was 'Dussala'. She was married to Jayadratha, king of Sindh.

One day Pandu left his wife Kunti and the children in a hermitage and roamed in the forest with his wife Madri. He became passionate and caught her by force. Madri remembered the curse pronounced upon her husband by the Rishi and also resisted him to the best of her power but it was of no avail. Pandu could not control his passion. He became a victim of lust and expired. Madri, the devoted wife of Pandu, burnt herself on the funeral pyre of her husband. This sad news reached Dhritarashtra and Bhishma. They went to the forest and the obsequies of Pandu were duly performed by his five sons. Then they brought Kunti and her sons to Hastinapura.

✿ ✿ ✿

Even during boyhood, while playing, the Pandavas exhibited great strength, valour, intelligence and skill in the use of arms. This produced jealousy and hatred in the heart of Duryodhana, against the virtuous Yudhishthira and his brothers. Drona, son of Bharadvaja, who was a profound scholar of the Vedas and a perfect master of the science of arms, was their preceptor. They became proficient in the use of all kinds of weapons, in horsemanship, in swordsmanship, in archery and in the weilding of mace, spear, etc. They had profound knowledge of the Vedas and other sacred scriptures.

Yudhishthira mastered the Vedas. He practised self-denial, self-restraint and was ever righteous in his conduct. He adhered strictly to the principles of Dharma, as laid down in the scriptures. He would not deviate, even a hair's breadth, from the path of virtue. He trained his brothers also in the path of righteousness.

Duryodhana wanted to kill the Pandavas. Therefore, he sent them to live in the palace built of lac by Purochana. Vidura divulged the plot to Yudhishthira.

Kunti one day fed many Brahmins of the neighbourhood in that house. A low caste woman with her five sons also came uninvited to the feast. They rested on the floor of that house on account of overeating. When Duryodhana had the house set on fire, the uninvited six guests were burnt to death. The bones of these six persons were found in the ashes and actually the Pandavas and Kunti escaped through a subterranean passage. Duryodhana and his men took the bones to be the remains of the Pandavas and their mother. They rejoiced very much at the thought that their enemies were dead.

Meanwhile the Pandavas and Kunti, who escaped through the subterranean passage, reached the forest, put on the garb of Brahmins and wandered from place to place, living on alms. Duryodhana later on came to know that the Pandavas and Kunti had escaped. He was very much afflicted at heart when his plot became a thorough failure.

The Pandavas and Kunti were passing through the forest. They were all very much fatigued. Kunti and the Pandavas, except Bhima, slept for a short time. Bhima guarded them. There was a great monster (Rakshasa) in the forest named Hidimba. He rushed towards Bhima who fought with the monster and killed him. Thereupon Bhima married Hidimbi, the sister of the monster, and had a son through her, Ghatotkacha by name.

The Pandavas left the forest and wandering in the guise of ascetics, reached the city of Ekachakra. This city was haunted by a monster (Asura) named Baka. This monster was a cannibal and ate every day a lot of foodstuff in addition to a few men and animals. He threatened to destroy the city to satisfy his monstrous appetite. Then all the citizens of the place jointly prayed to the monster to desist from his cruel destruction of human beings. They agreed to send him his daily food consisting of two buffaloes, one human being, one cart-load of rice and cakes. Each family in the city supplied this food to the monster. Whatever more food he required, he should make good by eating the wild animals of the forest like wolves, tigers, etc. The monster agreed to this arrangement.

In that city, the Pandavas lived in the house of a poor Brahmin. One day Bhima heard a piteous cry in the house. He asked the Brahmin, "What is the matter with you? Why do you all cry today?" The Brahmin replied, "O venerable guest! Today

I have to provide meal for the monster Baka. Today is my turn. It is not yet settled as to who should be sent for the monster's food. The children are crying for the sake of parents. The parents are crying for the sake of children."

Bhima at once offered to go himself as the monster's food. He went to the spot and began to eat the rice and cakes himself. Baka came at the usual time. He became indignant when he saw his victim eating his food. He gave severe blows to Bhima but Bhima did not move a bit. He continued to eat the food. The monster was burning with anger. He uprooted a big tree and hurled it against Bhima. Bhima finished his dinner, got up and caught hold of the tree with his hand and dashed it to pieces. He then jumped upon the monster and killed him. The monster fell dead. Bhima had a full meal for many a long day.

In due course, the Pandavas moved to Panchala. There they came to know through some Brahmins of the marriage of Draupadi to take place soon. They repaired to Drupadnagar with the hope of getting some wealth by way of charity. Arjuna bent his bow and hit the target of a fish high above, which was revolving with great speed, by looking at its reflection in a basin of water below. Raja Drupada came to know that these five were the five Pandavas and the man who hit the target was Arjuna. So he won the hand of Draupadi.

Drupada: Let Arjuna marry today my daughter with all due rites. Today is an auspicious day.

Thereupon the virtuous-minded king Yudhishthira replied, "O great king! I shall also have to marry."

Drupada: Then take the hand of my daughter yourself. Or give Draupadi in marriage to him whom you like.

Yudhishthira: Draupadi shall be the queen of all of us. It has been thus ordained by our mother. Your jewel of a daughter has been won by Partha (Arjuna), O king! We must equally enjoy a jewel that we obtain. This is our rule. We are not willing to break that rule. Draupadi shall be the wedded queen of all of us. Let her take our hands before the fire, one after the other, according to our age.

Drupada: O Yudhishthira! It is ordained that a husband can have many wives but I have never heard that a wife can have many husbands. You are pure and you know the rules of morality. You should not commit an act that is sinful and opposed both to the Vedas and usage.

Yudhishthira: O king! Morality is subtle. We do not know its course. Let us, therefore, tread on the path that was trodden by the illustrious men of former ages. My tongue never utters an untruth. My mind never turns to that which is sinful. It has been ordered by our mother and I approve of it. It is certainly conformable to virtue. Therefore, act accordingly without any scruple. Fear not in the matter.

Drupada: Consult with Dhrishtadyumna and Kunti once more and settle the matter amongst yourselves. I shall do what is proper tomorrow.

These three conferred on the subject. At that very time Vyasa came there.

Drupada: O venerable and wise sage! How can one woman become the wife of many men without being tainted by sin? Tell me truly in detail all about this matter. I am very eager to hear on this point.

Vyasa: What is your opinion in this matter?

Drupada: In my opinion this practice is sinful as it is opposed to both the usage and the Vedas. There is nowhere a wife with many husbands. The practice appears to be of doubtful morality. How can the elder brother, if he is at all of good character, approach the wife of his younger brother? I will never agree that Draupadi should become the wife of five husbands.

Yudhishthira: I have heard in the Puranas that Jatila, a lady of the Gotama race, the foremost of all virtuous women, married seven Rishis, altogether; so also the daughter of an ascetic married ten brothers who all had the same name of Prachetas and who were all ascetics. It is said that obedience to superiors is a cardinal virtue. Of all superiors the mother is the foremost. She has commanded 'Enjoy all of you that which you have obtained as alms today.' Therefore I consider this act to be virtuous.

Kunti: It is so, as the virtuous Yudhishthira has said.

Vyasa: I shall tell you how this practice has been established and why it is to be considered as old and eternal. What Yudhishthira has said is quite conformable to virtue. There is no doubt of this. In the olden days, the celestials performed a great sacrifice in the Naimisaranya forest. Yama, the son of Vaivasvata, became the slayer of animals. As he was employed in that sacrifice, Yama did not kill any human being. Therefore, the number of human beings greatly increased. The celestials, Soma, Sakra, Varuna, Kubera, the Sadhyas, the Rudras, the Vasus, the twin Asvins—these and other celestials went to Prajapati and the following dialogue took place.

Celestials: We are alarmed at the increase of human beings. We ask your protection.

Brahma: You have no fear from human beings. You are all immortal. You should not be afraid of the mortals.

Celestials: The mortals have all become immortals. There is now no difference between them and us. We should have some distinction from men.

Brahma: Yama is now engaged in the great sacrifice. That is the reason why the human beings are not dying. When this sacrifice is over, he will start his work of killing with redoubled energy and will sweep away hundreds of thousands in no time. Do not be afraid, O gods!

Vyasa continued, "Then the celestials went to the place of sacrifice. They saw a golden lotus in the Bhagirathi. They were very much astonished. Indra went to find out where it grew. He went to the source of the Ganga. There he saw an effulgent lady. The lady was bathing in the Ganga and was weeping. The drops of tears that fell from her eyes were changing into golden lotuses."

Indra: O blessed lady! Why are you weeping? Tell me everything. I wish to know the truth.

The lady: You will know who I am and why I am weeping. Come along with me. You can then see why I weep.

Then Indra followed her and saw a beautiful youth with a young lady. They were seated on a throne on the peak of the king of mountains and were playing dice.

Indra to the Youth: 'O handsome youth! Know that this world is under my sway.' The youth did not pay any attention to the words of Indra. Again Indra said, 'I am the lord of this Universe.'

The youth was none else than Lord Siva. When he saw that Indra became angry, he cast a glance at Indra and smiled. Indra was at once paralysed. He stood on the spot like a statue.

When the game of dice was over, Lord Siva said to the weeping woman. 'Bring Indra here. I shall teach him such a good lesson that pride will not enter his heart again.'

The woman touched Indra. Immediately Indra fell down on the ground. Then Siva said to him, 'O Indra! Never behave like this again. Remove this big stone, enter the hole and remain there with others who are like you.

Indra removed the stone and saw the cave in the great mountain. He saw four others resembling himself in the cave.

Siva: O Indra! Enter this cave at once, because you have insulted me before my very eyes out of your vanity. Those who are puffed up with pride like you can never obtain my grace. The four in the cave were like you at one time. Enter the cave without delay and remain there for some time. The fate of you all is the same. All of you will have to take birth in the world of mortals. Having achieved many difficult feats of virtue, righteousness and sacrifices, you will regain the region of Indra by your own merits.

The four old Indras: We shall go to the world of men. But let the celestials—Dharma, Vayu, Maghavata (present Indra) and the twin Asvins—beget us out of our would-be mother. After fighting with men with celestial weapons we shall again come back to the region of Indra.

Indra: O Lord Siva! Instead of going myself, I shall create myself, with a portion of my energy, a person who will be able to do my task. He will be the fifth among these old Indras.

Visvavaka, Bhutadharma, Sivi, Sauti and Tejasvin—these are the five Indras of old. Thereupon Lord Siva granted the five Indras the cherished desire of their hearts and ordained that the exceedingly beautiful lady, who was none other than the celestial Lakshmi herself, to be their common wife in the world of men.

Lord Siva went to Lord Narayana along with these Indras and told Him everything. Narayana approved of everything. The Indras took births in the world of mortals. Lord Narayana took up two hairs from his body; one of them was white and the other black.

Those two hairs entered the wombs of the two ladies of the Yadu race named Devaki and Rohini. The white hair became Baladeva and the black hair became Krishna.

Those Indra-like ones who were kept in the cave of the mountain, are the five sons of Pandu. Arjuna is a portion of the present Indra.

Those who were at one time Indras were born as the sons of Pandu and the celestial Lakshmi herself is the beautiful Draupadi. She rose from within the sacrificial fire by virtue of your sacrifice. How could she, whose effulgence is like that of the Sun, whose fragrance spreads over miles around, take birth in any other but an extraordinary manner?

O Drupada! I give you the divine sight. Behold the sons of Kunti now possessing their old celestial forms. Thereupon Vyasa gave to Drupada divine sight. Then the king saw the Pandavas possessing their former forms. He saw them with celestial bodies, golden crowns, celestial garlands, celestial robes and ornaments. Each of them resembled Indra himself. Drupada was struck with amazement. He saw Draupadi as a celestial maiden with great effulgence and splendour. He thought that Draupadi was really worthy to be the wife of those celestial beings. Drupada touched the feet of Vyasa and said, "O venerable sage! There is nothing hidden from you."

Vyasa: There was in a certain forest a great Rishi. He had a daughter who was extremely beautiful and chaste but she did not get a husband. She did severe Tapas and propitiated Lord Siva. Lord Siva appeared before her and said, 'I am pleased with your penance. Tell me what you want?' The maiden said five times to Lord Siva, 'I wish to have a husband who is endowed with all accomplishments.'

Lord Siva: O blessed girl! You will have five husbands.

The girl said, 'I wish to have only one husband with all accomplishments.'

Lord Siva: You have addressed me five times saying, 'Give me a husband.' Therefore you will have five husbands. It shall be as you have asked. All this will happen in one of your future births.

O king Drupada! This daughter of celestial beauty is that maiden. Draupadi had been preordained to be wife of five men.

The celestial Lakshmi has risen, out of the great sacrificial fire, to be the wife of the Pandavas. After severe penances, she is born as your daughter. She has been created by Brahma for this purpose. Hearing all this, do what you desire, O king Drupada!

Drupada: O great Rishi! I am fully convinced now after hearing from you the full account of the births of the Pandavas and Draupadi. I will act as you have said. As draupadi had repeatedly asked, in her former life, five times saying, "Give me a husband," Lord Siva had granted the boon accordingly. He himself knows the right or the wrong of this. When the Lord has fixed this ordinance, I can have no objection. Thereupon let these heroes take, as ordained, the hand of Draupadi according to all due rites.

When Duryodhana came to know that the Brahmin who won the hand of Draupadi was no other than Arjuna, his heart was consumed with jealousy. The Pandavas now became very powerful after the marriage. Raja Drupada became their powerful ally.

Bhishma, Vidura and Drona advised Dhritarashtra to send for the Pandavas and give half the kingdom to them and said that this measure would remove the root cause of quarrel and dissension once for all. Dhritarashtra thought over this matter for some time and at last decided to send Vidura to Drupadnagar to bring the Pandavas back to Hastinapura.

Dhritarashtra asked Vidura to go to Drupadnagar and bring the Pandavas and Kunti back to Hastinapura along with Draupadi. Vidura at once proceeded to the capital city of king

Drupada and appeared before the king and conveyed to him the message of Dhritarashtra. Drupada requested Vidura to speak to Yudhishthira. Yudhishthira requested Drupada to allow him to return to Hastinapura. Drupada gave them permission. The Pandavas, Kunti and Draupadi started for Hastinapura. On their arrival near Hastinapura, they were given a hearty reception by Dhritarashtra. The people were extremely happy when they saw the Pandavas. They all exclaimed with joy, "Yudhishthira is our protector and benefactor. Let him immediately be crowned as king. May he rule till eternity. May the Pandavas live till eternity. We are blessed, indeed, as the Pandavas have returned to Hastinapura."

Yudhishthira then appeared before Dhritarashtra with his brothers and paid due obeisance to him. Then they repaired to the palace assigned to them. They took rest there. Then Dhritarashtra called Yudhishthira and said, "Live with your brothers at Khandavaprastha. This will stop the dispute between you all and my son Duryodhana. This will be a wise agreement."

Yudhishthira agreed to what the king said and proceeded to the forest with his brothers, mother and Draupadi. Khandavaprastha was a fearful forest. Yudhishthira soon converted the forest into a city of beautiful palaces, gardens and lakes. The city came to be called Indraprastha. In a short time the city became densely populated.

All the subjects lived there most happily. "As is the king, so are the subjects." Therefore, they were very virtuous. They followed the principles of Dharma. Even Lakshmi dwelt there. Yudhishthira led the life of an ideal king and worked hard for the welfare of his subjects. There was peace and prosperity everywhere. Misery, poverty, cruelty, impiety, hatred, selfishness, greed, oppression, injustice and all sorts of evils were unknown in his blessed reign.

Yudhishthira ruled for many years wisely and justly. He wished to perform Rajasuya Yajna. So he sent his heroic brothers in various directions to conquer all the other kings. One can perform this Yajna, only if he brings hundred kings under his sway. Bhima conquered and imprisoned many Rajas. He entered into a wrestling match with Jarasandha of Magadha and crushed him to death with his mighty mace. This victory over Jarasandha made Raja Yudhishthira lord of many kings.

❁ ❁ ❁

All the brothers conquered many Rajas and returned to Indraprastha with immense wealth, jewels, gems, ornaments, pearls, diamonds, elephants, camels, horses, chariots, weapons, coats of mail, armours, etc.

Then the brothers made grand preparations for the performance of the Rajasuya Yajna. All materials were collected. Vyasa became the Brahma in the sacrifice. Many temples were erected. A vast sacrificial ground was prepared. Around the sacrificial ground royal tents were pitched. Royal messengers were sent to different Rajas inviting them to the Yajna at Indraprastha. Nakula repaired to Hasthinapura to invite Dhritarashtra, Bhishma, Drona, Vidura, Duryodhana and his other cousins, to witness the grand Yajna. All the Kauravas arrived at Indraprastha. Hundreds of Rajas and Kshatriyas came from different directions with valuable offerings and precious gifts.

Among the distinguished royal guests were Suvala, Sakuni, king of Gandhar, Karna, Salya, Drona and his son Asvatthama, Kuntibhoja, Sisupala, Kanaka, Vasudeva, king of Paundras, the kings of Vanga, Kalinga and Kashmir, the Rajas of Chola and Pandya. Some presented a thousand elephants with tusks, some presented hundreds of jars of gold, some gave many golden dishes. Some gave thousands of servants.

Rich presents were given to the Brahmins and priests. Hundreds of thousands of Brahmins were sumptuously fed daily. Everyday meals were served to thousands of Brahmins in golden plates. They drank water in golden cups. The plate and cup became their property of each Brahmin after he took his food.

Duryodhana was in charge of the royal treasury. He spent the money extravagantly. He threw away money uselessly with the evil object of emptying the treasury and thereby bringing dishonour and disgrace to Yudhishthira. A wicked man always does wicked acts only, wherever he goes. Just as the shadow follows a man, so also the evil intentions and the evil thoughts of a malicious man follow him wherever he goes.

Duryodhana had a boon that, the more he squandered wealth, greater it grew. He forgot all about this boon. Lord Krishna, who is the Antaryamin, the Inner Ruler, the knower of all secrets, informed Yudhishthira of this marvellous boon which Duryodhana was endowed with. Therefore he was placed in charge of the treasury. Though Duryodhana wanted to ruin the Pandavas, by his wicked act of spending the money extravagantly, yet he was only increasing the wealth of Yudhishthira.

On the last day of sacrifice, Bhishma said to Yudhishthira: "Let Arghya be given to deserving persons in order of merit and age." Yudhishthira said, "O venerable grandsire! Kindly tell me who is the greatest man here, to whom the Arghya should be offered first?" Bhishma said, "Lord Krishna is the Supreme Being. He is the first of all, on account of his wisdom, strength, piety, love, courage and beauty. Offer him the first Arghya." Yudhishthira asked Sahadeva to offer the first Arghya to Lord Krishna. Sisupala, the king of Chedi and a cousin of Lord Krishna, who was always jealous of Lord Krishna, made a protest against the offering of the first Arghya to Krishna. Sisupala abused Lord Krishna and insulted him bitterly. Lord Krishna bore all the insults patiently. Sisupala went too far. At last, Krishna assumed his divine form and cut off Sisupala's head. A light emanating from the body of king Sisupala, entered the body of Lord Krishna. This strange phenomenon was witnessed by the whole assembly of kings present at the Yajna.

Sisupala attained oneness with the Lord when he left the physical body. He was devoted to the Lord through Vaira Bhakti (enmity). Sisupala was the attendant of Lord Narayana in Vaikuntha. By a curse given to him by the boy-saints Sanaka, Sanandana, etc., he had to take three births in Mrityuloka before he attained union with the Lord.

The place was again purified and the sacrificial rites were continued for many days. When the ceremony was over, all the kings took leave of the Pandavas and repaired to their respective kingdoms.

Lord Krishna and Vyasa blessed Yudhishthira and his brothers and left the place. Vyasa said to Yudhishthira before leaving, "The house of Bharata would be visited by calamity for full thirteen years. You will be the cause of destruction of all Kshatriyas, owing to the wicked conduct of Duryodhana, on the termination of the period of thirteen years. Your brothers would be instruments of their destruction. Be bold. Be not afflicted in your heart. What is destined must come to pass."

Yudhishthira was overwhelmed with sorrow. He informed his brothers all that Vyasa said and addressed them, "I do not wish to live any longer, as I will become the cause of destruction of all Kshatriyas. Life has no charm for me. Let me die to save my country and nation from destruction."

What a magnanimous speech and lofty sentiment? Yudhishthira wished to give up his life for the sake of saving his subjects and relatives. What a great spirit of self-sacrifice he had? Marvellous indeed!

His brothers comforted him and said, "O venerable brother! Do your duty as a king. Resign yourself to the Lord. There is no room for lamentation and despair. We always stand by your side with devotion and earnestness to serve and protect you."

Yudhishthira said, "I take a solemn pledge now that, as long as I am alive, I will not speak a harsh word to my brothers or any of the kings of the world or anybody. I will be ever faithful to my kinsmen. I will constantly practise virtue. I will make no distinction between my sons and those of others, between my brothers and other people. I will develop equal vision. I will give equal regard and equal treatment to all. Thereby I shall remove discord, disunion, rupture, disagreement, quarrels and dissensions. I am fully aware that disagreement is the root cause of war. I shall please and serve others whole-heartedly. I shall ever perform what is agreeable and pleasant to others. Then I may possibly avoid war altogether and lead a very peaceful and virtuous life. Nobody will have any cause to blame me."

The spirit of justice, universal love and equal vision, breathes in every word of Yudhishthira's speech to his brothers. What a magnanimous and large heart Yudhishthira had! He always cared to maintain law, order, peace and righteousness in his kingdom. That is the reason why he is called as 'Dharmaputra' or 'Dharma Raj.' This world has not witnessed up till now a just king like Yudhishthira and will not see in future also. This is a hard truth.

❁ ❁ ❁

One day, during the great Rajasuya Yajna at the palace of Yudhishthira, Duryodhana stumbled down in the lake which he took for a piece of land and on another occasion, drew up his clothes when he walked along a piece of crystal land which appeared like water. Bhima, Nakula, Sahadeva and some other servants laughed and jeered at Duryodhana. Draupadi taunted him with the sarcastic remark that the son of a blind man was bound to be blind. This incident and the wealth and greatness of the Pandavas produced acute jealousy in the heart of Duryodhana.

He and his uncle Sakuni persuaded Dhritarashtra to allow them to play dice with Yudhishthira. Sakuni had devised a loaded dice. Duryodhana knew pretty well that he could not gain victory over the Pandavas through fair play. Therefore he resorted to this foul means. Sakuni was an expert in the game of dice. He knew all kinds of tricks. Sakuni encouraged Duryodhana that he would get the kingdom of the Pandavas for him through foul play at the game.

Thereupon Dhritarashtra sent Vidura to invite Raja Yudhishthira for the dice play. Vidura appeared before Yudhishthira and gave him the message of Dhritarashtra. Yudhishthira said to Vidura, "O Vidura! I will not gamble. Gambling is the root cause of destruction of nations and men. Gambling leads to disagreement, dissension, difference of opinion, fighting, great misery and sorrow. The results of gambling are dreadful. No good has ever come out of it. As Dhritarashtra has invited me, I will go to Hastinapura but I will not play dice; but if Sakuni challenges me, I will have to take up the challenge as a true Kshatriya."

Yudhishthira, along with his brothers, Vidura and Draupadi

went to Hastinapura. Sakuni said, "O Yudhishthira, take up my challenge. Come to play with me dice." Yudhishthira was forced to accept the challenge though he had no desire at all to play the game. Sakuni played with Yudhishthira. Duryodhana supplied the stakes. Everytime Sakuni won the game, as he used foul means and as he was deceitful and treacherous. Yudhishthira lost all his estates and wealth.

Vidura persuaded Dhritarashtra to cease the play. He said that Duryodhana was a jackal in his house and that he would bring the destruction of all the members of the family. His words did not produce any effect. Yudhishthira's brothers bit their lips in anger when they saw that he lost everything; but dared not dissuade their brother from gambling in a reckless manner. Yudhishthira staked all his brothers, one by one, then himself, then Draupadi and lost all in the game. All became slaves of Duryodhana.

Vidura: Draupadi cannot become a slave. She was staked by Yudhishthira when he was no more his own master. This is my candid opinion.

Duryodhana: O Pratikamin (messenger of Duryodhana)! Bring Draupadi. Let her sweep our house. Let the woman of unvirtuous conduct live with the servant women. Vidura speaks against us. He is never our well-wisher.

Pratikamin: O Draupadi! Duryodhana has won you. Therefore enter the house of Dhritarashtra. I shall take you to do menial work.

Draupadi: Will any king stake his wife in a game? Have you ever heard of this? Ask the gambler in the assembly, "Did you first lose thine own self or me?"

The messenger went to the gambling hall and conveyed to Yudhishthira the very words of Draupadi. Yudhishthira became unconscious. He became like a dead man. He did not say a word in reply.

Duryodhana: Let Draupadi come here and ask the question. Let all hear what she and Yudhishthira have to say.

He then said to Dussasana, "This charioteer is afraid of Bhima. Catch hold of Draupadi yourself and bring her here. The

Pandavas cannot do anything to you since they have lost their freedom. They are our slaves now?

Dussasana: O Draupadi! Come now. You have been won righteously. Come to the hall and meet Duryodhana. Leave your bashfulness.

Draupadi ran to the place where the ladies of the king Dhritarashtra were. Dussasana caught her by the hair.

Draupadi: I am not well. I have got only one garment. Do not take me to the hall.

Dussasana: I do not care whether you are unwell or whether you remain with single dress. You have been won at gambling. You are now a slave. Live amongst our slave women.

Draupadi: You are doing an improper act. You are dragging a woman who is unwell in the midst of the warriors of the Kuru house. Nobody is condemning your wrong action. They endorse your attitude. Drona, Bhishma or even the wise Vidura and king Dhritarashtra are keeping quiet. Do they not notice this terrible Adharma? Is there no good sense in them? How can they allow Dussasana to do such an act of impropriety?

Dussasana laughed and called Draupadi, "Slave". Karna was highly pleased. Sakuni praised Dussasana for this remark. They were all rejoicing.

Bhishma: O blessed lady! The course of morality is subtle. Even the wise persons are not able to understand it always. What a strong man says in this world as morality is considered as such by others, though it may not be really so; while what a weak man says as morality is not regarded as such, even if it be the highest morality. Whether king Yudhishthira could have rightly staked and lost you, after losing himself, I am not able to give a definite and positive answer, as it is an intricate and subtle matter. One who is not a master has no power to wage another's property. But a woman is subordinate to her husband. When I consider this, I am unable to determine the truth of this question on account of the subtle nature of Dharma. Yudhishthira is just and virtuous. He will relinquish his whole kingdom but will not abandon Dharma. He has said that he has been won. Therefore I am unable to determine this.

Drona and others who are wise and conversant with morality sit with head down like men who are dead. Yudhishthira is an authority on this question. He is the proper person to declare whether you are won or not.

Vikarna (a virtuous son of Dhritarashtra): I shall speak the truth now. This irreproachable and virtuous Draupadi is common to all the Pandavas. She was staked by Yudhishthira, who himself was no longer free. Sakuni wanted Draupadi as the wager. Draupadi was mentioned by Sakuni as a bet. Considering all this, I think, Draupadi has not been won.

Those who assembled there praised Vikarna and considered the treacherous Sakuni as an embodiment of cheating.

Karna: Draupadi was mentioned by name. The Pandavas accepted her as stake. On what ground is she considered by you as not won? If you think that she has been unrighteously brought to the hall with a single dress, just listen to my words. A single husband is ordained by the gods for a woman, but this woman lives with five persons. She is certainly a whore or a base hireling. There is nothing amiss in bringing her to the hall. This is my candid opinion.

Duryodhana: O Dussasana! Catch hold of the clothes of the Pandavas and Draupadi. This Vikarna is a playful child, though he talks like a wise man.

The Pandavas threw away their upper clothes. Then Dussasana forcibly pulled the cloth of Draupadi in the assembly. Draupadi prayed to Lord Krishna. Lord Krishna provided her with inexhaustible length of cloth. Dussasana was tired of pulling. He sat down in shame with head down.

Karna: O Dussasana! Take the slave Draupadi into the house.

Dussasana dragged Draupadi. Duryodhana made gestures to Draupadi and asked her to sit on his thighs.

Draupadi: O evil Duryodhana! As you point your thigh to me, you will have death in your thigh. As Dussasana torments me thus, Bhima will drink his blood. Arjuna will kill this evil-minded Karna and his sons. Sahadeva will kill in battle this mean-minded Sakuni.

When Draupadi spoke thus, there was a rain of flowers from the Heaven.

Arjuna caught hold of his bow, jumped and looked at his enemies. The righteous and merciful Yudhishthira said, "Arjuna! Do not be impetuous and rash. Control your wrath for the sake of the world. Let not reputation die. I can burn these gambler sinners in the twinkling of an eye but I cannot deviate even a hair's breadth from the Truth and Righteousness."

At this time in the sacrificial hall of Dhritarashtra a jackal yelled at the top of its voice and donkeys also responded. The wise Vidura and Gandhari informed the king of this evil omen. Then Dhritarashtra spoke sweetly to Draupadi and gave her two boons. The Pandavas were made free.

Thereupon Duryodhana approached his father once more and took Sakuni, Karna and Dussasana to support him. He requested his father to allow them to gamble once more. He said, "This time those who are defeated should go to exile in the forest for twelve years and spend one year in disguise in some inhabited part of the country and if they are recognised during that period they should again live in the forest for another term of twelve years." Dhritarashtra yielded to his wish.

Again the Pandavas were called upon to gamble. They lost the game this time also. They were forced to enter the forest in exile. When they left the city for the forest, Bhima stretched out his strong arms and swore revenge. Draupadi spread her locks and took a vow that she would never tie them till the villain who had dragged her by the hair was punished.

The Pandavas repaired to the forest of Kamyaka. After some time they lived by the side of a sacred lake in Dvaitavana. They led a very simple life. They slept on beds of grass and subsisted on fruits of the forest. Draupadi served them with intense faith and devotion. She regarded serving her husbands as serving the Lord Himself. She considered that the serving of her lords would lead to highest bliss.

During their sojourn in the forest, Surya or Sun God, was much moved when he saw the hardships of Draupadi and the

Pandavas and presented Draupadi with a golden bowl (Akshayapatra) that possessed the miraculous power of giving as much food as they needed.

The brothers and Draupadi tried to persuade Yudhishthira to go back to Indraprastha and get back the kingdom. They said, "O noble brother! We were cheated by the treacherous Sakuni. We should pay them in the same coin. We will have to teach them a bitter lesson for their dishonest dealings. It is not binding on us to keep faith with those who were treacherous and fraudulent."

Yudhishthira: It is quite true that we were cheated by them, but I shall keep faith even with rogues and dishonest persons. I am to blame for all that has befallen you. Wise persons should not lament for what is past and gone. I accepted the stake. Therefore we are bound to spend the stipulated period of twelve years in the woods. I should stick to my word at the cost of my life. I will never think of breaking it even if I may get the kingdom of the seven worlds by so doing. I prefer to die rather than gain a kingdom by breaking my word. Be patient. Better days will soon come. I tell you once more that my 'word' is dearer to me than my 'life'. I can never break it, even though my ruin was brought about by fraudulent means. 'Honour' is more precious than 'life'. Dominion, sons, fame, wealth and even life itself are nothing before 'truth'. I am as adamant as a rock. I will stick to truth. Nothing in the three worlds can make me break my word.

The brothers and Draupadi were tongue-tied when they heard the stirring and soul-elevating speech of Yudhishthira. They did not speak a word. They drew inspiration from his masterly discourse. They also made up their minds to stick to 'truth' at all costs. They learnt a valuable lesson from the speech of Yudhishthira.

The Pandavas roamed from place to place in the forest and thus spent the twelve years.

Yudhishthira called his brothers and said, "We have spent twelve years in the forest. Now we have to spend the thirteenth year in some inhabited country without being recognised. What do you propose to do? Let us put on disguise and live in a distant part of the country. The Kurus will not be able to recognise us." They finally decided to take refuge under king Virata in the kingdom of the Matsyas. They entered the service of the king in different capacities. Yudhishthira assumed the name of 'Kanka', a Brahmin expert in dice and gambling. He was appointed as a courtier to amuse the king. Bhima assumed the name of 'Ballava' and obtained employment in the royal kitchen as a cook. Arjuna became an eunuch, assumed the name of 'Brihannala' and got the job of teaching the king's daughter dancing and singing. Nakula was in the management of the king's stable. Sahadeva put on the guise of a cowherd and was employed as king's herdsman. Draupadi got employment as a maid-servant under the name of 'Sairandhri'. She was to prepare unguents and garlands for the king as also needle work. They all so managed not to create any suspicion in the king or other people of their real identity.

Kichaka, the brother of the queen, fell in love with Draupadi. Draupadi complained of this to Bhima in secret. Bhima secretly murdered Kichaka. Bhima and Arjuna performed many feats of strength and skill. The Pandavas kept their real selves a secret with great difficulty.

The Kauravas tried their level best to find out the whereabouts of the Pandavas. All their attempts were of no avail. The Kauravas came to know that Kichaka, the king's reputed general, died. They invaded the kingdom of Virata. They were defeated with the help of the five brothers and were put to flight. The wonderful feats of Bhima and Arjuna created suspicion in the Kauravas. The identity of the Pandavas was thus revealed; but the thirteenth year was completed by that time.

Yudhishthira with his brothers and Draupadi came back to Hastinapura after the thirteenth year was past and demanded back his lawful share of the kingdom. Duryodhana declined to give him the share and said that he would fight for every inch of ground.

War became inevitable, although Yudhishthira tried to maintain peace. The famous war of the Mahabharata began. It lasted for eighteen days. Ultimately the Pandavas became victorious as they fought for a just and righteous cause. 'Where Krishna is, there is victory.'

After the war was over, the Pandavas did the ceremonial rites of all their relatives. Yudhishthira then assumed rulership of his kingdom. He ruled the country peacefully and justly for a number of years.

When Lord Krishna, who was the chief support and the mainstay of the Pandavas passed away to his original abode in the Heavens, the whole world lost its charm for Yudhishthira. The Pandavas and Draupadi made preparations for their journey towards Heaven. They took leave of all and marched towards the Himalayas. A faithful dog which could not bear the separation from them even for a second also followed them. They were clad in birch-bark and walked barefooted. They reached the snowy regions of the Himalayas. All save Yudhishthira fainted on the way and died.

Yudhishthira alone proceeded on his journey, followed by a dog. Even Yudhishthira felt slightly the pang of death when he remembered the one falsehood he had unconsciously uttered during the whole period of his life.

Drona was as invincible as Bhishma. Arjuna found it impossible to defeat Drona in the war. Then Krishna found out a device. Drona was very much attached to his son Asvatthama. Drona had declared, on one occasion, that he would fight as long as his son was alive. So an elephant with the face of Asvatthama was made out of clay. It was placed in front of Arjuna. Arjuna aimed his arrows at the elephant and shot. It was declared by the people of the Pandava army that Asvatthama was killed. The news reached the ears of Drona. Drona was shocked to hear the news of the demise of his son. He would not believe it. He said that he would believe, if it came out of the mouth of Yudhishthira. Yudhishthira said, "*Asvatthama hatah kunjara*—the (clay) elephant Asvatthama is killed." But at the exact moment when Yudhishthira uttered the word "*kunjara*", there was the sound of conch blowing drowning the last word. So, Drona heard only the first two words meaning that Asvatthama died. Drona in spite of his better knowledge believed it. He did not hear the word "*kunjara*." Drona laid down arms and was thus defeated.

Yudhishthira felt that he was responsible for this partial lie. So he had to pass through the Hell on his way to Heaven.

Yudhishthira saw that a celestial light was moving towards him. In the midst of the celestial light was Indra, the god of Heaven, in his chariot approaching to welcome him.

Indra: O noble Yudhishthira! You have got the rare privilege of entering Heaven in your human form, as you led a virtuous and untainted life. Please ascend this chariot which will take you at once to the abode of Heaven.

Yudhishthira: I have no desire to enter the Heaven without my brothers and Draupadi by my side. They should also accompany me. Even Heaven itself is not worthy of attainment, if its realisation meant separation from one's beloved persons who have been allotted to remain in the region of pains and sufferings. Really I do not want such a Heaven which could separate me from my devoted brothers and devoted wife.

Indra: O Yudhishthira! Ascend the chariot and come to Heaven. You will find them there. Be assured.

Then Yudhishthira accepted the invitation and allowed the dog to go first into the chariot.

Indra: O king! You have won immortality. Enjoy the happiness of Heaven. Send away this dog. There is no place for a dog in Heaven. It will pollute the place. You left your brothers and Draupadi behind dying, as you were ascending the Heaven. Is a dog worthier than them? Can you not renounce this dog?

Yudhishthira: The scriptures have impressed on us that to spurn a suppliant is equal in sin to the murder of a Brahmin. Therefore, not even for the bliss of the highest Heaven, I am prepared to forsake, O Mahendra, this poor faithful dog, who has no hope or friend other than me, so helpless, and has taken shelter with me—me, who, among men, was called steadfast and just. As for my brothers and my beloved Draupadi, it is well known that none can hurt or help the dead. They, my dear ones, who died would not have arisen even if I had turned—therefore I did not turn. I would have turned back if it would have helped them. The dog has been my faithful companion throughout its life. How can I renounce this faithful dog who has ever followed me like a shadow and has helped me in my adversity? This is unworthy of a true Kshatriya. It will surely bring me a bad name. It will bring a great taint on my character and the virtuous life I had led. I will be an object of contempt even in my own eyes. I will be charged with selfishness and ingratitude. To abandon such a dog, at a time when I am about to enjoy the Highest Bliss, is a great sin and crime indeed. There are four sins, O Sakra,— grievous sins—the first is making a suppliant despair, the second is to slay a nursing wife, the third is spoiling Brahmins' goods, the fourth is injuring an ancient friend. But even these four, I consider, not as worse as the sin of abandoning a humble comrade on coming out of woe to weal. Therefore I am determined not to enter the Heaven itself, if I am not permitted to take this dog with me.

The dog disappeared and Yudhishthira saw in its place Lord Yama—lord of Dharma—the god of Righteousness. He said, "O Yudhishthira! You renounced even the Heaven itself for the sake of a dog. Thrice blessed art thou! There is no one in Heaven who is equal unto thee. Regions of eternal bliss are thine." Yudhishthira thus ascended the Heaven in his mortal frame.

All welcomed Yudhishthira. They eulogised him very highly for his truthfulness and righteousness. But he was not happy. He did not find his brothers and Draupadi there. He said that he would leave the Heaven and go to the place where his brothers and Draupadi were. He said to Indra, "Take me to the place where my brothers are, be it Heaven or Hell. I do not wish to live anywhere else." He turned hither and thither in order to find his brothers and Draupadi; but he saw Duryodhana and his brothers. Indra advised him to cast off the mortal chains as he was one of themselves—a god! This was Heaven. Yudhishthira continued: "I cannot live, even for a moment, without those souls I love best. My place is by their side. Keep Heaven for such as these (pointing to Duryodhana), if they can come here. I do not wish to stay where my loved ones are not and where he is, whom I hated justly as he was a covetous prince, whose actions were responsible for the slaughter of countless brothers and friends."

Other saints of Heaven intervened to pacify Yudhishthira.

Narada consoled him in soft words and advised him not to question the justice of the gods. 'Those who come here lay aside all their enmities of the Earth. Duryodhana is here because he has expiated his sins. He is here in his own right as a king who lived and died in virtue's path and yielded his breath on the holy field of Kurukshetra. Forget your former relations! Forget your past wrongs and enemies in this Heaven which is free from hatred.'

Yudhishthira was not consoled, however. He said: "If Duryodhana has attained Heaven by his own merits, I have no quarrel with that. You are all gods and, therefore, just. You have granted him Heaven. I accept it. But show me the place where they dwell, my noble brothers who were loyal to me even in adversity, who have never moved away from the path of virtue. Where is my brother Karna—the hero-hearted? Where are those noble kings who fought for me and died a noble death? I see them not, neither kings Drupada, Virata, Panchala nor his sons, nor Abhimanyu the unconquerable and a hundred others whom I knew well. Do they dwell here? If they be unworthy, neither am I, nor is my soul willing to stay here without them. Though I am in Heaven now, I am afflicted with grief, remembering the words of my mother Kunti when I was pouring water for the dead at Kurukshetra: 'Pour for prince Karna, my son'. I did not know then that he was of her blood, my blood. I crave to see Karna and embrace him and Bhima who is dearer to me than my own life, the god-like Árjuna, Nakula and Sahadeva—twin lords of war—and my tenderest Draupadi."

Show me these souls!

I cannot tarry where I have them not
Bliss is not blissful, just and mighty ones
Save if I rest beside them. Heaven is there
Where Love and Faith make Heaven. Let me go!

Indra commanded the celestial messenger to show Yudhishthira his brothers and Draupadi. The messenger took the king to the region of Hell. Yudhishthira, however, did not find his brothers there. Slowly he turns his back to return and as he does so, piteous lamentations break out all around him beseeching him to stay yet a while as his very presence soothed their torments. They all cried out in one voice "Please stay—even if it is for just one moment." Thereat, the high-souled Yudhishthira, moved by compassion for the sufferers' cries, asked, 'Who are you?' and received replies, 'I am Karna', 'I am Drona', 'I am Arjuna', 'I am Bhima', 'We are Nakula and Sahadeva', 'I am Draupadi', 'We are the sons of Draupadi'. On hearing these familiar voices, the monarch's spirit broke and he loudly exclaimed 'What doom is this? How have my beloved ones deserved death with the damned or a life more loathful than death in the deepest Hell? Were the sins of Karna so deep, or those of Bhima, Arjuna, the twin brothers or of the sweetest and best of women, Draupadi? Duryodhana, the root cause of death and misery to so many, sits in Paradise in the midst of Mahendra and the gods, while these, my loved ones, are in Hell. What were their sins as compared to his?'

> For if they slipped, it was in Virtue's way
> Serving good laws, performing holy rites
> Boundless in gifts and faithful to the death.

For a moment, Yudhishthira could not contain himself on account of righteous indignation and he well-nigh cursed the gods. But he restrained himself in time and softly addressed the escorting angel thus:

> Go to those thou servest;
> Tell them I come not thither. Say I stand—
> Here in the throat of Hell and here will bide—
> Nay, if I perish—while my well-beloved
> Win ease and peace by any pains of mine!

O Yudhishthira! O noblest soul! O Prince without parallel!

In a moment there was a sudden change! A cool refreshing breeze began to blow. Light dawned. The horrible scenes of Hell disappeared. Yudhishthira found himself amidst gods. They said, "O virtuous king! Ascend to Heaven now. Every king must see Hell. If the good actions of a man outnumbers his evil actions, he suffers first and enjoys afterwards. He is a blessed person indeed. You and your brothers have witnessed the Hell for a short space of time only. Your eternal home is Heaven, because your good actions far outweigh the evil ones. Join

Karna and your brothers and Draupadi in the blessed realms of Heaven. Lord Krishna Himself is waiting to welcome you. Your lot is doubtless enviable."

When Yudhishthira had taken his seat among his brothers and Draupadi and his friends, Dharmaraja,—Lord of Righteousness—exclaimed, addressing him—"O my son! I am well pleased. Hail to thee! Worthy, wise and firm! Thy faith is full, as also thy virtue, patience, truth and self-mastery. Thrice I tried you—once in Dvaita's forest when all your brothers were lying as if dead, you asked for Nakula's life and not of Bhima or Arjuna, because he was Madri's son. Next, after your brothers' and Draupadi's death, you were faithful to the meanest friend, the dog in whose guise I followed you to the gates of Heaven. Here was the third and the hardest test—that you should hear the cries of your brothers in Hell and you stood by them firm like a rock. Thou art fortunate, pure and past trials now." Dharmaraja thus praised his son and requested him to bathe in the celestial Ganga, in order that he may cast off his human body and assume a heavenly form.

Such is the brief sketch of the career of Yudhishthira, who was an embodiment of patience, forbearance, truthfulness, learning, justice and righteousness.

He who reads this great story becomes self-controlled. He is blessed with sons and grandsons. He lives for a hundred years. He who thoroughly understands the story is never inclined towards unrighteousness, breaking friendships, misappropriating other people's property or violating other people's wives. He never entertains evil thoughts.

May Yudhishthira's noble life awaken in you noble thoughts! May his life inspire you with truthfulness and righteousness! May his example inspire in you ambition of following in his footsteps and may you succeed with the blessings of the Lord!

YUDHISHTHIRA AND YAKSHA

Once when the Pandavas were wandering in the forest, they were all fatigued and were thirsty. Yudhishthira said to Nakula,

"O son of Madri! Climb this tree and look around in order to find any signs of water in the neighbourhood. Your brothers are fatigued and thirsty."

Nakula soon ascended a tree and looked carefully all around. He said to Yudhishthira, "O king! I see numerous trees and also hear the cries of the Sarasa birds and cranes. Therefore, surely, water must be somewhere near."

Thereupon, Yudhishthira said, "O Nakula! Go there and soon bring water in the quivers." Nakula quickly proceeded towards the spot where the water was and soon reached it. He also was very thirsty. He at once stooped down to drink some water. A mysterious and invisible voice addressed him. This was the voice of a Yaksha, who was in the form of a crane. "O child! Do not drink the water. I am in possession of it. First answer my questions and then drink the water and carry it away. Such is the law of the pool. If you break it, you will surely meet with death." Nakula was so thirsty that he did not care for the mysterious warning. He drank the cool water. But as soon as he drank it, he fell dead.

Seeing Nakula's delay, Yudhishthira said to Sahadeva, "O Sahadeva! Our brother has been long out. Go and bring him and also water." Sahadeva went to the spot. He also heard the same voice which Nakula heard. He disregarded the words, drank water and fell dead.

Yudhishthira sent Arjuna and Bhima to fetch water. They also shared the same fate as that of Nakula and Sahadeva. Thereupon, Yudhishthira himself went to the spot. He then saw his brothers lying dead on the ground. As he was very thirsty, he bent down to drink water. At once the Yaksha, who presided over the pond, in the form of a crane, addressed him thus, "I am a crane. It is I who have caused the death of your brothers. You shall be the fifth victim if you attempt to drink water before you have answered my questions."

Yudhishthira: Who are you, O crane? It is not possible for a bird to have done this! You must be a Devata. Are you the foremost of the Rudras?

The Crane: I am a Yaksha. I am not an aquatic bird. It is I who caused the death of your energetic and powerful brothers.

The Yaksha assumed his original huge shape and stood before Yudhishthira in all his majesty.

Yudhishthira: O Yaksha! I shall answer your questions according to my knowledge. Ask me.

The Yaksha: What is that which makes the Sun rise? Who remains near him? What is it that makes him set? In what is he established?

Yudhishthira: It is Brahma who makes the Sun rise. The celestials remain near him. Dharma makes him set. He is established in Truth.

The Yaksha: What makes one learned? By what does one attain to what is very exalted?

Yudhishthira: By the study of the Vedas one becomes learned. By asceticism one attains to what is very exalted.

The Yaksha: What is the divine attribute of the Brahmanas? What virtuous practices of theirs resembles those of the pious? What is their human attribute? What practices of theirs resemble those of the impious?

Yudhishthira: The study of the Vedas is their divine attribute. Their asceticism resembles the virtuous practices of the pious. Death is their human attribute. Slander by them resembles the behaviour of the impious.

The Yaksha: What is the divine quality of the Kshatriyas? What practice of theirs is like the behaviour of the pious? What is their human attribute? What practice of theirs is like that of the impious?

Yudhishthira: The arrows and weapons constitute their divinity. The sacrifices they perform resemble the virtuous practices of the pious. Fear is their human attribute. The forsaking of the distressed resembles the practice of the impious.

The Yaksha: What is that one thing which is the sacrificial Soma? What is that which constitutes the sacrificial Yaju? What is that without which sacrifices cannot be performed?

Yudhishthira: Life is the sacrificial Soma. Mind is the sacrificial Yaju. Sacrifices cannot be performed without wealth.

The Yaksha: What thing is the best for the agriculturists? What is of the greatest value to those who want to attain prosperity? What is of the greatest value to those who bring forth?

Yudhishthira: Rain and seed are the best things for the agriculturists. Cow is the best thing to those who wish to attain prosperity. Son is of the greatest value to those who bring forth.

The Yaksha: Is there any person gifted with intelligence, worshipped by the world, honoured by all men, who though enjoying the objects of the senses is dead?

Yudhishthira: That person who does not propitiate the gods, the guests, the servants, the Pitris (ancestors) and his own self, though living, is dead.

The Yaksha: What thing is weightier than the Earth? What is higher than the Sky? What is swifter than the Wind? What is more numerous than the Grass?

Yudhishthira: A mother's love is weightier than the Earth. The father is higher than the sky. The mind is swifter than the Wind. The thoughts are more numerous than the Grass.

The Yaksha: What is that which sleeps with eyes open? What does not move after birth? What is it that has no heart? What is it that swells with its own force?

Yudhishthira: Fish do not close their eyes while sleeping. Eggs do not move after birth. A stone has no heart. A river swells with its own force.

The Yaksha: Who is the friend of an exile? Who is the friend of a householder? Who is the friend of a sick person? Who is the friend of a dying person?

Yudhishthira: The friend of an exile is his companion. The friend of a householder is his wife. The friend of a sick person is the doctor. The friend of a dying one is 'charity'.

The Yaksha: Who is the guest of all the creatures? What is Amrita? What is the eternal religion? What is this whole world?

Yudhishthira: Agni is the guest of all creatures. The milk of the cow is Amrita. Homa with Amrita is the eternal religion. Air is the whole world.

The Yaksha: What is it that wanders alone? What is it that is born again after its birth? What is the antidote to cold? What is the largest field?

Yudhishthira: The Sun wanders alone. The Moon is reborn after her birth. Heat caused by fire is the antidote to cold. Earth is the largest field.

The Yaksha: What is the refuge of religion, of fame, of heaven, and of happiness?

Yudhishthira: The refuge of religion is liberality. The refuge of fame is charity. The refuge of Heaven is truth. The refuge of happiness is righteousness.

The Yaksha: What is the soul of a man? Who is that friend given to him by destiny? What is his chief support? What is his best refuge?

Yudhishthira: The soul of a man is his son. The wife is his friend given by destiny. The clouds are his principal support. Charity is his best refuge.

The Yaksha: What is the best of all praiseworthy objects? What is the best of all sorts of wealth? What is the most important of all gains? What is the best of all kinds of happiness?

Yudhishthira: Dexterity is the best of all praiseworthy objects. Knowledge of the Vedas is the best of all wealth. Health is the most important of all gains. Contentment is the best of all happiness.

The Yaksha: What is the highest virtue? What religion always bears fruits? What is that thing, by controlling which, man never experiences misery? With whom does friendship never break?

Yudhishthira: Absence of cruelty is the highest virtue. The religion of the three Vedas always bears fruit. If the mind is controlled, man never experiences misery. Friendship with the righteous persons never breaks.

The Yaksha: What is it, the renunciation of which, makes one dear? What is that which, if abandoned, does not make one miserable or unhappy? What is that, renouncing which, one becomes rich? What is it, the renunciation of which, makes one happy?

Yudhishthira: The abandonment of pride makes one dear. Giving up of anger never leads a man to misery. Relinquishment of desire makes one rich. Renunciation of greed makes one happy.

The Yaksha: Why does one give wealth to the Brahmanas? Why does one give money to the Natas and the dancing people? Why does one give money to the servants? Why does one give wealth to the kings?

Yudhishthira: One gives to the Brahmanas money for religious purpose. One gives to the Natas and the dancing people for acquiring fame. One gives to the servants for getting services. One gives to kings to save himself from fear.

The Yaksha: What envelops the world? Why a thing cannot discover itself? Why friends are abandoned? Why one cannot go to Heaven?

Yudhishthira: The world is enveloped by ignorance. A thing cannot discover itself on account of spiritual darkness. One abandons his friends on account of greed. One cannot go to heaven on account of his attachment to the world.

The Yaksha: Why is a person is regarded as dead? Why a kingdom becomes dead? Why a Sraaddha becomes dead? Why a sacrifice becomes as dead?

Yudhishthira: A poor person is regarded as dead, though he is alive. A kingdom without a king becomes dead. A Sraaddha performed by an ignorant priest becomes dead. A sacrifice in which nothing is given is regarded as dead.

The Yaksha: What is the path one should follow? What is spoken of as water, as food, as poison? What is the proper time for Sraaddha?

Yudhishthira: One should follow in the footsteps of the righteous. The firmament is spoken of as water, the cow as food and request as poison. A Sraaddha may be performed whenever an able priest or Brahmana may be secured.

The Yaksha: What are the characteristics of asceticism, self-control, forgiveness and shame?

Yudhishthira: The characteristic of asceticism is sticking to one's own religion; that of self-control is control over the mind; that of forgiveness is the endurance of enmity; and that of shame is refraining from all vicious deeds.

The Yaksha: What is real knowledge? What is serenity? What is the greatest kindness? What is real simplicity?

Yudhishthira: Knowledge of Brahman is real knowledge. Peacefulness of the mind is serenity. A desire to do good to all is the greatest kindness. Evenness of the mind is real simplicity.

The Yaksha: Who is the unconquerable enemy of man? What is his incurable disease? Who is regarded as honest? Who is dishonest?

Yudhishthira: Anger is the unconquerable enemy. Greed is the incurable disease. He who is friendly to all beings is honest. He who is cruel is dishonest.

The Yaksha: What is ignorance? What is pride? What is idleness? What is grief?

Yudhishthira: Absence of knowledge of Brahman is ignorance. Too much thinking of one's own self is pride. Paying no attention to religious life is idleness. Ignorance is grief.

The Yaksha: What is spoken of as steadiness by the Rishis? What is patience? What is true ablution? What is true charity?

Yudhishthira: Resting in one's self or remaining firmly in one's own religion is steadiness. Control over passion is patience. Purification of the mind is true ablution. Preservation of all creatures is true charity.

The Yaksha: Who is a learned person? Who is an atheist? Who is an ignorant person? What is desire? What is envy?

Yudhishthira: He who is versed in religion is a learned person. An ignorant person is an atheist. He who has no knowledge of his own self is an ignorant person. Desire is longing for the worldly objects. Envy is grief of the heart.

The Yaksha: What is pride? What is hypocrisy? What is said to be the grace of the gods? What is wickedness?

Yudhishthira: Pride is ignorance or stupidity. Hypocrisy is the putting up of a false show of the banner of religion. The fruit of charity is the grace of gods. Slandering others is wickedness.

The Yaksha: Virtue, profit and desire clash against one another. How can these be united together?

Yudhishthira: When Virtue and wife are in harmony with each other, i.e., when a wife does not prove a hindrance to religious duties, then these three things can exist together.

The Yaksha: Who is doomed to eternal damnation?

Yudhishthira: He who calls a poor Brahmin for alms and says that he has nothing, is doomed to eternal hell. He who says that the Vedas, the religious books and the gods are false, goes to eternal hell. He who has wealth but who never enjoys it, nor gives it, through greed, in charity, and says he has nothing is doomed to eternal hell.

The Yaksha: Whether by birth, good character, study of the Vedas, or learning or by what a person becomes a Brahmana?

Yudhishthira: Neither birth nor learning makes one a Brahmana. Good character alone makes one a Brahmana. One, especially a Brahmana, should very carefully maintain his character. He who has a strong character is never weakened. He who has lost his character lost himself. If teachers and students who study the scriptures do wicked deeds, they should be regarded as ignorant and not as Brahmanas. He who does meritorious actions and is learned is a Brahmana. But a Brahmana who has a wicked conduct is a Sudra, even if he has studied the four Vedas. He is lower in rank than an honest Sudra. He who performs Agnihotra daily and who has controlled his passion, is a Brahmana. He who practises what he knows to be good is the true Brahmana.

The Yaksha: What is the best habit? When does the individual soul find perfect peace and happiness? Who is the man that lives though he is dead? Which is the most profitable conduct?

Yudhishthira: A life of righteousness is the best habit. Knowledge of truth or Brahman gives perfect rest to the individual soul. He whose memory is cherished for his meritorious acts is alive even after he is dead. Respect for elders and superiors is most profitable conduct.

The Yaksha: What does a person of sweet and agreeable speech gain? What does he gain who acts with deliberation? What does he, who has many friends, gain? What does a virtuous person gain?

Yudhishthira: A person of agreeable speech is dear to all. He who acts with deliberation obtains much. He who has many friends lives happily. A virtuous person attains an exalted state.

The Yaksha: Who is really happy? What is wonderful? What is the proper path? What is the interesting news? Answer the four questions, O king! I will restore to life your four dead brothers.

Yudhishthira: He who cooks in his own house a little vegetable in the fifth or sixth portion of the day, but who is neither in debt nor exiled from home is really happy.

In this world innumerable beings die daily, yet those who remain, desire immortality here. What can be more wonderful than this?

Discussions do not lead to definite conclusions. The Srutis are divided in opinion. There is not a single Rishi whose opinion can be accepted as conclusive. Truth about religious matters is concealed in caves. Therefore that path which has been followed by great men is the proper path.

In this cauldron of the world, which is full of great ignorance, the Sun is the fire, the days and nights are its fuel and the months and seasons are its wooden ladle. Time is cooking all creatures. This is the interesting news.

The Yaksha: O king Yudhishthira! You have correctly answered all my questions. Now tell me who can be called a man and which man is enriched with all sorts of wealth?

Yudhishthira: The report of a man's meritorious acts reaches both Heaven and Earth. He is called a man so long as that report continues. That man to whom, the pleasant and the unpleasant, joy and sorrow, pleasure and pain, the past and the future, are all alike, is enriched with all sorts of wealth.

The Yaksha (pleased with the reply): Let one of your brothers, whomsoever you wish, be restored to life.

Yudhishthira: O Yaksha! Let this Nakula be brought back to life.

The Yaksha: This Bhima is very dear to you. This Arjuna is your chief support. Why, then, O king, do you wish for the life of Nakula, who is only a step-brother of yours?

Yudhishthira: He who sacrifices virtue is himself destroyed. He who preserves it is himself preserved. Therefore, I do not sacrifice virtue. Refraining from cruelty is the greater virtue and, in my opinion, greater than the greatest desirable object. I prefer that virtue, viz., non-injuring or non-violence. People call me the just and the righteous. I will never swerve from my duty. It is my wish that both Kunti and Madri have sons. As Kunti is to me, so also is Madri. I do not make any distinction between them. I wish to behave equally towards my two mothers. I cannot bear the sight of Madri being childless. Therefore, O Yaksha, let Nakula be brought back to life.

The Yaksha: As abstention from cruelty is, in your opinion, superior to both profit and desire, as you are wise, noble and just, let all your brothers be restored to life. Depart in peace.

Thereupon, the dead four rose up at the words of the Yaksha.

Yudhishthira: O crane, who stands on one leg in the lake, what god are you? I cannot believe that you are a Yaksha.

The Yaksha: O child! I am your father, Dharma. Fame, truth, self-control, purity, simplicity, modesty, renown, firmness, charity, asceticism and Brahmacharya are my limbs. Absence of cruelty, impartiality, tranquillity, asceticism, purity and want of pride are so many avenues for attaining me. You are always very dear to me.

You have practised the five virtues, viz., evenness of mind, self-restraint, forgiveness, abstinence from sensual indulgence and Yoga. You have conquered the six, viz., hunger, thirst, sorrow, delusion, decrepitude and death. Of these six, the first two manifest themselves in the first stage of life; the second two in the middle stage; and the last two in the last part of life in order to make creatures go to the next world. I came here to test you. I have been pleased with your spirit of mercy. I will grant you boons.

Yudhishthira: May the Agni of the Brahmana, whose fire sticks were carried away by the deer, be not extinguished. This is the first boon I crave.

Dharma: I took away the fire sticks of that Brahmana in the form of a deer. I did this in order to test you. I grant you this boon. I bless you. Ask for another boon.

Yudhishthira: The twelve years of our forest life have passed away and the thirteenth year has come. May no one recognise us in the course of this year wherever we may live.

Dharma: I grant you this boon also. Even if you wander in the world in your own form, no one in the three worlds will be able to recognise you. Through my favour you will lead a secret and incognito life in the city of Virata during this thirteenth year. Whatever form every one of you wishes to assume, you will be able to assume that form at will. O best of men! Accept a third boon.

Yudhishthira: May my mind be always inclined towards charity, asceticism and truth. May I be free from greed, anger and delusion.

Dharma: O my beloved son! You are, by nature, endowed with all these virtues. You are the very embodiment of virtue itself. However, may you again have what you desire!

With these blessings, Dharma vanished.

(Vana Parva, Ch. 311-313)

ARJUNA THE MIGHTY BOW-MAN

Arjuna was not only one of the greatest warriors of his time but also pre-eminently fit to receive spiritual instructions from Lord Krishna Himself. He was indeed a blessed soul; for Sri Krishna instilled into him the knowledge of Atman in the battlefield to remove his doubts and delusion. Arjuna got initiation into the mysteries of Kaivalya from Krishna and attained Brahma Jnana. These instructions are embodied in what is known throughout India as the Bhagavad Gita. He was the only fortunate person who had a direct cosmic vision or Visvarupa Darshan. Lord Krishna Himself says, "This rare vision cannot be had by charity, study of the Vedas or penance. I have shown this only to you as you are very dear to me and as you are the only person qualified to have such a magnanimous vision."

He had not to retire into caves for obtaining the knowledge of the Self. He possessed all the qualifications of an aspirant. He showed to the world that the knowledge can be had, even in the battlefield, that the knowledge is not the sole monopoly of recluses, hermits and Sannyasins alone who lead a retired life or the Nivritti Marga or the path of renunciation. He showed to the world that the knowledge can be attained by a man while discharging his duties in the world, amidst bustle and turmoil.

His heroic deeds are marvellous. He obtained rare weapons from gods on account of his rigorous Tapascharya. He was a great Tapasvin. He stuck to his promise and vow with an iron will and fiery determination. What a tremendous and terrible vow he took! "I will kill Jayadratha before the next sunset or I will burn myself in the flames."

He led the life of truth, devotion and love. His affection and devotion to his brothers and reverence for Yudhishthira was unique. He said to Indra, "I do not want the happiness of Heaven. My happiness lies in serving my brothers and alleviating their pain and sufferings and protecting them from the attacks of enemies, even at the risk of my life." What a magnanimous thought! He exhibited great power of self-restraint in Indra's palace when he resisted the charms of Urvasi. He fought single-handed against the Kauravas when delivering the cows of king Virata from their custody.

Arjuna was the greatest exponent of the art and science of archery. He showed many strange and dexterous feats in the exhibition held by Drona; so also at the Svayamvara of Draupadi. All spectators were struck with wonder.

❁ ❁ ❁

As children, Drona and Drupada were thick friends but when Drupada succeeded to his father's throne, he abandoned all friendship with Drona and turned Drona away and insulted him. Drona wanted to teach Drupada a bitter lesson.

It was the custom in India in ancient days for pupils to pay their teacher according to his demand when their academic career terminated. Drona called the Pandavas and the Kaurava princes and said, "Go to Drupadanagar, the capital of the country of Panchala, and bring the king Drupada bound hand and foot to me. This alone is my fee."

The sons of Dhritarashtra proceeded to fight with Drupada but they were severely beaten by Drupada's men. In the end Arjuna marched forward and defeated Drupada and carried him in chains to Drona. Drupada remembered his past misbehaviour towards Drona and repented very much. Drona removed the chains and pardoned Drupada. Drupada took a vow in Drona's presence that he would beget a son who would kill Drona and a daughter to marry the hero Arjuna. He performed a great sacrifice. From the sacrificial fire came up Draupadi and Dhrishtadyumna.

On their way to Panchala, the Pandavas were nearing a holy place called Somasrayana. It was dark as the night was approaching. They could not see the path clearly. Therefore Arjuna used a torch.

A Gandharva named Chitraratha, the friend of Kubera, was bathing in that holy place with his family. He rebuked Arjuna as he was coming to the spot with a torch in his hand. "Who are you, bold intruders? Stop. Otherwise you will lose your heads."

Arjuna replied, "Thank you very much. Strength is no monopoly of the celestials. Who knows whether you will lose your head or we?"

This retort exasperated the Gandharva who showered arrows on Arjuna immediately. Arjuna defended himself with his shield. He then took a fiery arrow and shot at the Gandharva. Chitraratha fell down senseless from his chariot. Arjuna caught hold of his curls and dragged him to Yudhishthira.

Yudhishthira was moved with pity and said, "O Arjuna! Set the Gandharva free." Chitraratha was immensely pleased at the noble treatment and taught Arjuna the mysterious art by which one could see all objects far and near at will. He gave to Arjuna one hundred horses. In return Arjuna gave Chitraratha Brahmastra. Chitraratha embraced Arjuna and told the Pandavas to select the Brahmin Dhaumya, who lived at Utkochaka, as their priest, and took leave of the Pandavas.

❁ ❁ ❁

Years passed and Draupadi grew up into lovely womanhood. The day of Svayamvara came at last. Many kings were present. Krishna and Balarama also attended. The Pandavas seated themselves among the Brahmins, as they were in the guise of Bramins. Princess Draupadi with her maids appeared on the scene.

Then Dhrishtadyumna, the son of king Drupada and brother of Draupadi, came forward and declared, in a loud voice: "Whoever in the assembly shoots down the mark with his bow would win the princess Draupadi." The mark was a golden fish suspended high up in the air and revolving with great speed. There was a basin of clear water in which the reflection of the golden fish could be seen. The successful aspirant for the hand of Draupadi was to look at the reflection, shoot at the golden fish and bring it down.

Then the contest began. Princes came forward one by one but few of them could even bend the bow and string it. All the Kshatriya princes failed to hit the mark. Then Arjuna stepped forward in his Brahmin garb. He strung the bow quite easily and hit the arrow into the eye of the golden fish and brought it down.

The success of this Brahmin roused the jealousy of all Kshatriya princes. They cried, "This maiden is a Kshatriya and must not be given to a Brahmin." They joined together and opposed the king when he was about to give his daughter to the winner. But Arjuna with Bhima resisted the princes successfully and left the place with Draupadi.

The five brothers returned to their cottage. The door was shut. They shouted to their mother from outside: "Beloved mother! We have come with the most precious alms we ever had." Kunti replied from within the cottage, "Share ye all what you have got." When Kunti came out and saw Draupadi she was very much troubled at the thought, 'How the five brothers could share the same bride without sin attaching to Draupadi?' Vyasa himself appeared on the spot, explained to them how Draupadi was destined to be the wife of five husbands, and the course of conduct which they had to adopt. Then they were all satisfied. The king gave his daughter to the five princes. The Pandavas with Draupadi went to live at Khandavaprastha. Sage Narada, in order to maintain unity amongst the brothers, made them to abide by the condition that Draupadi should live with each brother by turns and that when she was in the company of any brother, any of the others interrupting them should go into exile for one year.

❁ ❁ ❁

One day a thief came and stealthily took away the only cow of a Brahmin. The poor Brahmin came to Arjuna and said, "I have lost my only cow. I earn my livelihood through this cow. I am ruined." Arjuna was greatly moved. He said, "Fear not, O Brahmin! I shall get back the cow for you." He immediately ran to the room where his weapons lay.

At that very moment Yudhishthira was sitting in conversation with Draupadi in that room. Arjuna entered the room, caught hold of his bow and ran after the thief at once. Arjuna wanted to be true to the promise given to the Brahmin. He determined to relieve the distress of the Brahmin even at the cost of the penalty of being exiled for breaking the condition.

Arjuna regained the cow and delivered it to the Brahmin. He then came to Yudhishthira and said, "I became an intruder. The vow has been broken. Therefore allow me to go into exile for one year." Yudhishthira shed tears and said, "Beloved Arjuna! You entered the room in order to relieve the distress of a poor Brahmin. Here was nothing wrong in your conduct. Therefore you need not go into exile."

Arjuna replied, "O revered brother! It was you who taught me that it is a crime even to do a virtuous deed by breaking a vow." Yudhishthira then gave him permission to leave the kingdom.

❁ ❁ ❁

Arjuna wandered in the forest. He put on the garb of an

ascetic and visited many holy places. One day Arjuna was taking his bath in the Ganga. He was carried deep down through the waters into the regions of the serpent-king by Ulupi, the daughter of the king. She took him to the royal palace and forced him to marry her. Arjuna had to yield to her wishes. He married her and stayed there for some time. Then he came back to the Earth and continued his wanderings.

He reached the land of Kalinga. Chitrabhanu was the king there, Manipur was his capital. The king had a beautiful daughter named Chitrangada. Arjuna fell in love with her. He told the king his name. The king gladly gave him his daughter in marriage. Arjuna spent some time at Manipur. Thereupon he proceeded to some holy places on the banks of the Ganga. These places were deserted as river was infested with crocodiles. But Arjuna was absolutely fearless. He dipped his legs in the water. A huge crocodile caught hold of one of his legs. At once he jumped back to the bank and dragged the crocodile ashore. The crocodile assumed the form of a beautiful maiden. Arjuna asked, "Who are you, O maiden?" The maiden replied, "I am a celestial nymph. My name is Varga. There are four others like me who are now living as crocodiles in four other ghats. We rebuked a saint and on account of his curse we were transformed into crocodiles. The holy saint told us, 'You will be free from my curse as soon as any man would drag you to the bank from the water.' Therefore we have been living here all the time, catching hold of every human being who descends into the water, but no one could ever drag any of us to the shore till now. You have delivered me. Please deliver my friends also."

Arjuna plunged into the water of the four holy ghats and delivered the celestial maidens from the curse. The five maidens blessed Arjuna and flew to Heaven immediately.

Arjuna at last came to Prabhasa, a sacred place, which was situated within the domain of Krishna. Krishna heard that Arjuna had come to Prabhasa. Krishna wanted to give Subhadra in marriage to Arjuna. Therefore he announced that a great fair would take place at Prabhasa for three days. All the Yadavas including Krishna and Balarama attended the festival. Subhadra was also taken to Prabhasa.

Subhadra had heard about the great heroic feats of Arjuna and desired to marry him. She had once expressed her desire to Krishna also.

When Krishna, Balarama and Subhadra were coming round the fair, they saw an ascetic in meditation. Krishna recognised this ascetic as Arjuna. Balarama was attracted by the ascetic and took him to his house.

Subhadra was asked to attend on the ascetic (Arjuna) and help him in his worship and prayers. One day after usual prayers were over, Subhadra enquired of the ascetic whether he knew anything about Arjuna. Arjuna smiled within himself and at last revealed his identity. The same night Arjuna eloped with Subhadra with the previous consent of Krishna.

The Yadava chiefs and Balarama heard this news and ran immediately after Arjuna. Krishna intervened and said, "Arjuna has not done any wrong. He has done what a Kshatriya should do. He is a mighty warrior. You cannot conquer him. You should all cordially welcome him." Arjuna was married to Subhadra with great pomp and eclat. Arjuna, Krishna, Subhadra and Balarama returned to Khandavaprastha.

✿ ✿ ✿

One day Krishna and Arjuna were sitting on the bank of the Yamuna. A Brahmin approached them and said, "I am hungry. Will you appease my hunger?" Arjuna said, "What do you wish to eat?" The Brahmin replied, "I am Agni. I have long cherished the desire of consuming the forest of Khandava. But Indra is putting obstacles in my way, because the serpent Takshaka, who is the friend of Indra, lives in the forest. Whenever I try to burn the forest, Indra sends a good downpour of rain to extinguish me. I pray that you will be graciously pleased to stop the showers of Indra and fence in all the beasts of the forest. If you can do this I will surely enjoy a sumptuous meal."

Arjuna replied, "We are quite ready to help you; but we have neither weapons nor chariots." Then Agni brought the mighty bow known as 'Gandiva' from Varuna, a quiver of inexhaustible arrows and the chariot named 'Kapidhvaja' and gave them to Arjuna. He also gave Krishna two terrible weapons of destruction, viz., a disc named 'Sudarshana' and a club known as 'Kaumudaki'.

Thereupon Arjuna and Krishna agreed to help Agni. Agni started his work immediately. The whole forest was ablaze. Many beasts were burnt. Indra tried his best to put an end to the conflagration but failed. He hurled his thunder and huge rocks on Krishna and Arjuna but the arrows of Arjuna dashed them to pieces. Indra failed but was pleased to see the skill and courage of the son of Kunti, born with his blessings.

The whole forest was burnt within a short space of time. A demon named Maya was spared by Arjuna. Agni was highly satisfied. He blessed Krishna and Arjuna and went away.

Then the demon Maya came to Arjuna and said, "You have saved me from the flames. Tell me, what I can do for you?" Arjuna replied, "I want nothing in return for what I have done. I have been able to save you. This will suffice." But the demon persisted in his prayer. Arjuna said, "Do what Krishna commands you to do." Krishna said, "Build a magnificent palace for the king Yudhishthira, the like of which was never seen or will be seen on the surface of this Earth."

This Maya was a marvellous architect. He built a crystal palace, studded with pearls and gems, within a period of fourteen months. The beauty of design and grandeur of the mansion was beyond description.

The Pandavas, while spending their twelve years of exile, met Vyasa in the Dvaita forest. Then Vyasa said to Yudhishthira, "I shall teach you the art of celestial science of weapons. Teach it to Arjuna and then send him in search of powerful weapons from the gods." He taught the art to Yudhishthira and went away.

Yudhishthira taught this art to Arjuna. Arjuna repaired to the forest with his bow and quiver of arrows, to practise penance. He crossed the Gandhamadana peak and came to the Indrakila mountain. Here he saw an ascetic. The ascetic said, "Who are you?

This is a peaceful abode of saints. Bow and arrow have no use here. Throw them away." But Arjuna stood silent. He did not pay any attention to the words of the ascetic.

The ascetic was no other than Indra. Indra was very much pleased with the bravery of Arjuna and revealed his true form to Arjuna and said, "O Arjuna! Ask me a boon."

Arjuna replied, "O celestial lord! Give me mighty weapons to fight with the enemy." Indra said, "My child! Why do you want these meagre weapons? I shall open to you the very gate of the kingdom of Heaven. Go there and enjoy eternal bliss."

Arjuna said, "Bliss! I do not know any other bliss than the happiness of my brothers. I do not care for the happiness of the Heaven, when my brothers undergo severe hardships in the forest." Indra was very much moved when he came to know of the intense affection and love which Arjuna had for his brothers. He said, "Practise penance and propitiate Lord Siva. Your desire will be fulfilled." So saying, Indra disappeared.

✿ ✿ ✿

Thereupon Arjuna came back to the Himalayas, practised severe penance for four months and worshipped Siva with great devotion. One day a huge boar rushed towards him. Arjuna took his bow at once to shoot it down. But he saw at the very moment a hunter (Kirata) running after the boar with his bow and arrow. The hunter said, "I aimed at the animal first. Therefore, it is not proper for you to shoot at it." But Arjuna did not pay any attention to the words of the hunter. He discharged an arrow at the same time and claimed the animal as his own.

A big quarrel arose between Arjuna and the hunter. Arjuna became angry. He thought that a man of low birth and meagre strength was behaving towards him in an arrogant manner. Therefore, he began to shower arrows on him. The arrows did not produce any injury on the hunter. The hunter stood firm and smiled. Arjuna was about to throw his mighty bow on the hunter. But the hunter quietly snatched it away. Then Arjuna hit him on the head with a sword. The sword broke into pieces. Then he hurled big stones on the hunter. The stones were broken into pieces. They did not cause any injury to the hunter.

Then Arjuna began to wrestle with the hunter and pressed him with all his strength. The hunter stood unmoved and Arjuna fell senseless on the ground.

Arjuna regained his senses. He was not able to understand who this mysterious hunter was. He immediately sat down to worship Lord Siva in a clay idol. He offered a garland of flowers to the idol. The garland instead of falling on the idol twined round the neck of the hunter.

Arjuna at once thought that the hunter was no other than Lord Siva Himself. He ran towards the hunter and prostrated at his feet and said, "O Lord! Kindly pardon me. I struck Thee without knowing that Thou art Lord Siva. Thousand prostrations unto Thee! Forgive! Forgive! I am Thine."

Lord Siva replied, "O Arjuna! Thou art a real hero and a brave warrior. I am highly pleased with thee. Now ask a boon." Arjuna said, "O Lord! Grant me the weapon called Pasupata." Lord Siva gave him the weapon at once with instructions how to use it, returned to him the Gandiva, which He had snatched away awhile ago and disappeared. Many other gods also appeared on the spot and presented him with mighty weapons.

❁ ❁ ❁

Then Arjuna went to Heaven. Indra took him there and presented him many rare weapons. The gods taught him the use of those weapons. In return, Arjuna killed a demon there who was doing much harm to the gods.

Arjuna learnt here the science of music from a Gandharva named Chitrasena. His character was put to test here. Urvasi, the celestial nymph, tempted Arjuna in a variety of ways. One night she put on a gorgeous dress, appeared before him and offered herself. But Arjuna stood unmoved and showed his purity of character and remarkable self-restraint. He prostrated himself before Urvasi, calling her, "Mother! Mother!" Urvasi was disappointed in her attempt and pronounced a curse on him, that he should become an eunuch.

Indra knew of the curse and said to Urvasi, "O Urvasi! I myself brought Arjuna to kill the demon and you have given him this curse. It is not proper." Then he said to Arjuna, "O

Arjuna! Do not be afraid of her curse. Her curse will do you more good than harm. You can utilise this whenever you wish to become an eunuch."

Thereupon Arjuna returned to his brothers who had left the Kamyaka forest and lived now on the Gandhamadana peak. The brothers greeted Arjuna with great joy. The Pandavas repaired to the Dvaita forest and lived there happily in a hut by the side of the lake.

❁ ❁ ❁

The wicked Duryodhana wanted to behold the distress of the Pandavas with his own eyes. So he went with his men to the place where the Pandavas lived in exile. On the way he had to pass through the beautiful garden of Chitrasena, the chief of the Gandharvas. The army of the Kauravas entered the garden for taking rest. They plucked the flowers and uprooted plants. The Gandharvas became infuriated. A formidable fight ensued. Many heroes on the side of the Kauravas fled. Duryodhana and his brothers could not find time to escape. They were made captives by the Gandharvas.

The Pandavas knew nothing of this incident. Some of the soldiers of the Kauravas ran to Yudhishthira and appealed to him for help. Yudhishthira at once sent Bhima and Arjuna to the spot. A serious fight ensued. The Gandharvas were defeated. Chitrasena himself surrendered and said, "O Arjuna! I am defeated, I am your friend." Then they embraced each other. Chitrasena was the same Gandharva who taught music to Arjuna.

Duryodhana and his brothers who were captives were brought before Yudhishthira. Yudhishthira pardoned and released them, although Chitrasena had told him the evil intention of Duryodhana in coming to the forest. The wicked Duryodhana, who was saved by the mercy of the Pandavas, and who was not successful in his evil design, became more jealous of the Pandavas. He was not able to forget the shame and humiliation of the day for a very long time. His pride, vanity and haughtiness were crushed in this memorable incident. As he was puffed up with vanity, the kindness of his cousins was not endurable. He did not recognise their extreme good nature and righteous conduct towards him, despite his malicious and treacherous nature.

❁ ❁ ❁

When king Virata was away from his capital with his army, Duryodhana suddenly invaded his kingdom with a big force and carried away sixty thousand cows. The news reached prince Uttara. He said, "Duryodhana did a cowardly act. If I have a man to drive my chariot, I will teach him a good lesson." This news reached the ears of Sairandhri (Draupadi). She said to the prince, "Brihannala, the music teacher of your palace, is a good charioteer. He is a brave warrior too. He will be very serviceable to you."

The prince asked Brihannala (Arjuna) to be his charioteer for the day. Brihannala readily agreed and drove the chariot by the side of the big Sami tree whose leaves concealed the bow and the quiver of arrows of Arjuna.

Prince Uttara saw now the big army of Duryodhana and got frightened. He said to Brihannala, "How can we fight with such a big army? My head reels. Drive the chariot back to the palace."

Brihannala: "What will people say if you go back without taking the cows? I will never return till I win them back."

Uttara jumped out of the chariot and ran with great speed. Brihannala also jumped out of the chariot, followed Uttara, caught hold of him and placed him on the chariot again. He drove the chariot to the spot where the Sami tree stood. He asked the prince to climb up the tree and bring down the weapons. Uttara had never seen such mighty weapons. He was astonished. He asked, "To whom do these belong, O Brihannala?"

Brihannala: They belong to the Pandavas.

Uttara: If these weapons belong to the Pandavas, please tell me where are the Pandavas now?

Then Brihannala informed the prince that he was none other than Arjuna and how his brothers and Draupadi had been living in disguise in the palace of king Virata, the father of the prince.

Uttara drew courage now. Arjuna told the prince that he

himself would fight and asked Uttara to drive the chariot. Then prince readily agreed.

Arjuna threw away his eunuch's dress and wore armour and mounted the chariot. There was a terrible fight. The Kaurava chiefs were defeated. Duryodhana fled to his capital to save himself. Arjuna got back all the cows and returned with prince Uttara to king Virata's capital. Arjuna told the prince not to disclose the secret for some time.

Later on, king Virata came to know that the Pandavas and Draupadi had taken shelter with him in disguise. He was immensely pleased with the valour and heroism of Arjuna. So he offered the hand of his daughter to Arjuna. Arjuna declined to marry as he was her tutor. Then she was wedded to Abhimanyu, the son of Arjuna, who was as powerful as his father.

❁ ❁ ❁

The year of concealment was over now. The Pandavas were entitled to get back the kingdom they had lost. But Duryodhana refused to give them back the territory. Both the parties prepared for war.

Both parties were eager to get the help of Lord Krishna. Duryodhana and Arjuna went to see Krishna at Dvaraka. They reached Dvaraka and found Krishna lying asleep in his bed. Arjuna stood at the feet of Krishna. Duryodhana sat by the side of the head of Krishna. As soon as Krishna awoke, he saw first Arjuna standing at His feet. He gave Arjuna the choice of either having Himself or His army of a hundred million men to help him. Arjuna said, "I want You only, O Krishna!" Then Duryodhana got Krishna's army.

The two parties assembled on the plains of Kurukshetra, close to the river Hiranvati.

❁ ❁ ❁

After the fall of Bhishma in the great battle of Kurukshetra, Drona became the commander. Abhimanyu, the son of Arjuna, a lad of eighteen years, fought with great bravery and skill. Even Karna and Kripa could not stand against him. He gained the secrets of archery and fighting when he was in his mother's womb.

One night Arjuna was speaking to Subhadra about the various kinds of warfare. He related to her the secrets of Padmavyuha (Chakravyuha). He was describing to her how a soldier enters the Padmavyuha and fights with his enemies. At this stage Krishna discovered that Subhadra was actually sleeping and that the child in her womb was responding to Arjuna's speech. Immediately Krishna took away Arjuna outside. Therefore Abhimanyu could not know the secret of coming out of the Padmavyuha.

Seven generals united together to attack Abhimanyu. Jayadratha, who had married the sister of Duryodhana, was one of the seven generals. He bore great grudge against the Pandavas. Abhimanyu fought with great fury and courage. His bow was cut, the horses of his chariot were killed and his driver was also killed; yet he fought on with shield and sword. His sword and shield were broken and at last he fell unconscious and while in this condition Dussasana's son struck Abhimanyu on the head and the boy of 'heroic arms' expired.

Arjuna came to know of the death of his son. He took a vow either to kill Jayadratha before sunset the next day or to enter the flames himself. The news of the terrible vow of Arjuna soon reached the Kauravas. Jayadratha trembled with intense fear. He wanted to retire. But Duryodhana encouraged him and said, "We will save you. Be not afraid."

Six great warriors guarded Jayadratha on all sides. But Arjuna fought with great fury and heroism. The six warriors were pierced all over their bodies with the arrows of Arjuna. Jayadratha himself was badly hurt but it was difficult for Arjuna to kill him as he was protected by the six generals.

The day was drawing to a close. The sun will go down within a couple of hours. If Jayadratha lives till that time, Arjuna must enter the flames. It was a critical juncture.

Just then Krishna covered the Sun with Sudarshana Chakra. A black cloud covered the Chakra. The Earth was enveloped as if in twilight. The Kauravas rejoiced that the sun had set and

Arjuna must now enter the flames. Jayadratha thought that he was quite secure. He came out of his hiding place, raised his head and looked hither and thither. Arjuna appeared before him and shot an arrow. His head was cut. It fell on the lap of Vriddhakshetra (father of Jayadratha).

Now the dark cloud vanished and the Sun, which was about to set, appeared on the firmament. The Kauravas saw that Arjuna had kept his word.

The great Drona also died. Then Karna became the commander. He killed thousands of soldiers of the Pandavas. Karna and Arjuna fought furiously. The wheels of Karna's chariot stuck into the earth and yet he fought with great vehemence, but the wheels sank deeper and deeper into the ground. He jumped down and tried to draw them out but all in vain.

In this hour of danger, Karna said to Arjuna, "O Arjuna! You are brave and righteous. Wait a bit. Let me pull these wheels out." Arjuna kept silent. Krishna said, "It is shameful for you to talk of justice and righteousness at this hour of peril. Pray, tell me, where did this sense of justice remain when you joined with the Kauravas to injure the Pandavas? Where did you abandon the sense of justice when the boy Abhimanyu was killed? Think of your cruel and unjust acts. Be prepared to die now."

These words of Krishna made Karna more furious. He sent a fiery arrow at Arjuna. The latter fell senseless in his chariot. In the meantime, Karna tried to pull the wheels from the ground. But all his efforts were of no avail. The wheels sank deeper and deeper into the ground every moment. Arjuna regained his senses and sent a terrible weapon towards Karna. In the twinkling of an eye the head of Karna fell rolling to the ground. The fall of Karna was like a bolt from the blue to Duryodhana, for he relied on Karna alone for his final victory.

❁ ❁ ❁

Salya took the command. He also fought furiously and killed many soldiers of the Pandava army. But he was killed by Yudhishthira. Bhima killed all the brothers of Duryodhana.

Sahadeva slew Sakuni. Only Duryodhana, Kripa, Kritavarma and Asvatthama, the son of Drona, survived.

Duryodhana fled from the field to save himself and hid in a lake. But the Pandavas soon found out his hiding place and challenged him to fight. Duryodhana also was a great warrior. He had great skill in wielding clubs or mace like Bhima. He came out of the lake and fought with Bhima with the club. Bhima broke his thighs. Duryodhana fell on the ground.

Then Asvatthama became the commander. He went to the camp of the Pandavas along with Kripa and Kritavarma but returned in despair to a forest nearby. Asvatthama entered the camp of the Pandavas at night. The five Pandavas, Draupadi and Satyaki had been out that night. Asvatthama went into the tent and killed the five sons of Draupadi. He killed many soldiers also. Kripa and Kritavarma were watching at the gate. They returned to Duryodhana and informed him of what they did. Surely this is a mean and cowardly act. To kill people at night when they were sleeping is a dastardly, unworthy and despicable action. But Duryodhana smiled when he heard of the deed done by these great and remarkable heroes!

Yudhishthira performed Asvamedha Yajna or horse sacrifice. The sacrificial horse was let loose under the protection of Arjuna. Any prince or Raja who seizes the horse must show his strength by actual fight. Arjuna got victory over many princes. At last he came to the kingdom of Manipur. Previously during the wanderings, Arjuna came to this place and married Chitrangada, the princess. He had a son named Babhruvahana by her. He was on the throne now.

Babhruvahana came with his ministers and courtiers to give a royal reception to his father. But Arjuna scolded him, "I have come to fight with you. You are greeting me with warm reception. Such an act is unworthy of the race. It gives me shame." Ulupi, the step mother of Babhruvahana, the daughter of the king of Nagas said, "My son, fight with your father. It is quite proper for you. This is the best way to gratify him. He has come with the horse of Asvamedha Yajna."

Thereupon Babhruvahana ordered his men to seize the horse. He marched with a large army to fight against his father. He fought very bravely. Arjuna was not able to hit his son but Babhruvahana hit Arjuna on the head. Arjuna fell down on the ground in a senseless condition. Then Chitrangada and her son scolded Ulupi. Ulupi ran to her father's place in the kingdom of Nagas and brought a gem. The gem was placed on Arjuna's breast. Then he came back to consciousness. Arjuna was immensely pleased with his heroic son. He invited him, his mother and Ulupi, to the sacrifice and went away.

Then Arjuna got victory over Meghasaudhi of Magadha, the grandson of the mighty Jarasandha and the son of Sakuni, king of the territory of Gandhara.

Arjuna returned to Hastinapura in triumph. The horse sacrifice was performed with due pomp and splendour. Many kings attended. Much wealth, gold and jewels were distributed to the Brahmins and the priests.

King Yudhishthira was on the throne for fifteen years. Dhritarashtra expressed his desire to retire into the forest. He repaired into the forest and lived there with his wife for some years. On one occasion, the Pandavas visited the cottage of Dhritarashtra. The sage Vyasa also came there and said, "You are all mourning over the death of those heroes who were killed in the war. I shall show them to you now." They all took bath in the Ganga and stood on the bank with eagerness. Suddenly a great noise was heard. Those who were slain in the war rose one by one in front of them. Vyasa temporarily bestowed eyesight to the blind old king who now saw his sons for the first and the last time.

Once Arjuna visited Dvaraka. He paid due respects to Sri Krishna and they were both conversing with each other on some important subject.

Interrupting their speech, a Brahmin fell down weeping at the feet of Sri Krishna. Sri Krishna made him sit and enquired the cause of his grief. The Brahmin related his sorrowful story, how he lost all his nine children as soon as they were born. Krishna kept quiet over the matter. When he could not get a reply from Krishna, the Brahmin was enraged and blamed Krishna and said, "When the Devas are displeased with the king's rule, calamities occur in the country. Brahmins are put to various sorts of difficulties. Famine prevails in the land. There is untimely death. Anarchy prevails. These are the signs of the displeasure of the Devas. Therefore, O Krishna! The responsibility of restoring back life to my sons rests with you. The king should protect his subjects from theft, untimely death, famine, etc." Thus the Brahmin blamed Krishna. Even then Krishna was silent.

Arjuna who was sitting by his side was moved to pity and promised to save the tenth child of the Brahmin. The Brahmin was not sure of the abilities of Arjuna and said, "How can I depend on your strength alone? I have lost nine sons previously." Arjuna said, "O Brahmin! Know me to be Arjuna, the beloved brother of Yudhishthira. I have got great powers and skill in archery. I have got many divine weapons. I have stopped rains from falling on the earth when Agni was consuming the Khandava forest. I have won the great battle of Mahabharata. I have conquered many demons and men of great prowess. To save a child of yours is no impossible task for me. Have confidence in my great powers. If I fail to save your child, I shall immediately prepare a big fire and perish in the consuming flames."

The Brahmin was convinced of the great strength of Arjuna and promised to intimate to him when his wife was about to give birth to the child. Then the Brahmin returned home.

After some days the Brahmin came to Arjuna and appraised him of the time of birth of his child. Arjuna immediately followed the Brahmin and put a cage of arrows around the room in which the Brahmin's wife was lying, to prevent Yama's messengers entering the room to take away the Prana of the newborn baby. The Brahmin's wife duly gave birth to a child and immediately the child disappeared. On previous occasions, at least the Brahmin could see the dead body of the child but this time he could not see even that. The Brahmin fell down in a swoon.

According to his promise, Arjuna made ready a big fire and was about to jump into it when suddenly Krishna appeared on the spot and stopped him from his terrible act. Krishna and Arjuna took leave of the Brahmin saying, "Be not troubled. All your sons will be restored to you soon."

Krishna took Arjuna to Vaikuntha immediately where Lord Vishnu received them warmly and said, "O Arjuna! O Krishna! Nara and Narayana! I have been much pleased with your various actions in the world. I had a great desire to meet you and therefore, I brought the sons of the Brahmin to my abode as soon as they were born. Here are the boys. Take them back safely."

Krishna and Arjuna took leave of Vishnu after paying him due respects. They reached Dvaraka and visited the Brahmin's house and returned the ten children. The Brahmin was overjoyed and praised Krishna and Arjuna for their kindness and mercy on him.

The Yadavas at Dvaraka became unruly and frivolous. They played with the ascetics and rebuked them. They dressed a boy like a woman and stuffed some clothes and rags underneath the dress. They took the boy, who was in the disguise of a woman, to the ascetics and enquired of them when she would give birth to a child and that whether it would be a male or a female. The ascetics knowing the truth of the case, said, "She will give birth to an iron club and your race will be totally destroyed by that."

An iron club came out of the stomach of the boy. The Yadavas were much afraid of their annihilation. They reduced the iron club to powder and threw it into the sea. On one occasion the Yadavas went to visit the holy temple at Prabhasa. They drank too much wine on an empty stomach and began to fight amongst themselves furiously. The Yadavas got hold of the weeds that grew on the shores of the sea and began to fight with the reeds. These reeds contained the iron pieces that were thrown into the sea. These harmless reeds became transmuted into iron rods. All died, except Krishna, Daruka and Vajra, Krishna's grandson.

Krishna sent Daruka to Hastinapura to convey to Arjuna the news of the destruction of the Yadavas. He himself went to search Balarama and found him sitting underneath a big tree in the forest. He witnessed a huge serpent coming out of the mouth of Balarama. It had one thousand heads. The serpent came out and moved towards the sea. It was the soul of Balarama. The mortal frame was found on the ground as a corpse.

Krishna stretched himself on the ground on account of exhaustion. Jara, a hunter, from a distance took Krishna for a deer and shot an arrow at him. The arrow hit the sole of Krishna's feet. The hunter ran to the spot and found Krishna there instead of a deer. His heart was filled with remorse and he begged Krishna's pardon. Krishna pardoned him and said it was not his fault and then left for Vaikuntha. The last piece of the iron club hit Krishna's feet in accordance with the curse of the ascetics on the Yadavas.

❁ ❁ ❁

Arjuna and his brothers lost all charm for this world after Krishna departed from it. Then the Pandavas ascended the summits of the snowy Himalayas. Arjuna fainted on his way and reached the Heaven.

Such is the short life sketch of Arjuna, a mighty hero, who stuck to his ideal and vows at the risk of his life, who showed extraordinary skill in the battlefield in the use of arrows and weapons, who was loyal and devoted to his brothers, who was a master musician and who was, at the same time, a Brahma Jnani. We are extremely grateful to him because on account of him only, we have got the priceless book 'Gita' which contains an inexhaustible treasure of divine knowledge.

If there had been no Arjuna, this world would not possibly have seen this marvellous book 'Gita'. So long as this world lasts, the name of Arjuna will remain. He has immortalised his name, not because of his heroic deeds, not because of his excellence in the science of archery, not because of his virtuous qualities, but because of his discourses with Lord Krishna which are handed down to us to guide us in the spiritual path, which serve as a beacon light to the weary pilgrims of this world, giving them solace and peace and which serve as a nectar to eradicate the dire disease of birth and death with its concomitant evils.

May the noble life awaken within us noble thoughts and inspirations! May he throw light on us from his new abode of Immortality! Glory to Arjuna, whose life generates a mighty holy thrill in our hearts when we remember his name and his mighty superhuman deeds!

KARNA THE MUNIFICENT

Karna is famous for his liberality. He is the son of the Sun-god. Kunti received a Mantra from Rishi Durvasa for begetting an offspring. The Rishi said to Kunti, "Repeat this Mantra after you attain proper age and you will get a son through the grace of Sun-god." Kunti was hasty and curious. She wanted to test the power of the Mantra. Therefore, she recited the Mantra, before the proper time, when she was a virgin. She begot a son. The child was born with ear-rings (Kundalas) and armour. This son was Karna. To hide her shame, she put this son in a box and floated it in the river.

Adhiratha, the charioteer of Dhritarashtra, found the box. He and his wife Radha reared the child. No one knows this. He sent Karna to Parasurama for learning archery. Karna told a lie and informed Parasurama that he was a Brahmin by birth, because Parasurama took only Brahmin students for teaching archery. One day Parasurama kept his head on the lap of Karna and slept soundly. A Rakshasa assumed the form of a bee and bored the thigh of Karna. There was profuse bleeding. Karna did not even shake his body a bit, because he thought that his preceptor's sleep would be disturbed. The stream of blood gushed along the head of Parasurama. Parasurama woke up and said to Karna, "O vile wretch! You are certainly not a Brahmin. You are a Kshatriya. As you have told me a lie, you will forget the secrets of archery just at the time when it is most needed."

Karna came back to Radha's place. He became a friend of Duryodhana. There was rivalry between Karna and Arjuna. From the very beginning, Karna was friendly towards Duryodhana and inimical towards Arjuna. For his loyalty to Duryodhana, the latter made him king of Anga, thus removing from him the inferior status of the son of a charioteer. Duryodhana relied on Karna's prowess and skill in archery and his invincible armour or coat of mail to defeat Arjuna.

Arjuna was the son of Indra, and Karna the son of the Sun-god. Karna could only be defeated by Arjuna if the former were deprived of his armour and ear-rings. Therefore Indra appeared before Karna in the disguise of a Brahmin to get the armour and the ear-rings, when the twelve years of exile were over and the thirteenth year began.

The Sun-god knew the evil intention of Indra. He appeared in the form of a Brahmin in a dream to Karna and said in order to protect him, "O Karna! Indra himself is coming to you in the guise of a Brahmin to beg of you your ear-rings and armour. Do not give them to Indra. You cannot be killed by your opponents in the battlefield so long as you have the ear-rings and armour."

Karna said, "Who are you, sir? You seem to be much interested in my welfare." The Brahmin replied, "O Karna! I am the Sun-god (Surya). Do what I have told you. This will bring you supreme good."

Karna said, "I entreat you. Do not check me in doing what I desire. If Indra comes to me, I shall give him my ear-rings and armour. I will achieve great glory by offering the gift to him in the prescribed manner."

The Sun-god said, "What is the use of glory when one is dead? Only if you are alive, you can enjoy the glory. I again repeat what I have said. If you have the ear-rings and the coat of mail Arjuna cannot defeat you in battle, even if Indra himself becomes an arrow to hit you. These ear-rings and the armour will make you invincible in battle. Therefore do not give these to Indra."

Karna replied, "You are certainly caring for my good. Kindly forgive me. I do not fear death so much as I fear ungraciousness. If Indra comes for begging, I will give him even my life."

The Sun-god said, "If you wish to give Indra the ear-rings and the armour, give them to him on this condition. Ask him to give you in return the Sakti weapon which destroys all enemies." After saying this the Sun-god vanished.

Karna woke up from his sleep and thought deeply about the dream. He made a determination not to ask anything in return from Indra, for 'a gift is no gift if conditionally made.' Karna valued Truth much more than even his life.

Indra assumed the form of a Brahmin and approached Karna. Indra said to him, "O virtuous Karna of great liberality and fame! Give me alms."

Karna: O Brahmin! Shall I give you beautiful women who wear gold necklaces or wealth? I shall give you whatever you want.

The Brahmin: I do not wish to have these things. Cut the ear-rings and the coat of mail from your body and give them to me if you are devoted to Truth.

Karna consented to give Indra his coat of mail and the pair of ear-rings. He took the knife and proceeded to cut the coat of mail from his body.

Indra stopped him and said, "O Karna! I simply admire your liberality. There is none on the surface of this Earth who is equal to you in liberality. I am immensely pleased. Ask any boon you like. Do not hesitate."

Karna: O lord of gods! I do not want any boon in return. It is my duty to give you whatever you ask. This is my vow in life.

Indra: My child! Your selfless sacrifice and liberality excite my admiration and reverence for you. Pray, do ask any boon, you like. This is my duty to give you, as you are a high-souled personage.

Karna: Grant me, O noble one, that boon by which my liberality will increase daily. Let me not refuse to anybody anything that lies in my power to give.

Indra: O amiable Karna! You are already an embodiment of liberality. I grant this boon also. 'Let it be so.' Further I give you my Sakti weapon with which you can overcome one strong and heroic opponent. Here it is, my noble child! Take this.

Karna accepted this from the hands of Indra with joy. Then the generous-hearted and valiant Karna took a sharp knife, cut from his body the invulnerable coat of mail and gave it, wet with blood, to Indra. Thereupon he cut from his ears the ear-rings and gave them also to Indra. Indra was immensely pleased with Karna. He made Karna famous and resplendent among men and thought within himself that he did a very great service indeed to the Pandava brothers.

What a large and generous heart Karna had! He was famous for making gifts and so he had immortalised his name. He was willing to give even his life to the Brahmin (Indra), though the Sun-god advised him not to give the armour and ear-rings. He loved Truth more than his life. He stuck to the Truth even at the risk of his life. When he removed the coat of mail by cutting his limbs, even the stones would have melted. All who witnessed the act of Karna would have shed profuse tears.

O noble Karna! How did you develop such a generous and liberal heart! Certainly you have this heart through the grace of your father Surya and the Tapas of your mother Kunti. Ages have rolled on, centuries have passed and yet you live in our hearts. What Tapas did you do to obtain the grace of Surya?

Karna's valour was unparalleled. He would have killed Arjuna had it not been for the support of Lord Krishna. Karna was in no way inferior to Arjuna. Karna even excelled Arjuna. Glory to Karna, the superman of heroism and liberality, whose name will not be forgotten as long as this world and Mahabharata exist. He had earned undying fame and glory.

Yudhishthira thought that he was a very liberal man on the surface of the Earth and was puffed up with a little pride. Lord Krishna came to know of this as He was the Inner Ruler of all beings. He wanted to teach Yudhishthira a good lesson. One day he took Yudhishthira and Karna by the side of the Himalayas and converted two mountains into pure gold, through His Yogic power. Lord Krishna gave one mountain of gold to each of them and told them to use it in any manner they liked.

Yudhishthira was immensely pleased with the gift from Lord Krishna. He at once engaged some workmen to dig the mountain and distributed with his own hand, some gold daily for some months to all those people who came to him to get gold.

Karna hit upon another good plan to distribute his portion of the mountain of gold. He made a proclamation in the city that any one desiring to have gold could go and dig out from the mountain as much as he liked. The whole mountain was cleared within ten days.

Yudhishthira was still keeping his own share of gold. He was a bit niggardly. He did not possess that liberal heart which Karna had. When he saw that Karna's mountain of gold was distributed within ten days, he bent his head in shame. He found out that Lord Krishna wanted to test both and remove his pride.

He prostrated himself before Lord Krishna, admitted his fault and declared openly that Karna was an embodiment of liberality and that he himself was nothing before Karna with regard to this virtue.

✿ ✿ ✿

Karna was a great warrior. He was not, in any way, inferior to Arjuna. He fought furiously in the great battle of Mahabharata and killed countless soldiers and warriors. He aimed at Arjuna Naga Astra; Krishna saved Arjuna by sinking the chariot. Eventually he was killed by Arjuna but Karna is not dead—except in the physical sense. He still lives in the hearts of all souls, as the greatest generous man of all times.

Karna had no ambition for himself and was a selfless man. All throughout the struggle between the Kauravas and the Pandavas, he sided and strongly supported Duryodhana because, in his first serious contact with the Pandavas, the latter taunted him about his low birth and Duryodhana immediately made him king of Anga and removed the taint of low birth. As king of Anga, he could have withdrawn from the struggle between the Kauravas and the Pandavas and quietly ruled in his kingdom but his sense of loyalty urged him to support Duryodhana through thick and thin.

Again, after the thirteen years' exile of the Pandavas, Lord Sri Krishna Himself went to the Kauravas as ambassador to urge them to give their kingdom to the Pandavas but failed. Just when He was returning after the failure of His mission, He called Karna to Him and took him a brief way in His chariot and related to him, for the first time, the real truth about his birth,—how he was born and why he was abandoned. Lord Krishna reminded him of his real mother Kunti and of the fact that he was, in truth, the eldest of the Pandavas and that he would now take him to them and reveal the story of his birth. Gladly would they bow down to him, as their monarch; all the Pandavas would follow him; the kingship of the whole world would be his and the devotion of his younger brothers. Calmly, but firmly, Karna declined the offer of honour and happiness. Kunti had abandoned him and he could not, at that late stage, take up the broken ties of relationship between him and his brothers. Besides, he owed everything to Adhiratha and his wife Radha. They cared for him in his infancy, protected him in his childhood, guided him in his boyhood and trained him in his youth. He had married in the race of Adhiratha and had children. Family ties, affection and loyalty bound him to his adopted father and mother. He could not forsake them for anything Lord Krishna offered. He added 'I must not also forget my obligation and gratitude to Duryodhana. He made me a king long ago. He is largely depending on me in this cruel war and I have been elected to meet Arjuna. In these circumstances, O Lord! I must, humbly but firmly decline the honour. But not a word of this to the Pandavas. They must not know the story of my birth; else they will never fight against me or accept the kingdom. Besides, even if the kingdom were offered to me, I must again give it back to Duryodhana owing to my allegiance to him. Yudhishthira is in everyway a worthier king than Duryodhana and, with you on his side, the kingdom is practically theirs. I realise that Duryodhana, Dussasana, I, all of us, are bound to die in the great sacrificial battle.' With one humble prayer, he ended, 'O Lord, let this mighty host of

Kshatriyas die on that most sacred of all battlefields, Kurukshetra. And may Thou accomplish, on this spot, what Thou hast in mind and may the whole race of Kshatriyas attain to Heaven.'

A great man! Will there ever be another?

DRAUPADI—THE SYMBOL OF VIRTUES

Draupadi is a well known historical figure in the Mahabharata and is a familiar name in every Hindu household. She is cited even now, after five thousand years, as the embodiment of duty, charity, truth, devotion to Bhagavan, chastity, righteousness—in short, as the symbol of all the virtues. She lives in the mind and heart of every virtuous and dutiful woman of India as a model to follow and in that glorious galaxy of the most famous women of ancient India—Sita, Rukmini, Anasuya and a host of others—Draupadi has a prominent place. The story of Draupadi will bear repetition for ever.

Draupadi was the daughter of king Drupada. Her real name was 'Krishna.' She was really the incarnation of Goddess Shri (Lakshmi). In her last birth, she performed penances and when Mahadeva appeared before her and offered to grant her, her desire, she asked for the boon of a husband worthy of her; but she repeated this quickly five times. Mahadeva decreed that in her next birth she should have five husbands.

When Drona, through his disciples the Pandavas, deprived Drupada of half his kingdom as a punishment for his arrogance, Drupada performed a great sacrifice to obtain a son who would conquer Drona. At the sacrifice, as soon as the priest poured the sanctified butter on the fire, a boy sprang from the flames; and a voice cried 'This prince has been born for the destruction of Drona.' Then a lovely girl arose from the centre of the sacrificial platform and the same voice cried, 'This dark-complexioned girl will be the best of women and she will be the cause of the destruction of many Kshatriyas.' The boy was 'Dhrishtadyumna', the commander-in-chief of the army of the Pandavas at Kurukshetra, and 'Krishna' the beautiful, became the wife of the Pandavas.

After the Pandavas escaped from the house of lac, prepared by Duryodhana for their destruction and set on fire by Purochana, they became fugitives and for a time lived in the house of a Brahmana. It was here that Vyasa came to the princes, told them the history of Draupadi and advised them to go to the capital of Drupada, king of Panchalas. The Pandavas thus proceeded to Drupada's palace in the guise of Brahmanas and attended the Svayamvara of Draupadi.

Drupada had set up the most difficult feat in archery for the hero who would aspire to the hands of Draupadi. Great was the crowd of kings assembled to take part in the contest. The competition began. King after king failed even to fasten the string to the bow, while Draupadi looked on seeking her future lord. At last Karna rose, bent the bow, fastened the string and placed the arrow on the string. But at this juncture, Draupadi exclaimed 'I will not marry a *Suta*—son of charioteer as Karna was known to be.' Karna had to retire crest-fallen. Then Arjuna, who with his brothers was sitting among the Brahmanas, rose—a stripling—yet attractive and tall—fastened the string without effort and drawing it lightly sent five arrows with lightning speed to the mark. Flowers dropped from the sky, and while musicians and bards broke into soft music, Draupadi, royally clothed and smiling, approached Arjuna and garlanded him as her husband. The other warriors interposed and raised an objection that a Brahmana cannot marry a Kshatriya princess and they were on the point of rushing on the Pandavas; but Lord Krishna, who was in the company, reminded the guests that Draupadi had been won in a fair contest.

King Drupada had always intended that his daughter should marry Arjuna and when he learnt that the hero of the day was really Arjuna, his joy knew no bounds; but when he learnt that actually she should be the wife of the five brothers, he raised objections. A great discussion arose. Vyasa who arrived just then pacified Drupada by relating to him the past history of his daughter and how, through the blessings of Mahadeva, she was destined to be the wife of the Pandavas. Drupada at last agreed and sent back his sons-in-law with great wealth. In the meantime, Dhritarashtra on the advice of Bhishma, Drona and Vidura, allowed the Pandavas to have half the kingdom. They thus left the palace of Drupada for Khandavaprastha—the capital—with Draupadi.

One day, Narada came to see them at their new palace, advised them about maintaining unity among brothers and in order that there may not arise any quarrels amongst them, through having common wife, asked them to accept a rule that she should live with each of them by turn, and that when one of them was in her company, others should not interrupt them—the penalty being self-imposed exile into the forest for a year. Actually one of the brothers—Arjuna—had to undergo this penalty. As regards Draupadi, she conducted herself towards the brothers in such a way that none of them felt themselves slighted by her. Her devotion to all of them was impartial and exemplary.

While the Pandavas were living happily at Khandavaprastha, Yudhishthira performed Rajasuya Yajna which was attended by all kings and princes—including his cousins Duryodhana and the Kauravas. Duryodhana seeing all the prosperity of the Pandavas became jealous of them, then angry at them on account of some jokes played against him, plotted with his uncle Sakuni for their downfall. On the advice of Sakuni, he challenged Yudhishthira to play at dice. As is well-known, the noble prince lost everything, his wealth, kingdom, his brothers, himself and at last even his queen Draupadi to Sakuni, the wily gamester. All at once, the wicked Kauravas insulted Draupadi openly in the court, taunted her, humiliated her and heaped untold contempt on her. Dussasana went so far as to drag her by the hair, and attempted to outrage her modesty by pulling off her clothes. She was helpless—as all who were there assembled felt. Was she? No! She had yet one unfailing source of help—no less than Lord Krishna Himself! She appealed to Him, prayed to Him: "O Govinda! Thou that dwellest at Dvaraka—O Krishna!" Lord Krishna came immediately to her help, and standing hidden from all, covered her with clothes faster than Dussasana could pull them off. At last even Dussasana became tired and ashamed and sat down. Draupadi, a real Pativrata was saved through the grace of Lord Krishna!

Bhima unable to see the plight of Draupadi took a terrible oath, "Hear these words of a Kshatriya and having spoken them, if I do not accomplish them hereafter, let me go to hell! Tearing open the breast of this wicked Dussasana in open battle, if I do not drink his blood, let me not attain the path of my ancestors!" But Draupadi's ordeal was not over. Duryodhana insultingly uncovered his left thigh and invited her. Again Bhima shouted, "Let Bhima not attain Heaven if he does not break that thigh of Duryodhana in the great conflict." At last, wiser counsels prevailed and Dhritarashtra ordered the Pandavas to go into exile for twelve years and remain incognito for one year. Draupadi—a princess born and brought up—followed then unhesitatingly and willingly as her privilege. She never even cared to consider the hardships she would have to bear. She was urged by only one thought—service and duty to her husbands. She thus confirmed what Sita had initiated more than a thousand years before when she accompanied Sri Rama to the forest for fourteen years.

Thus began the twelve years of exile into the forest for the Pandavas and Draupadi. On the way, Draupadi, who had not tied into the usual knot her hair since Dussasana dragged her by them, covered her face with the dishevelled hair and wept—not for herself but for the wives of her enemies, who in fourteen years would be bewailing their husbands on that same road. Yudhishthira while in the forest was very much in grief because, as in the days of his kingship, he could not feed the Brahmins. He stood on the bank of the Ganga and prayed to the God, as revealed in the Sun, as the Giver of all in the world. Sun-god appeared before him and gave him a golden bowl which should never be empty of food so long as Draupadi held it in her hands without partaking of its contents. From thence onwards, the anxiety of Draupadi, about feeding the Pandavas, was removed and Yudhishthira was pleased that he could feed Brahmins to his heart's content. Everyday, when all had taken their food and Draupadi last of all, the bowl was empty. Everybody was reconciled to the hardships of the exile; but not Draupadi! She smarted under the insults heaped on her by the Kauravas and could not bear to see the Pandavas—whom she loved more than her own self—bear all these hardships and lead a life of idleness which she knew they hated inwardly.

At this time, Lord Krishna visited them and explained why He did not come to prevent the game of dice. To Him, Draupadi made a most piteous and reproachful appeal that she had been forsaken, during that awful ordeal in the court of Duryodhana, by her husbands, friends and everybody. 'Nor have I Thee, O Thou slayer of Madhu, for Ye all, beholding me treated so cruelly, sit still unmoved.' Lord Krishna consoled her and solemnly promised that she should again reign as queen. 'The heavens might fall or the waters of all the oceans dry up—but take it from Me—My words shall not fall to the ground.' But Draupadi, as an ally of Lord Krishna in the matter of destruction of the wicked Kshatriyas of the world, could not remain patient, knowing her husband Yudhishthira too well as all-forgiving even to his enemies. She must keep alive in his breast the fire of the wrongs done to her by the Kauravas and, therefore, you find her still urging him not to forgive the wrongs they had suffered, to wreak vengeance on his enemies, to secure for their sons the rightful heritage which would still have been theirs but for the treachery of Sakuni. This drew forth from Yudhishthira an admirable discourse on forgiveness, on charity, on the practice of virtues for their own sake, which everybody in these days would do well to learn by heart and repeat and practice everyday.

During the period of twelve years of exile, many learned and famous ascetics and sages like Vidura, Vyasa, Lord Krishna, Markandeya, Narada, etc., visited the Pandavas, and made their exile pleasant and happy as far as possible. The Kauravas, of course, tried their level best in the other direction but all their efforts came to nothing. During all this period, Draupadi served the Pandavas unhesitatingly, devotedly and placed their happiness and comfort above her own. One incident is worth recording here as an indication that Lord Krishna was ever watching her interests and of the Pandavas. Duryodhana managed to obtain the good graces of the great sage Durvasa by devoted service and sent him with all his numerous disciples to the Pandavas unexpectedly at dead of night. Durvasa arrived. Yudhishthira welcomed him with due respect and requested him to take bath in the river nearby and be ready to break their fast after the long and arduous journey. In the meantime, Yudhishthira went inside and consulted Draupadi regarding the arrangements for feeding hundreds of ascetics who had accompanied Durvasa. But Draupadi had already partaken of the food and bowl given them by the Sun-god was empty. Yudhishthira got frightened that he would fail in his word to Durvasa and in his duty to feed the Brahmanas and guests. But Draupadi rose to the occasion and advised him not to worry. She earnestly prayed to Lord Krishna to come to her help in this hour of need. He came, asked for the bowl and found a very minute particle of food sticking to the side. This satisfied Him and at once the sage and his retinue felt abundantly fed. How would it be otherwise when the Lord Himself was satisfied?

When the twelve years passed, the time came for one more year's exile in secret. The Pandavas decided to take service, under different disguises, in the palace of Virata, king of Vidarbha. Draupadi became a Sairandhri—a superior maid-servant and companion—and cheerfully prayed Yudhishthira not to worry about her. Here more than ten months passed uneventfully.

One day as she was plucking the flowers in the garden, Kichaka, the brother-in-law of Virata saw her and fell madly in love and would not listen to wiser counsels. In vain, Sairandhri implored him to desist, as she was the wedded wife of Gandharvas and to love her was courting disaster. At last Kichaka persuaded his sister, queen Sudeshna, to send Draupadi to his house on some pretext. Draupadi refused. Sudeshna insisted. Draupadi, at last, after praying to Surya to protect her, went to Kichaka's house and when the latter began to molest her, she ran away to the king's court for protection. Kichaka followed her and dragged her by the hair and kicked her in the very presence of the king. A demon appointed by Surya to protect Draupadi, however, flung Kichaka away and thus Draupadi was saved.

But what were the Pandavas doing all this while, when Draupadi was being molested in their presence? Yudhishthira was playing dice with Virata in whose presence all these events had occurred; but he remained unmoved. Bhima—who was passing as Ballava the cook—became furious and forgetting that he would be betrayed, went out to uproot a tree to kill Kichaka. Yudhishthira calmed him and cried to him 'Are you looking for faggots for fuel, O cook! If so, please look for them in the forests.'

Draupadi now addressed the king himself and reproached him for allowing her to be insulted in this way in his very presence. Virata, however, who was afraid of Kichaka and partly because he was Sudeshna's brother, took up a neutral attitude. The courtiers were on the side of Kichaka and began to praise the beauty of Sairandhri. But Draupadi's words, though addressed to the king, were really intended for Yudhishthira. He knew it and therefore thus gravely rebuked her: 'O Sairandhri! It is not meet that you stay here. Go and take shelter in the apartments of the queen who will surely protect you. The wives of heroes cheerfully bear affliction for the sake of their husbands, whatever their faults. Your Gandharvas, of whom you are the wedded wife, will surely and, in due course, avenge your present wrongs. It seems to me that they are of opinion that the present is not the opportune time to interfere. O Sairandhri! You are ignorant of the timeliness of things and therefore you are now interrupting the king in his play. Go now. The Gandharvas, in their own time, will surely take the life of him who has insulted you.'

Draupadi, unable to bear the insults of Kichaka and the indirect but none-the-less the bitter rebuke of Yudhishthira, replied passionately: 'It seems to me that, they who have wedded me are very kind to others only and as the eldest of them is given to the play of dice, I am to bear all these insults and oppression.'

That night she secretly went to Bhima, roused him from sleep and poured out to him, in bitter terms, all her grievances—"How can I bear this life, seeing my husbands—born princes, rulers and great heroes as they were—in menial occupations in a stranger's house? I myself was born the daughter of a king and am the queen; but look at my hands—all bearing the marks of hard toil and of pounding unguents for a far lesser queen." Bhima took her sweet hands and clasped them to his face, bewailed his own helplessness and passionately implored her to control her grief for a short while and said: 'For only a half a month be patient.' But Draupadi knew quite well that even in this remaining fortnight, she would not be safe from Kichaka and declared sternly, 'Unless Kichaka is killed, I am never safe and if you don't kill him, then tomorrow I will kill myself and so preserve my chastity which you, my husband, are not prepared to protect. There is no other course open to me. In either case, there is blame coming to you—whether Kichaka tries to molest me—because you could not protect me—or I kill myself because you thought your own safety more precious than my life!' Bhima promised to do all he could to protect her and bade her to make an appointment with Kichaka in a deserted temple outside the city.

The next day, Bhima met him and strangled him to death. Draupadi, with pretended tears, gave out that, while she was keeping the appointment with Kichaka, her Gandharva husband came and killed him.

In due course, the Pandavas could again, after thirteen years, come forth and take their place in the world. Almost at this stage, it may be thought that Draupadi's active part in the destruction of the wicked Kauravas closed. By her constant reminders and urgings to the Pandavas, she had so far kept alive in their hearts the wrongs of the Kauravas and set them firm in their resolution to demand that the Kauravas keep to their promise to give them half the kingdom. She knew, in her heart of hearts, that Duryodhana would not yield and they would have to wage a war to put finally an end to the wickedness of the Kauravas. She knew that, while her husbands and sons were fighting with their lives at stake, her duty was by their side to help them, encourage them and comfort them. Thus, the famous battle of Kurukshetra began and ended in a glorious victory for the Pandavas and Draupadi could again reign as queen!

Sometime after this, she met Satyabhama—the pet spouse of

Lord Sri Krishna and—and in an earnest discussion between them regarding the duties of an Arya consort, she set forth in a discourse which is even today handed down from mother to daughter as an ideal which every women should aspire to attain. Thus, both by example and precept, throughout her life, she led a life of virtue, chastity, truth, righteousness and devotion to duty and to the husband in a manner unparalleled in this world and entitles her to sit in the galaxy of other famous Arya women of this world.

India is honoured by such women and India is still the land where the ancient holy traditions of Aryans have survived on account of such women as Draupadi. Draupadi did not perform any Tapasya, any sacrifice or penance in the accepted sense of the terms; but her life combined all the three. Hence in her dire needs, Lord Krishna Himself ran to her help, once in the court of Dhritarashtra and again in the forests when Durvasa came to visit the Pandavas. On numerous occasions, He constantly saw her and encouraged and advised her. A woman whom Lord Krishna honoured is worthy of honour universally.

APPENDICES

MORALS

Mahabharata is one of the greatest books of the world. Its greatness is in all directions—it is great from the point of view of Ethics, from the point of view of Philosophy, from the point of view of Literature. It is not proposed to discuss here the merits of the epic as a monument of literature. From the point of view of philosophy, it stands unique as it contains what is now known as the 'Bhagavad Gita'—which brings together the essence of the 'philosophy of life' of the ancient Aryans and stands as the foundation of the Hindu religion of the present day. Many books and commentaries of excellent merit are written on this subject. There remains another side of the picture as presented by the Mahabharata—the merits from the ethical point of view. The stories from Mahabharata given in the foregoing chapters of this book give some of the important moral lessons of conduct and behaviour, in different circumstances of life. Here it is proposed to classify them according to virtues.

Throughout the Mahabharata, the one dominating idea is to inspire into the reader the IMPORTANCE OF ONE'S DUTY in different circumstances of life. But duty is a very general term. In short, duty may be defined as one's conduct in life. As everybody knows, one's duty varies in its relation from person to person. All of us have our duty towards our father, mother, towards our Guru, towards persons we generally come across in our everyday walk of life, towards wife, children, towards the king, etc. Each of the duties are called by a different name—each of them is a Virtue.

You have all read the Bhagavad Gita and know the circumstances of its origin. Arjuna, at the last moment, when his chariot was in the midst of the opposing armies, wanted to throw away all his weapons and retire from the field rather than fight his own grandfather, Bhishma, his Guru Drona and his cousins. Above all, he felt for Bhishma. Arjuna loudly lamented: "He is my grandfather—he on whose lap I used to climb in my days of childhood and call him 'father'—I cannot fight this high-souled and illustrious grandfather. What is the worth of victory to me if they perish—my dear ones— Bhishma, Drona, etc." Lord Krishna reminded him: "O Dhananjaya! Do not forget the eternal duty of the Kshatriyas that they should fight, protect their subjects and perform sacrifices—*all without motive.*" That is the keynote running through the whole of Mahabharata—DO YOUR DUTY. Do not consider your own feelings, your selfish motives, your own life. Do your duty without looking to the fruits or consequences of your actions and God will be with you.

The one outstanding example of this guiding principle is Bhishma, who stands above all in this respect. Was God with him? Let us see. When after the great battle of Kurukshetra, Yudhishthira was crowned king, he had one occasion to go to Sri Krishna. He found the Lord seated in meditation—all abstracted and quite unaware of the presence of Yudhishthira or his worship. After waiting a long while Krishna saw Yudhishthira who asked Him why He should have to practise Yoga and meditation. Kesava gently replied: "No, no! It is not Yoga or meditation in the ordinary sense. Far away, on the battlefield of Kurukshetra, Bhishma was thinking of Me. Hence my mind was also concentrated on him!" What a glorious thought and reward! When a worshipper fixes his mind and his thoughts on God, God thinks of him! When, at last, the time of Bhishma's departure from this world came, Lord Krishna himself was present and Bhishma addressed Him thus: "Save me, O God of gods! I humbly surrender myself to Thee! Do Thou give me permission to depart from this world. If Thou permit me, I shall attain the highest Heaven." Lord Krishna sweetly replied: "I willingly give thee leave, O Bhishma! You will attain the highest Heaven you desire, O thou of great splendour, who hast not been guilty of a single transgression in this world." How many of us are worthy of this certificate from the Highest? Yet there is no mention of Bhishma ever doing Tapascharya in a forest, or undergoing penances on the bank of the Ganga or practising Yoga and meditation. Still, he was the only one whom Lord Krishna himself considered as worthy of the highest form of praise: "Not guilty of a single transgression in this world." The simple explanation is that the whole life of Bhishma—every action or conduct in life embodied the practice of Yoga. Keeping perfect faith in God, he performed his duty in all circumstances without exception. That is Duty.

Let us consider Mahabharata from this aspect and review some of the incidents in the lives of the personalities in that epic.

Filial Piety: While Santanu, Bhishma's father, wanted to marry Satyavati, Bhishma agreed willingly to renounce his title to ascend the throne after Santanu; not only this—he vowed: "I have with great pleasure given up my right to the throne. I shall now settle the question of my children. O fisherman! From today, I shall for ever and ever observe, both in spirit and to the letter, the vow of celibacy and may God help me in keeping to the vow!" The heavens cried: 'This is Bhishma (the Terrible)!' Yet, Bhishma at the very threshold of life was giving up what most men hold most precious and incidentally beginning the life 'without a single transgression in this world.'

True to Vow: When several years later, both the sons of Satyavati died without children and the line of Bharata was on the point of extinction, Satyavati—broken-hearted—begged Bhishma to take the throne and marry the widows of his step-brothers. His friends, ministers of state and relatives begged him. The crown and wedded happiness were at his feet begging him to pick up. No. His vow stood between him and the crown. Only his vow! But to Bhishma, truth was more than his own life. He replied: 'O Satyavati! Indeed, your advice is no doubt binding on me and it is also prescribed by our scriptures. But you know my vow and the circumstances in which it was taken by me. I repeat the vow I took then. I am prepared to renounce the three worlds, Heaven itself or anything greater than that; but TRUTH I shall never renounce.' A great temptation was before Bhishma—which few could have resisted—but he was proof against it.

Resistance to Temptation: This is a great virtue. Bhishma had it in full measure. So also Karna, Yudhishṭhira, Drona, etc., in the same degree. After Lord Krishna had failed in his mission to the Kauravas to induce them to give half the kingdom to their cousins, He took Karna a part of the way in His chariot and revealed to him his real origin—and if he so wished he could reign as the eldest brother of the Pandavas instead of

Yudhishthira. Karna refused: "For good or evil, for better or worse, I have cast my lot with the Kauravas and I cannot forsake them, O Govinda, in their direst need on the battlefield of Kurukshetra."

Yudhishthira had also to pass through similar tests. Once, when, while the Pandavas were passing their lives in exile in the forests, Duryodhana who had come there in order to persecute them was himself caught as prisoner by the Gandharvas. But Yudhishthira sent Arjuna and Bhima to liberate him. Chitrasena, the king of Gandharvas, explained to Yudhishthira that Duryodhana had come to humiliate the Pandavas. Yet Yudhishthira, instead of allowing the Gandharvas to destroy him, set him free and said, 'O brother, never again do such mean things. Go back to your kingdom and reign in peace.' Yudhishthira knew that he had taken the vow of passing thirteen years in exile and could not reign as king by destroying Duryodhana without breaking his vow. Nor was it his nature to take undue advantage of his foe's helpless position. If he had to fight Duryodhana, he would do it on equal terms.

On three distinct occasions, gods themselves put heavy temptations in his way in order to test his virtues. Once, when all his brothers had been killed by the Yaksha he chose that Nakula should live rather than his own brothers—Bhima and Arjuna—'I choose that Nakula, son of Madri, should live because abstention from injury is the highest virtue and therefore I do desire that neither of my father's wives should be childless.' The Yaksha was so pleased that he revived all the brothers. Again at the gate of Heaven, Indra—Lord of the heavens—prohibited a poor dog accompanying Yudhishthira. 'Why, O Yudhishthira! Do you care so much for a *dog*? You have attained immortality and a condition equal to mine even—the unparalleled success—and there are now before you all the joys of Heaven!' Yudhishthira gently replied: 'There is no pleasure for me in the happiness and joys purchased at the expense of a dog. It is given that the abandonment of one that is devoted is as much sinful as the sin of slaying a Brahmana. Not even for the sake of my own happiness shall I cast away this dog.' The dog was no other than god Dharma himself—who then blessed his son. But the gods had not finished with Yudhishthira. A third temptation was before him, viz., a sight of Duryodhana sitting in the Heaven while his own brothers Karna, Bhima, Arjuna, etc., his queen Draupadi, Draupadi's sons, were nowhere to be seen. He insists on taking his abode by their side—wherever it be. When at last he finds them in the dark regions, undergoing unbearable agonies and when he hears them, all praying him most piteously to stay there just for one moment longer—because his presence eased their torments—he coolly told his guide from Heaven: 'Return to them who have sent you here and tell them that I shall not return to them but shall stay here, since by my presence here, my beloved ones are comforted. What is Heaven to me where *they* are not? *This* is my heaven. *That* is not.' A more steadfast courage there never was! Courage to resist such temptations even at the expense of one's own welfare!

Truth: To pick and choose all the incidentals pointing to this great principle is almost an impossible task. It is reading the great epic itself. Still, a few instances may be given. 'Be true to yourself' is the one and the most sacred message of Mahabharata.

Bhishma spoke the Truth in his advice to Yudhishthira in this wise. Listen to his noble words: "Truth is an eternal duty. One should reverentially bow to Truth. There is nothing like truth as the highest refuge. Truth is duty. It is penance. It is Yoga. It is the eternal Brahman. Truth is considered as a sacrifice of a very high order. Everything is based on truth. The forms of truth are: impartiality, self-control, forgiveness, modesty, endurance, goodness, renunciation, contemplation, dignity, fortitude, compassion and abstention from injury. There is nothing higher than truth and no sin more heinous than an untruth. In short, truth is the very foundation of righteousness. Once upon a time, a thousand sacrifices were weighed against 'truth' and 'truth' weighed heavier than all the thousand sacrifices put together." Bhishma was a monument of truth and therefore his words about 'truth' should count against all.

When Arjuna transgressed the rule laid down by Narada that, when Draupadi was in the company of any of the Pandavas, the other brothers should not interrupt them, he—according to the rule—had to undergo the penalty of an exile in the forests. Yudhishthira realising that Arjuna broke into his room out of sheer necessity, advised him to desist from the purpose and not to go. Arjuna replied to him: 'I have heard from yourself that quibbling is not permitted in the discharge of duty. I cannot depart from Truth, even if it means as exile from you for a long period. Truth is my weapon.' For the sake of 'truth', he willingly went into exile.

After the Pandavas had been sent to the thirteen years' exile, Bhima urged Yudhishthira they should regain their kingdom instead of wasting their time in the forests. 'Virtue is not enough' he said. 'It is the duty of Kshatriyas to fight. Let us wage war against Duryodhana and reconquer our kingdom. This is infinitely better than sitting in the forests instead of in our palace which you have lost.' Yudhishthira replied: 'I fully know that I am to blame for all your misfortunes. I know that I lost self-control and brought you to ruin. But I have given my word to stand by the result of the dice-play and I must stick to this. My promise can never be untrue. I regard the virtue of truth as higher than life or Heaven itself. Kingdom, sons, fame, wealth—they do not come up even to a fraction of truth.' Yudhishthira preferred thirteen long years of exile to an untruth.

Loyalty: When the war between the Pandavas and Kauravas became inevitable, it tried the conscience of Bhishma and Drona and Karna also very sore. But they never wavered. Bhishma knew that righteousness was on the side of the Pandavas. They had carried out their part of the contract. They also were far better in their conduct of life than the wicked Kauravas. How could they fight against Pandavas? As Drona piteously said, Arjuna was dearer to him than his son. Bhishma, above all others, felt it very much. He had to fight against his own grandsons. Above all he was devoted to Lord Sri Krishna. How could he raise his arm against Him? He (Bhishma) was an embodiment of duty, righteousness and justice, which were all on the side of the Pandavas and it was ordained that he should fight against them. Yet the example of Bhishma, as a monument of duty, never shone more brightly than in this struggle. Drona knew that in the war he would have to fight against Arjuna whom he himself had trained and loved above all. Karna—after he was made aware of the real origin of his birth had an opportunity—a most tempting one—to go to the Pandavas and he also knew that if he stuck to the Kauravas, he would have to fight his own brother Arjuna. But none of them hesitated for a moment. To them, DUTY was of supreme importance. And for the Kshatriyas, the duty to fight for their king was the supreme law. Because all the three had sworn allegiance to their king Dhritarashtra and his sons,—their bodies, their might, skill in weapons,—all these—were at the disposal of the Kauravas. They must repay, even with their lives, the debt which they owed to the king. But their feelings, their love, inclination, were with the Pandavas and Lord Krishna. They never hesitated, even though they knew that they had to fight against Lord Krishna. Did they perchance hope that they might even fall on the battlefield at the hands of the Lord Himself and thus die? Nothing would be dearer to them.

Forgiveness and Virtues: Listen to these noble words of Yudhishthira on these two subjects. Draupadi bitterly resented the insults heaped on her by the Kauravas and after they had gone to the forests, she urged on Yudhishthira to take action to avenge her and never to forgive the Kauravas. This brought forth from Yudhishthira an admirable discourse on forgiveness, "If a man who has received abuses from another speaks to him in the same strain, if a man returns injury to injury, or a father kills his son or a son kills his father, how can there be any progress in this world where so much unrighteousness prevails? One should forgive every injury—no matter what kind—O Draupadi! That man is indeed a wise one who does not give way to anger, who shows forgiveness even when insulted, oppressed or abused by another. Forgiveness is Divine. Forgiveness is Truth. Forgiveness is potential ascetic merit. It is asceticism, penances and holy. Forgiveness is the foundation of the world. The man of wisdom should ever forgive—when he is capable of forgiving everything—for he attains Brahman."

But Draupadi was not satisfied with this kind of barren merits of virtue. She asks, 'What is the use of virtue, if the virtuous are to suffer while the wicked prosper?'

Gently, but none-the-less firmly, Yudhishthira answers her: "O Draupadi! You speak hastily without realising what you say. Your question looks as if it might have come from godless persons. Never, never act with a desire to get the suitable fruits out of your actions. I give away because it is my duty to give. I act because it is my duty. I sacrifice for the sake of duty. I act virtuously, not because I desire the fruits of virtue, but because I do not wish to transgress the ordinances of the Vedas and thereby I follow the path trodden by the holy men. O Draupadi! The man who wishes to reap the fruits of his actions is a trader in virtue. He is by nature mean. Never allow such a blot on your good name. It is true that every act has its own consequences, results and fruits and therefore if you act virtuously, the results must be good and, in the long run, must end prosperously to the virtuous. But who knows of the divine dispensation of God? Therefore though you may not see the fruits of virtue, they may be blessings in disguise. You should not doubt God's actions. You should perform your sacrifices with a will, practise charity and forgiveness with modesty and without insolence. Acts in this world have their fruits and virtue is eternal. Therefore dispel all your doubts about virtues. Reflecting upon all this, do not give way to scepticism—doubts regarding the merits of virtues. Acquire faith in them. Above all, do not slander God who is the Lord of the universe. Strive to know Him. Bow down to Him humbly, O Draupadi! Never disregard that Supreme Being through whose divine grace alone man may acquire immortality through piety."

Devotion to the Guru: This is a holy duty enjoined on all Hindus and it was one of the most prominent features of our ancestors. Devotion to the Guru has great merits. When the Kauravas and Pandavas were placed under Drona, Ekalavya—a son of a neighbouring king—came to Drona who however refused to take him as his pupil on account of his low birth. Nothing daunted, Ekalavya, far from being angry, reverently touched the feet of Drona and went into the forest. There he made an exact image of Drona, worshipped it as his Guru and practised before it the use of such weapons as he desired. He acquired thus, by his reverence to his Guru and devotion to his purpose, such skill that he surpassed even the royal pupils (princes) of Drona.

To the same degree was the reverence of Arjuna towards Drona and also devotion to his purpose. That is why Drona had a fond affection for Arjuna. Much can be achieved by diligent devotion to a purpose. One day Drona asked his pupils to shoot at a bird seated in a tree. First Yudhishthira took up the bow. Drona asked him: 'What do you see?' The reply was 'I see the tree, the leaves, fruits, you, my brothers and the bird.' Drona rejoined: 'You are not fit to shoot at the bird.' Thus in turn he asked all of them and—invariably— about the same reply was given. Then came the turn of Arjuna. 'What do you see?' 'I see only the head of the bird.' 'Shoot', commanded Drona, full of joy.

Devotion to Husband: You have all, probably, read the story of Draupadi, Savitri, Damayanti and other great women, who attained to this glory through their devotion to their husbands. To make the picture complete, Gandhari is an example of most supreme devotion to her husband. When she learnt that she was to marry Dhritarashtra—the blind king of the Kauravas—she blind-folded her eyes and did not open them to the last. As a result of this ascetic life, she had acquired such powers that she could see without opening her eyes. There is a scene in the Mahabharata in which Gandhari, with the aid of clairvoyance, piteously described to Lord Krishna how, step by step, both the sides of battle of Kurukshetra lay slaughtered, how the bodies of her sons were burning on the funeral pyre and vehemently asks the Lord why He did not prevent the slaughter of the Kurus. Unable to bear the agony at the loss of her sons, at last she raises her voice and denounces Him. Such is the power which ladies may acquire by devotion to their husbands.

Everyone should, if possible, read the two *Parvas* (parts) Santi Parva and Anusasana Parva of the Mahabharata—as they are the most important parts of the Epic. They contain the advices given by Bhishma to Yudhishthira. Some of the points are the highest order, contain the most profound thoughts and fundamental principles of Dharma. Many of them have already been given in the foregoing pages. Thus when he speaks of the duties of a king he warns Yudhishthira against oppressing the weak.

"God has given power in the hands of certain persons (like kings) in order to protect the weak. Please always regard, O Yudhishthira, the eyes of the weak, raised to you for help, as unbearable. Do not therefore come into hostile contact with the weak. The weak are always subject to humiliation. Take care that their eyes do not burn you. Weakness is, in the long run, more powerful than the greatest power, because if you do not come to their help and relieve them, it is a sin on you. If a person who has been humiliated or oppressed fails to obtain protection and relief, divine chatisement overtakes those who, having the power to do it, did not go to the help of the weak. Do not, therefore, while in enjoyment of power and wealth, oppress the weak or take away their wealth. The tears shed by weeping men, afflicted by falsehoods, destroys those who utter the falsehoods."

The greatness of Bhishma, as a teacher of the first order, lies in his capacity to distinguish between reality and appearance, the permanent and transient, in his shrewed observations regarding the path to success in life and other cognate subjects.

Penances: He says, 'Vedas say that penances are higher than sacrifices. What are penances? Listen to me, O prince! Abstention from injury, truthfulness in speech, action and thought, benevolence, compassion,—these are considered as penances and not the emaciation of the body.' He gives the story of King Janaka and Sulabha and points out the moral in the words of Janaka: 'Outwardly I am a king, enjoying wealth and pleasure which are considered as bondage; but I have cut them off by the sword of renunciation.' A man may renounce only outwardly and not inwardly which is more difficult. A Sannyasin is to be recognised not by his saffron-coloured cloth but by his steady mind and destruction of all desires. A man may be a Yogi in any dress or any walk of life—a king like Janaka, a barber like Sena, a weaver like Kabir, a shoe-maker like Raidas, of more recent times. Surrounded by wealth, wife, children, he may be without attachment to them, except that of attachment as to any other person. Those only are honoured by God who are Yogis in heart. They are the true Sannyasins.

How may a man overcome difficulties? Asked Yudhishthira of Bhishma to which the relpy is: 'By not deceiving others, by restraining oneself by reasonable restrictions, by controlling worldly desires, one may overcome all difficulties. They who do not retaliate when injured or insulted by others, who give and never take, succeed in life. The successful men never commit any sin, either in word, thought or deed, always speak the truth—even at the risk of life—never deceive and always spend their wealth for the benefit of others.'

Fundamentals of True Religion: The practice of universal compassion is the true religion. That man, who regards all creatures as his own self, completely controls anger, greed, desires, never injures another and ever speaks the truth, is the follower of true religion and attains the highest happiness. This, in brief, is the rule of righteousness. Abstention from cruelty is the highest religion, highest form of self-control and highest gift. Gifts made in sacrifices, ablutions in sacred waters, gifts made according to scriptures—all these do not come to the standard of abstention from cruelty. The man who abstains from cruelty is the father and mother of all creatures.

When asked who is the God of the world, Bhishma, in reply, recited, THE ONE THOUSAND SACRED NAMES OF VAASUDEVA (Vishnusahasranama).

Lastly, the advice of Bhishma on the importance of a man doing his duty—whatever it be—and general conduct in life, are words which one should never forget even for a moment.

Concerning DUTY in general term, he gives the instance of a king who was seized by a Rakshasa. But the king defied the Rakshasa. He asserted: "In my kingdom, there are no thieves, no criminals, no drunkards, no sin or sinners. My people are engaged always in their respective duties as ordained by religion, scriptures and traditions and are content. I have always striven to support the helpless, the weak, the aged, the sick, the forlorn, the poor, the helpless widows and children. I have spent my life and shed my blood for the welfare of my people and for justice to them and I am happy to say that my people have blessed me. Though you have possession of my body for the moment, I defy you to hold me much longer." The Rakshasa immediately let him go. The king could fearlessly defy him because he had done his duty. A man who does his duty—however humble or exalted—need have no fear. It is only when you have forgotten or neglected to do your duty that any harm can come to you. People are timid or troubled, if they are guilty of wrong actions or thoughts. It is these who invite the enemy to take hold of you in your weak moments. Do your duty conscientiously and fearlessly and God will be with you for ever and ever. This is the message of Bhishma to Yudhishthira and the whole Mahabharata is a masterly exposition of this one great principle of life—DUTY. Do your duty and God will always be with you.

यत्र योगेश्वरः कृष्णो यत्र पार्थो धनुर्धरः ।
तत्र श्रीर्विजयो भूतिर्ध्रुवा नीतिर्मतिर्मम ॥

Wherever is Krishna, the Lord of Yoga, wherever is Partha the archer, there is also prosperity, victory and happiness and firm policy; such is my conviction.

Gita Ch. XVIII – 78

In short wherever is Righteousness (Arjuna), there is also the Lord Krishna, and there you will find prosperity, success and happiness.

WHO IS WHO IN MAHABHARATA

Abhimanyu: Son of Arjuna by Subhadra. He married Uttara, daughter of king Virata. He was the father of Parikshit. When he was a lad of eighteen only, he fought bravely against seven commanders single-handed. He was put to death by them while he was lying unconscious.

Adhiratha: The charioteer of the Kauravas and foster-father of Karna. He found Karna when he was a baby in a basket floating on the river and brought him up as his own son. His wife's name was Radha.

Amba: The eldest daughter of the king of Kasi. Bhishma brought her with her two sisters by force to be given in marriage to Vichitravirya. She was sent away at her own request to marry king of Salva. As however the king refused to marry her, she asked Bhishma to marry her. Bhishma also refused and hence she tried her best to compass the death of Bhishma. She was born as Shikandi in her next birth to king Drupada and fought on the side of the Pandavas and caused the fall of Bhishma.

Ambika, Ambalika: Daughters of king of Kasi and younger sisters of Amba. Both of them were married to Vichitravirya but since he died without leaving any issue, Satyavati their mother-in-law, summoned sage Vyasa and by Niyoga system begot Dhritarashtra and Pandu on Ambika and Ambalika respectively.

Angirasa: He was the father of Brihaspati. He was a Brahmarishi.

Arjuna: The third son of Kunti, begotten by god Indra, the bravest of the Pandavas, the best bowman and the brightest star in the galaxy of warriors. Most favourite pupil of Drona and constant companion of Lord Krishna. Beloved by Him so much that He gave His sister Subhadra in marriage and elected him to be the fittest person to hear the Gita and have the holiest *Visvarupa Darshan*. He won Draupadi at the *Svayamvara* by performing the most brilliant feat in archery. During his wanderings (self imposed exile owing to breach of a rule) he married Ulupi, Chitrangada and Subhadra. He lived incognito in the court of king Virata as an eunuch, teaching dancing and music to princess Uttara and was called 'Brihannala'. Bhishma and Karna, the two great warriors on the Kauravas' side, were killed by Arjuna.

Asvatthama: The only son of Drona. He had a jewel on his head. He is a Brahmachari and Chiranjeevi. He is a great warrior. He murdered Dhristadyumna and the five sons of Draupadi while asleep at night. He was put to disgrace for this inglorious act by being deprived of the jewel. On hearing the death of his father, Asvatthama wanted to make the Pandava line extinct. He discharged a terrible weapon into Uttara's womb. The child in Uttara's womb was saved by Lord Krishna by His Yogic powers. Hence the child was named Parikshit.

Babhruvahana: Son of Arjuna by Chitrangada. He seized the sacrificial horse of Yudhishthira (escorted by Arjuna) and slew Arjuna in battle. But afterwards Arjuna was restored to life by Ulupi.

Baka: A demon killed by Bhima.

Balarama: Elder brother of Krishna; an incarnation of the great serpent Adisesha. He vanished from the world in the form of a serpent which came out of his body and entered the ocean.

Bharata: Son of Dushyanta and Sakuntala. The Bharata race and the Epic Mahabharata takes its name from him. India is called as "*Bharatavarsha*" after his name. His decendants are called as Bharatas. Dhritarashtra, Pandu and the Pandavas, Parikshit and Janamejaya the great grandsons of the Pandavas are known as Bharatas.

Bhima: The second of the Pandavas begotten on Kunti by god Vayu. He was famous for his strength and swiftness and for his skill in the mace. The principal events of his life are his conquest of Jarasandha, the fearful vow uttered by him against Duryodhana and Dussasana and fulfilling the same to the letter in the great war and also his killing of Kichaka and Bakasura.

Bhishma: Son of Santanu and goddess Ganga. Grand-uncle of the Pandavas and the Kauravas. He was a saintly warrior, adviser, teacher, statesman and patriarch of the Bharata family. He was an embodiment of truth, justice, duty, loyalty and sacrifice. He was famous for his valour and lifelong celibacy. In fact the most outstanding figure in Mahabharata.

Chitrangada: Handsome daughter of Chitrabhanu, the king of Kalinga. Arjuna fell in love with her and married her during his wanderings and had a son by her known as Babruvahana.

Daruka: Charioteer of Krishna.

Daussasani: Son of Dussasana. He, with Jayadratha and others, fought with Abhimanyu.

Devaka: Brother of Ugrasena, who was the father of Kamsa; Krishna's maternal grandfather. He had a daughter by a Sudra wife who was given in marriage to Vidura.

Dhaumya: A Brahmin priest of the Pandavas.

Dhristadyumna: Son of king Drupada; brother-in-law of the Pandavas. He was the commander of the Pandavas army.

Dhritarashtra: The blind son of Ambika by Vyasa and the father of one hundred Kaurava brothers—Duryodhana, etc. Because he was blind, Pandu his younger brother became king and ruled over the kingdom.

Draupadi: Known as 'Krishna'. Incarnation of Goddess Shri. Daughter of king Drupada and the common wife of the Pandavas. She underwent difficult and various mental and physical sufferings, troubles and vexations with unrivalled fortitude and patience. She was a model of duty, charity, truth, devotion to Bhagavan, chastity and righteousness. She considered service and duty to her husbands as the foremost and unhesitatingly and quite willingly followed her husbands to the forest. During the period of incognito life, she lived by the name 'Sairandhri' in the palace of king Virata, as an attendant to the queen.

Drona: Son of Bharadvaja—a Brahmin. He was a master of

the Dhanurveda (the science of archery). Instructed the Pandavas and Kauravas in the use of arms. He was a partial incarnation of Brihaspathi, the preceptor of the Devas. He was absorbed unto him in the end.

Drupada: King of Panchalas. He was forced to lose half the kingdom at the hands of Drona—through his disciple Arjuna—for having offended Drona once. He performed a sacrifice and, as a result, secured a son, Dhristadyumna by name, to slay Drona and Draupadi a daughter to marry Arjuna.

Duryodhana: Eldest of the hundred sons of Dhritarashtra. From the very beginning he entertained hatred and jealousy towards the Pandavas and tried to do them as much harm as possible. He also tried to burn them alive but failed. He sought the help of Sakuni and defeated Yudhishthira in a game of dice; and when they (the Pandavas) were helpless, he openly, in court, in the presence of respectable elders and Rishis, insulted Draupadi. He forced Yudhishthira to go into the forest with his brothers and Draupadi for thirteen years. As the result of his denial of the legitimate share of the kingdom, when the Pandavas completed the exile, the war broke out. He was finally killed by Bhima.

Dussala: The only daughter of Dhritarashtra and Gandhari. She was wedded to Jayadratha, the king of Sindhus.

Dussasana: One of the brothers of Duryodhana. He went so far as to drag Draupadi by the hair and even attempted to outrage her modesty by pulling off her clothes. He was put to death by Bhima in the great war.

Gandhari: Daughter of king Gandhara. Wife of *Dhritarashtra*. She was so dutiful and devoted to her husband that she covered up her eyes because her husband was blind. She gave birth to hundred sons—Duryodhana and others and one daughter.

Ghatotkacha: Son of Bhima and Hidimbi. He joined the Pandavas with an army of demons. He was killed by Karna with his Sakti weapon.

Hidimba: A demon slain by Bhima.

Jarasandha: Son of Brihadratha. He became king of Magadha. When Yudhishthira performed the Rajasuya sacrifice, Bhima with Arjuna and Krishna went to the kingdom of Jarasandha in the guise of Brahmins and challenged him to a fight and killed him.

Jayadratha: Brother-in-law of Duryodhana. He bore great grudge against Pandavas and once he carried off forcibly Draupadi and was rescued by Arjuna. He was slain by Arjuna in the great war.

Karna: Eldest son of Kunti, begotten by the Sun-god while she was yet a virgin. He was born with invulnerable Kavacha and Kundalas. He was found by Adhiratha—the charioteer of Dhritarashtra—in the river and was brought up by him as his own son. When he was humiliated by Kripacharya by being disallowed to have a duel with Arjuna, as he was not having the requisite qualification of being a crowned king of any kingdom, Duryodhana took up the challenge and installed him thereupon as the king of Angas, for which magnanimous act, he ever afterwards became the intimate friend of Duryodhana. He was splendidly generous in nature and unparalleled in valour. He learnt archery under Parasurama. He was faithful and loyal to Duryodhana till the end.

Kichaka: Brother-in-law of king Virata. He wanted to violate the chastity of Sairandhri (Draupadi) when she was working as the attendant in the palace of king Virata during the period of her incognito life. He was put to death by Bhima when he had come for a clandestine engagement with Draupadi at midnight.

Kirata: Lord Siva in the form of a hunter with whom Arjuna fought and got Pasupata Astra.

Kripa: A Brahmin. He was the first preceptor of the sons of Pandu and Dhritarashtra; brother-in-law of Drona—one of the three survivors on Duryodhana's side in the great battle. He is a Chiranjeevi.

Krishna: Son of Vasudeva and Devaki. The eighth and full incarnation of Lord Vishnu. He evinced His divine character by many superhuman acts—even as a child. Beloved friend and charioteer of Arjuna in the great war. He was instrumental in marrying his sister Subhadra to Arjuna. He revealed his Visvarupa Darshana to Arjuna and disclosed the essentials of 'DUTY' (Dharma), of every order of life (Brahmacharya, Grihastha, etc.,) as also of every walk of life in his Gita which is universally accepted as the *vade mecum* of the principles of moral virtues and spirituality. But for His divine guidance, the Pandavas would not have won the war. After the destruction of the Yadavas at Prabhasa, he was unintentionally killed by a hunter who mistook him for a deer.

Kritavarma: The only Yadava chief who fought for Duryodhana. One of the survivors on the side of Duryodhana in the great battle.

Kunti: Otherwise known as Pritakunti or Pritha. Daughter of Sura, a Yadava chief. She was adopted as daughter by king Kuntibhoja, a cousin of Sura. She once pleased sage Durvasa by her devoted services to him and got a Mantra from him by the use of which she could invoke any god and get boons from them. She was the first wife of Pandu and mother of the first three of the Pandavas and Karna.

Kuru: An ancestor of the Bharatas. The race is named after him also. Dhritarashtra and his sons of the Epic are called Kurus or Kauravas.

Madri: Sister of Salya; second wife of Pandu and mother of Nakula and Sahadeva.

Mandavya: A sage who pronounced a curse on Yamadharma. On account of this curse, Yamadharma partly incarnated himself as Vidura.

Nakula: The fourth of the Pandava princes, son of Madri by the elder Asvin. He was famous for his wisdom.

Nara: An ancient sage, brother of sage Narayana, incarnated as Arjuna. He is partially identical with Narayana.

Pandu: The pale son of Ambalika by Vyasa. He was cursed by Rishi Kanva that he would die if he embraced his wife. As a result of the curse he died when he ventured one day to embrace Madri.

Parasurama: Son of Jamadagni by Renuka. As his father was slain by a Kshatriya, he cleared the earth of Kshatriya kings twenty-one times. Finally he was defeated by Sri Rama, after which he went to the Mahendra mountain and is believed to be practising Tapas even today. He was tutor of the science of archery to Karna. He imparted knowledge only to Brahmin students. He cursed Karna when he found out that he was not a Brahmin.

Parikshit: Son of Abhimanyu and Uttara; father of Janamejaya to whom Vaisampayana narrates the Mahabharata under the command of Vyasa.

Pratipa: Father of Santanu.

Prativindhya: Son of Yudhishthira and Draupadi.

Drupada: Father of Draupadi, king of the Panchalas. He was the son of king Somaka.

Purochana: Minister and ally of Duryodhana. Duryodhana entrusted him with the task of burning the Pandavas in the lac house at Varanavata. He was burnt in the same house while the Pandavas escaped.

Sahadeva: The youngest of the Pandava princes begotten on Madri by the yonger Asvin. He was proficient in astrology.

Sakuni: Son of the king of Gandharas; brother of Gandhari and uncle of Duryodhana; a great cheat and an adept in the art of gambling. He was killed by Sahadeva in the great battle.

Salya: Brother of Madri (second wife of Pandu); uncle of Nakula and Sahadeva. He was a great warrior. He was equal to Krishna in valour and in leading the horses. He wanted to join the side of the Pandavas but Duryodhana cleverly took him to his side. He drove the chariot for Karna and became the commander of the forces of Duryodhana after the death of Karna. He was killed by Yudhishthira.

Sanjaya: The charioteer, minister and messenger of Dhritarashtra. He narrated every event of the war to Dhritarashtra.

Satanika: Son of Nakula and Draupadi.

Satayupa: A Raja-Rishi (king who took to ascetic life). Dhritarashtra, Gandhari, Kunti, Vidura and Sanjaya stayed in his Ashram and got initiated into ascetic life.

Satyavati: Daughter of Uparichara Vasu; foster-daughter of the chief of the fisherman; mother of Vyasa by Parasara. She married Santanu.

Saubhapati: Otherwise known as king Salva. Amba wanted to marry him. Saubha is the name of his capital which was a huge Vimana which he could move at will in the air.

Sikhandi: Eldest son of king Drupada. He was originally a girl. There was sex-transformation in her. He was placed before Bhishma in order to kill him because Bhishma would not kill an eunuch, women or those who had been women once or those who bore the names of women. Bhishma laid down his arms when Shikandi faced him in the great battle.

Sisupala: King of Chedi. He was an enemy of Krishna. The Vidarbha princess Rukmini wanted to marry Krishna. But she was about to be given in marriage to Sisupala by her eldest brother Rukmi. But Krishna carried her away and married her. During the Rajasuya Yajna, he questioned the greatness of Krishna and insulted Him when the first *Arghya* was about to be given to Him. He was killed by Krishna.

Srutasena: Son of Sahadeva and Draupadi.

Subala: King of the Gandharas. Gandhari is his daughter. Sakuni is his son.

Sudeshna: Virata's queen.

Sura: A Yadava chief. Father of Vasudeva and grandfather of Krishna; father of Kunti.

Sutasoma: Son of Bhima and Draupadi.

Ulupi: Daughter of the serpent chief. Being attracted by Arjuna's beauty, she dragged him while he was bathing in the river Ganga and compelled him to marry her. When Arjuna was defeated in the fight with his son Babruvahana, she restored Arjuna to life.

Uttara: Son of king Virata. When the Pandava princes were living incognito in his father's court, Arjuna helped him in defeating Duryodhana when he carried away the king's cattle.

Vajra: Krishna's grandson. He was installed as king by Arjuna at Sakraprastha.

Valana: A servant of Duryodhana who helped Duryodhana to poison Bhima's food.

Vichitravirya: Son of Santanu and Satyavati. Married Ambika and Ambalika but died childless.

Vidura: Born of Vyasa by Niyoga to a Sudra maid servant of Ambika. He was the counsellor of Dhritarashtra. He was a partial incarnation of god Dharma. He was famous for his wisdom. He was absorbed in Dharma when he left his body.

Vikarna: The only righteous son of Dhritarashtra. He boldly proclaimed at the end of the gambling match, that Draupadi had not been made a slave.

Virata: The king of the Matsya. The Pandavas and Draupadi lived incognito at his palace for one year.

Vyasa: Son of Parashara by Satyavati. Half-brother to Bhishma and Vichitravirya. By his Yogic powers, he induced the birth of Dhritarashtra, Pandu and Vidura, out of Ambika, Ambalika and a maid servant.

Yavanadhipa: King of the Yavana people. He was defeated by Arjuna as soon as Yudhishthira was made Yuvaraja.

Yudhishthira: The eldest of the Pandava brothers begotten on Kunti by Dharma (Yama). He was known as the incarnation of Righteousness (Dharma) and was never known to utter even a single lie. Drona refused to believe when it was announced that his son Asvatthama died unless it came from the mouth of Yudhishthira. He was very patient and enduring under very great provocations even when his wife Draupadi was insulted by Duryodhana, Dussasana, Kichaka and others. But for his divine patience and endurance, his brothers Bhima and Arjuna would have been uncontrollable. He lost his kingdom and everything through the treacherous contrivances of Duryodhana and Sakuni. After thirteen years of great hardships in exile, he opened negotiations for the partition of the kingdom and being unsuccessful, undertook the great war. He was crowned emperor of Hastinapura after the great war and reigned justly for many years.

Yuyudhana: Son of Satyaka—a Yadava chief—relative of Krishna. He fought for the Pandavas.

Yuyutsu: Son of Dhritarashtra and his Vaisya wife. He joined the Pandavas in the great battle. He was appointed as regent for Parikshit by the Pandavas before they started on their journey to the Heaven.